Thinking Straight in a Crooked World

Other Books by Gary DeMar

God and Government: A Biblical and Historical Study

God and Government: Issues in Biblical Perspectives

God and Government: The Restoration of the Republic

Last Days Madness: The Obsession of the Modern Church

America's Christian History: The Untold Story

Surviving College Successfully: A Complete Manual for the
    Rigors of Academic Combat

"You've Heard It Said": 15 Biblical Misconceptions
    That Leave Christians Powerless

The Reduction of Christianity:
    A Biblical Response to Dave Hunt

The Debate Over Christian Reconstruction

Christian Reconstruction: What It Is. What It Isn't

To Pledge Allegiance: A New World in View

To Pledge Allegiance: Reformation to Colonization

War of the Worldviews

Last Days Madness

Is Jesus Coming Soon?

End Times Fiction

Thinking Straight in a Crooked World

A CHRISTIAN DEFENSE MANUAL

Gary DeMar

AMERICAN VISION
Powder Springs, Georgia

ISBN: 0-915815-39-7
Printed in the United States of America

01 02 03 04 05   5 4 3 2 1

For current information about all releases from American Vision, visit our website: www.americanvision.org
or write: American Vision
        Box 220
        Powder Springs, Georgia 30127

TABLE OF CONTENTS

Introduction

False ideas are the greatest obstacles to the reception of the
gospel. We may preach with all the fervor of a reformer and yet
succeed only in winning a straggler here and there, if we permit
the whole collective thought of the nation or of the world to be
controlled by ideas which, by the resistless force of logic, prevent
Christianity from being regarded as anything more than a harmless
delusion. Under such circumstances, what God desires us to do is
to destroy the obstacle at its root.[1]

When entering a battle, you had better be equipped with the
most effective weapons of the day, a winning strategy, a commitment to
prevail, and the assurance of victory. This is no less true for a spiritual
battle where eternal destinies are at stake. The Bible describes the conflict between the Christian worldview and all opposing worldviews by
using the metaphors of war (2 Cor. 10:3–6). Some might not like the
warfare analogy in this day of assassinations and school shootings, thinking that it's not "spiritual" to describe the Christian's walk with such
"worldly" examples.

Ideas have consequences. Some ideas have tragic consequences.
Consider the 1999 tragedy at Columbine High in Littleton, Colorado,
and the murder of Cassie Bernall by Eric Harris and Dylan Klebold. "A
girl was asked by one of the gunmen if she believed in God, knowing
full well the safe answer. 'There is a God,' she said quietly, 'and you

need to follow along God's path.' The shooter looked down at her. 'There is no God,' he said, and he shot her in the head."[2] Cassie's mother relates that "Most of the kids they killed—if not all of them—were Christian kids. . . . It was spiritual warfare. It's still happening. . . . [T]here was a young man walking in the mall wearing a black trench coat with a T-shirt that said, 'We're still ahead 13 to 2.'"[3] Larry Gene Ashbrook walked into the sanctuary of Wedgwood Baptist Church in Fort Worth, Texas, and opened fire, killing five. The gunman was intent on killing Christians.[4]

Of course, Christians are not told to take up arms to defend or advance the Christian faith. We are engaged in a war of ideas. The biblical image of war is designed to remind us that defending the faith is serious business (Acts 7:54-60; 12:2). We should not shy away from the war analogy since it is used by numerous groups to describe what is at stake in ideological battles:

> In all of this, the language of confrontation, battle, even war, then, is not merely a literary device but an apt tool to describe the way in which the many issues contested in American public culture are being settled. It is no surprise that many of the contenders on all sides of the cultural divide use the very same language to understand their own involvement. The national Organization for Women, for example, has a "War Room" in its national headquarters in Washington, D.C., a windowless room with charts, maps, a conference table, and a dozen or so telephones. Both sides of the new cultural divide could agree with the editor of *Publisher's Weekly* who declared that the controversy over the arts and publishing was a "war"—"a war that must be won." So, too, activists on both sides of the cultural divide could agree with James Dobson of Focus on the Family, who announced, "We are in a civil war of values and the prize to the victor is the next generation—our children and grandchildren." Another activist observed that this "is a war of ideology, it's a war of ideas, it's a war about our way of life. And it has to

be fought with the same intensity, I think, and dedication as you would fight a shooting war."⁵

While the Christian's weapons "are not of the flesh" (2 Cor. 10:4), the Bible uses battle weapons in a symbolic way to characterize the reality of spiritual warfare: armor, shield, breastplate, helmet, and sword (Eph. 6:10–17). The Bible shows Jesus at His coming with "a sharp sword" coming from His mouth "so that with it He might smite the nations" (Rev. 19:15). In addition, God's Word is described as "sharper than any two-edged sword, piercing as far as the division of soul and spirit, of both joints and marrow, and able to judge the thoughts and intentions of the heart" (Heb. 4:12).

A Modern Parable

God's Word functions *spiritually* in a manner that is similar to the way a soldier would wield his sword against an enemy in a flesh and blood battle. In order to modernize the biblical analogy and make it real for today's readers, I've changed the weapons and the setting to a more modern context. The following parable takes the Christian's worldview struggles seriously, showing that the way we do battle is just as important as the spiritual weapons we use.

It's ten o'clock at night. You're just leaving the library building. This is the third night this week that you've had to work on your research paper. Out of the shadows of the alley behind the library building a man appears. He attempts to block your path to the parking lot where your lone car sits under the dim reflection of a single light. He looks to be about six feet, four inches tall, probably weighing nearly two hundred and fifty pounds. He's holding a knife with a ten-inch blade. He starts to walk toward you. The campus is deserted. Screaming for help would be futile. You know he wants to run you through. He's not after money. He wants your life.

You panic for a moment. But you remember that you're armed with a .45 service automatic. The instructor at the survival school warned you there might be nights like this.

Your sweat-drenched hand reaches into your coat to grasp the handle of the gun. The campus menace is just a few feet away. You shout to him in a weakened voice:

"Stop! If you take one more step, I'll shoot!"

He laughs. Your seemingly calm demeanor turns to panic. Fear descends on you like a thick cloud. His mocking response sends an unfamiliar chill over you.

"I don't believe in guns," he mutters. "And I certainly don't believe in .45 service automatics."

His words startle you. Fear has now gripped you like a vise. You're confused. Your shooting instructor never covered this situation. You put the gun down and allow the brute to slash you to pieces.

Of course, this student's reaction is absurd. Nobody in his right mind would cease to believe in the effectiveness of his weapon just because some brute didn't believe in it. Let's repeat the scene, but with a different twist.

The mugger steps out from the shadows of the alley to block your path. His knife blade reflects the lone parking lot light, and the gleam from the polished metal catches your eye. The knife looks huge! You realize that he wants to slash you to pieces. You remain calm. You pull out your .45 service automatic and point it at the attacker. You shout to him in a confident voice,

"Stop! If you take one more step, I'll shoot!"

He laughs. He shouts back to you, "I don't believe in guns. And I certainly don't believe in .45 service automatics."

With that last word he lunges at you with death in his eyes. You make a believer out of him by emptying the clip of bullets into his lunging body.

In the second scene, the student had confidence in his weapon. The mugger's beliefs about the reliability of the .45 service automatic were irrelevant. His lack of belief in the power of the gun did not change the gun's effectiveness. But the student's beliefs about the reliability of his weapon were most relevant.

The student's life depended on his believing in the dependability of the weapon to do what he was told it could do. The gun remained a gun, and the bullets remained bullets no matter what the mugger or student decided to believe. In order for the student to appropriate the potential of his weapon, he had to unleash its power. Of course, the student's weapon had to be reliable. Believing that a water pistol will bring down an attacker is nothing more than wishful thinking at best and lunacy at worst.

The Bible is its own best defender. As Charles Spurgeon once said, "Defend the Bible? I would as soon defend a lion."[6] The lion needs no outside defenders. As the king of the beasts, he is quite capable of defending himself. If the lion needed another beast to defend him, then that creature would be the king of the beasts. In a similar way the Bible is its own best defender. It's the king of books because its words are the words of the King of kings.

How many times have you been confronted by someone who said he didn't believe in God, the inerrancy and infallibility of the Bible, the divinity of Jesus Christ, miracles, the resurrection, and other essential Bible doctrines? And when you were confronted with such unbelief, how many times were you cut to pieces because you acted as if the Bible were not true unless you could convince the skeptic of its truthfulness *on the skeptic's terms*? How often do you in practice deny the faith or its power because a skeptic does not believe the only authority that gives your faith validity—the Bible?

Let's take a final look at our mugging story. There is another methodology that a number of Christians use that betrays the Bible's self-authenticating authority.

The mugger sees your gun, but he is not convinced of its effectiveness. You consider his words of doubt and seek to persuade him that your gun is operative and lethal. You tell him about your gun's fire power and the latest ballistic tests. You inform him of your weapon's accuracy and its reliability under adverse conditions. You even recite a list of experts who agree with your statistics. While you are presenting your evidences, the attacker runs you through. You see, he doesn't believe your sources of information. In fact, he says your facts are all wrong. The experts? Well, they're just biased. They don't like knives. They never have. Those in the National Knife Association (NKA) have their own statistical data, and they refute the conclusions of the National Gun Association (NGA).

Evidences alone are not enough to convince the unbeliever of the reliability of the Bible or the existence of God. Evidences (facts) have meaning only when they are interpreted by some standard. Ultimately, facts are meaningful because God gives them meaning. Without God, if this assumption is pushed to consistency, facts are random and unintelligible.

Defending the Faith

Like the man with the knife who confronted the armed student, rival faiths are at work in the world. Often these rival faiths are consciously designed to stamp out all things Christian. Sometimes it's more subtle than that. Many people just ignore the Christian worldview. Because the Christian worldview is rarely discussed in secular contexts (except to be ridiculed), the implicit message is to disregard Christianity as a serious worldview option. Be on your guard. This is the most subtle and destructive tactic. If you can be convinced that you and your world can be defined and interpreted without reference to Jesus Christ and His Word, then Christianity has been rendered irrelevant, and you are on the road to skepticism or outright unbelief.

You may have tried to defend the Christian faith but found that the arguments were too difficult to handle. The next time someone questioned your beliefs, you remained silent. You may have felt guilty for not standing up for Christ, but you really didn't know what to say. After hearing the same arguments leveled against Christianity time after time, the walls of your own belief system started to crumble.

Maybe you were taught that Christians should not answer the critics. You just "believe." Well, that doesn't work for long. It gets to you in time. The Bible tells us as Christians that we are responsible to defend the faith. Defending the faith—giving an answer to those who ask what our hope is—is part of what it means to be a Christian. It's not an option.

The best way to handle attacks by skeptics is to have worked out an apologetic methodology. It's been said that the best defense is a good offense. Keep in mind that the Bible is like a loaded .45. The power to destroy all speculations raised up against the knowledge of God is inherent in God's Word. Yet many Christians either don't know how to use the Bible as a spiritual weapon or don't believe that it is effective in confronting "philosophy and empty deception" based on the "tradition of men, according to the elementary principles of the world" (Col. 2:8). A cogently presented, comprehensive, and consistent Christian worldview can stand up to and answer any hostile belief system. But it takes work to understand how skeptics think, believe, and behave. Your job is not finished until you are always "ready to make a defense to every one who asks you to give a reason for the hope that is in you" (1 Peter 3:15). This is what thinking straight in a crooked world is all about.

Notes

1. J. Gresham Machen, "Christianity and Culture," *Princeton Theological Review* 11 (1913), 7.

2. Nancy Gibbs, "In Sorrow and Disbelief," *Time* (May 3, 1999), 25.

3. Quoted in Wendy Murray Zoba, "'Do You Believe in God?'" *Christianity Today* (October 4, 1999), 33–40. The number 13 refers to the number of people Harris and Klebold killed. The 2 refers to their suicide.

4. David Van Biema, "Terror in the Sanctuary," *Time* (September 27, 1999), 42–43.

5. James Davison Hunter, *Culture Wars: The Struggle to Define America* (New York: Basic Books, 1991), 64.

6. Quoted in John M. Frame, *Apologetics to the Glory of God: An Introduction* (Phillipsburg, NJ: Presbyterian and Reformed, 1994), 17.

Part One
A Call to Defensive Action

1

Defending the Biblical Worldview

The Greek word *apologia* (from which we derive the English word
"apologetics") denotes a speech made in defense, a reply
(especially in the legal context of a courtroom) made to an
accusation. The word originated in the judicial operations of
ancient Athens, but the word occurs several times in the New
Testament as well. The difference between the Greek and Christian
methods of apologetics can be illustrated by contrasting the
Apology of Socrates (as Plato records it) with the approach of the
apostle Paul, who described himself as "set for the defense
(*apologia*) of the gospel."[1]

Apologetics does not mean saying you're sorry for being a Christian.
Christians are not called on to apologize for believing in God, the trustworthiness of the Bible, the reality of miracles, and the redemptive work
of Jesus Christ that saves sinners from final judgment. The Bible calls
on Christians to defend its truths with an intensity and proficiency
similar to the way a lawyer would defend a client who is on trial for
his life.

Some claim that Christians should not be involved in arguments
about the Christian faith because it's not "spiritual" or the loving thing

to do. Support for this opinion cannot be found in the Bible. In fact, Christians are *commanded* to defend the faith: "But sanctify Christ as Lord in your hearts, always being ready to make a defense to every one who asks you to give an account for the hope that is in you, yet with gentleness and reverence" (1 Peter 3:15). In Jude we are told to "contend earnestly for the faith which was once for all delivered to the saints" (Jude 3).

There are numerous accounts in the New Testament where such defenses—arguments and contentions—are made, even though there was a high price to pay. The apostles defended the faith and were beaten and imprisoned for their efforts (Acts 4). Stephen contended "earnestly for the faith," and his own countrymen stoned him to death (Acts 7). Paul offered his defense of Christianity before Greek philosophers (Acts 17:22–34), his own countrymen (Acts 22–23), and Roman civil officials (Acts 24–26). He was ready and eager to defend the faith before Caesar himself (Acts 25:11, 32).

Christians are called on to "examine everything carefully" (1 Thess. 5:21). John warns us not to "believe every spirit" but to "test" them "to see whether they are from God; because many false prophets have gone out into the world" (1 John 4:1). Notice that we are to examine *everything*, not just so-called "religious" issues. Furthermore, we are not to assume that just because a person has a string of degrees after his name or has compiled what he claims is "conclusive evidence" in support of his worldview that we should fail to put his dogmatic theories to the test. "Testing theories against the evidence never ends. The National Academy [of Sciences] booklet [on science] correctly states that 'all scientific knowledge is, in principle, subject to change as new evidence becomes available.' It doesn't matter how long, or how many scientists currently believe it. If contradictory evidence turns up, the theory must be reevaluated or even abandoned."[2]

Christian apologists give reasons as to why beginning with any presupposition other than the God of the Bible is impossible, irrational, and immoral. The audiences may vary—genuine seekers, skeptics, or hostile unbelievers—but the message and starting point are the same. The apologist's job, like a lawyer before a judge and jury, is to present sound arguments that testify to the truth.

Man in the Dock

But on what does the apologist stand to make his case? He cannot use himself as the standard or even the expert opinion of others. Furthermore, the Christian apologist must recognize that his opponent is not the final arbiter of truth. We should never entertain the thought that our philosophical foes are the designated cosmic judge and jury in determining whether God is just and His Word is true. Our task is not to present the Christian faith as a debatable hypothesis, a study in probability, or just one religious option among many. We should never say, "You be the judge." In a biblical defense of the Christian faith, God is not the one on trial. Modern man, however, does not see it this way, as C. S. Lewis points out:

> The ancient man approached God (or even the gods) as the accused person approaches his judge. For the modern man the roles are reversed. He is the judge: God is in the dock [the enclosure where a prisoner is placed in an English criminal trial]. He is quite a kindly judge: if God should have a reasonable defence for being the god who permits war, poverty and disease, he is ready to listen to it. The trial may even end in God's acquittal. But the important thing is that Man is on the Bench and God in the Dock.[3]

How can a finite, fallible, and fallen being ever be a qualified judge of eternal things? How is it possible that the creature can legitimately question the Creator? God asks Job: "Will the faultfinder contend with the Almighty? Let him who reproves God answer it" (Job 40:1). Job responded, knowing the limitations of his own nature, the only way he could: "Behold, I am insignificant; what can I reply to Thee? I lay my hand on my mouth" (40:4). God asks Job a series of questions that demonstrate how limited he is in knowledge and experience. God inquires of Job: "Where were you when I laid the foundation of the earth! Tell Me, if you have understanding. Who set its measurements, since you know?" (38:4). Job was trying to figure out the world and the way it works based on his own limited frame of reference. This is an impossible and immoral task.

The Neutrality Myth

The Christian apologist does not have the option of taking a so-called neutral position when defending the faith. Even if a Christian wanted to be neutral, he couldn't be, since neutrality is impossible. Even in the scientific field, where objectivity is thought to be synonymous with impartiality, neutrality is unobtainable. The following example describes what many scientists would claim as objective analysis:

> Louis Leakey, director of Kenya's Centre for Prehistory and Paleontology in Nairobi, described his discovery, together with his wife Mary, of a bit of skull and two teeth, in these words: "We knelt together to examine the treasure . . . and almost cried with sheer joy. For years people had been telling us that we'd better stop looking, but I felt deep down that it had to be there. You must be patient about these things." The time was July 17, 1959. This scene is a curious one on two accounts. First, the scientist Leakey knew what he had found before he examined it: he worked by faith, and viewed his findings by faith. He was finding "proof" for a theory already accepted, and he accepted his finding as "proof" on sight. Second, the intense emotionalism and joy sound more like a revival experience than a scientific analysis.[4]

Christians can never adopt the strategy that neutrality is possible, and they can never allow those who hold contrary worldviews to argue as if they are being neutral.

The Fool and His Folly

Given that neutrality is impossible, how is the Christian apologist to argue with someone who holds a contradictory set of presuppositions? The Christian apologist is commanded not to "answer a fool according to his folly." Why? He'll be "like him" in his misguided assumptions and will also be classified as a "fool" (Prov. 26:4). The Bible assumes that worldviews based on presuppositions that are contrary to the Bible are foolishness. This is why Scripture states emphatically and without apology that the professed atheist is a "fool" (Psalm 14:1; 53:1). How can an insignificant creature who is smaller than an atom when compared to the vastness of the universe be so dogmatic?

There's not much maneuvering room here. If we abandon the governing assumptions of the Christian worldview *from the start* and argue from a supposed neutral starting point, we place ourselves in the same category as the atheist, all in the name of "defending the Christian faith"! This means that the starting point in the Christian worldview is not subjective; it's not just one debatable opinion among many others.

Of course, the unbeliever doesn't like to hear this. It means that he is not in control. It's no wonder that the Apostle Paul explains the reality of unbelieving thought in stark and uncompromising terms:

> For the word of the cross is to those who are perishing foolishness, but to us who are being saved it is the power of God. For it is written, "I will destroy the wisdom of the wise, and the cleverness of the clever I will set aside." Where is the wise man? Where is the scribe? Where is the debater of this age? Has not God made foolish the wisdom of the world? For since in the wisdom of God the world through its wisdom did not come to

know God, God was well-pleased through the foolishness of the message preached to save those who believe. For indeed Jews ask for signs, and Greeks search for wisdom; but we preach Christ crucified, to Jews a stumbling block, and to Greeks foolishness, but to those who are the called, both Jews and Greeks, Christ the power of God and the wisdom of God. Because the foolishness of God is wiser than men, and the weakness of God is stronger than men (1 Cor. 1:18–25).

An apologetic methodology that claims a Christian should be "open," "objective," and "tolerant" of all opinions when the faith is defended is like a person who hopes to stop a man from committing suicide by taking the hundred-story plunge with him, hoping to convince the lost soul on the way down. No one in his right mind would make such a concession to foolishness. But Christians do it all the time when they adopt the operating presuppositions of unbelieving thought as if they were neutral assumptions about reality.

While the Bible maintains that the Christian apologist is prohibited from adopting the starting point of unbelieving thought, he is encouraged to show the unbeliever the end result of his foolish philosophical principles if they are consistently followed. As defenders of the only true faith, we are to "answer a fool as his folly deserves, lest he be wise in his own eyes" (Prov. 26:5). That is, we are to put the unbeliever's worldview to the test, showing how absurd it is when followed consistently. A world without God and moral absolutes leads to despair and moral anarchy.

Ted Turner, founder of CNN, had this to say about the Ten Commandments when he addressed the National Press Association in Atlanta, Georgia, in 1988: "We're living with outmoded rules. The rules we're living under [are] the Ten Commandments, and I bet nobody here even pays much attention to 'em, because they are too old. When Moses went up on the mountain, there were no nuclear weapons, there was no poverty. Nobody around likes to be commanded." Does Ted Turner really believe, for example, that laws against murder (sixth commandment) and theft (eighth commandment) are "outmoded rules"? I wonder how he would respond if some of his employees began to steal from him? What if one of his children was murdered? Would he feel that the perpetrator was justified by claiming that the Ten Commandments are "outmoded rules"? Philosopher Isaiah Berlin demonstrates how impossible it is to claim worldview neutrality.

> The world of a man who believes that God created him for a specific purpose, that he has an immortal soul, that there is an afterlife in which his sins will be visited upon him, is radically different from the world of a man who believes in none of these things; and the reasons for action, the moral codes, the political beliefs, the tastes, the personal relationships of the former will deeply and systematically differ from those of the latter. Men's views of one another will differ profoundly as a very consequence of their general conception of the world: the notions of cause and purpose, good and evil, freedom and slavery, things and persons, rights, duties, laws, justice, truth, falsehood, to take some central ideas completely at random, depend entirely upon the general framework within which they form, as it were, nodal points.[5]

There is no escape from the reality that all of life is evaluated in terms of an already adopted worldview.

We All Believe in Something

All worldviews are by definition belief systems. A person does not have to believe in God to be considered religious. John H. Dietrich, for example, admits that he is a religious humanist.

> For centuries the idea of God has been the very heart of religion; it has been said, "No God, no religion." But humanism

thinks of religion as something very different and far deeper than any belief in God. To it, religion is not the attempt to establish right relations with a supernatural being, but rather the unpreaching and aspiring impulse in a human life. It is the striving for its completest fulfillment, and anything which contributes to this fulfillment is religious, whether it be associated with the idea of God or not.[6]

Since we are all limited in knowledge and restrained by our inability to be everywhere (omnipresence) and know everything (omniscience), an atheist puts forth his claim that God does not exist in terms of a faith commitment. When the late Carl Sagan wrote, "The cosmos is all that is or ever was or ever will be,"[7] he was making a declaration of faith, a statement of his ultimate presupposition. There is no way he could be assured that God does not exist based on his limited knowledge and experience and the limited knowledge and experience of others. In the first line of the next paragraph of his best selling book *Cosmos*, Sagan admitted that "the size and age of the Cosmos *are beyond ordinary human understanding*."[8] Even so, Sagan was convinced that the material world was all that existed. He believed one thing to be true and dismissed any worldview that did not conform to it without having all the facts or the ability to understand fully what he did know. Sagan's assertions do not conform to reality. Greg Koukl writes:

> Everybody believes something, and even what appears to be a rejection of all beliefs is a kind of belief. We all hold something to be true. Maybe what you hold true is that nothing else is true, but that is nonetheless something you believe.
>
> Even if you are agnostic,[9] you believe that it is not possible to know things about ultimate issues like the existence of God. You believe in the justifiability of your agnosticism—your uncertainty—and you have a burden of proof to justify your unwillingness to decide. There is nowhere someone can stand where he or she has no beliefs.

> If you reject Christianity, there is something else that you
> end up asserting by default.[10]

Once a person rejects Christianity, he has not set himself free from the concept of faith. He has only transferred his faith to something or someone else.

For Sagan, the cosmos is god, a glorious accidental substitute for what he believed were ancient, pre-scientific beliefs about the deity and the origin and nature of the universe. The very idea of a *personal* God, in Sagan's worldview, is simply "the dreams of men."[11] Even so, Sagan's worldview is fundamentally religious. Sagan's starting point—his ultimate presupposition—evaluates all that he sees or doesn't see in the cosmos. There is no belief more fundamental. All that follows in the *Cosmos* worldview is measured by his one-sentence, presuppositional yardstick: "The cosmos is all that is or ever was or ever will be."

> When Sagan excludes even the possibility that a spiritual
> dimension has any place in his cosmos—not even at the un-
> known, mysterious moment when life began—he makes acci-
> dental evolution the explanation for everything. Presented
> in this way, evolution does indeed look like an inverted
> religion, a conceptual golden calf, which manages to reek
> of sterile atheism. It is little wonder that many parents
> find their deeper emotions stirred if they discover this to
> be the import of Johnny's education.[12]

While the Bible starts with, "In the beginning God" (Gen. 1:1), Sagan begins with, "In the beginning Cosmos." Sagan worships an eternal cosmos that he *presupposes* is an evolutionary substitute for the eternal God of the Bible who gives life and meaning to the cosmos. Sagan says it like this: "It is the universe that made us.... We are creatures of the cosmos.... Our obligation to survive and flourish is owed, not just to ourselves, but also to that cosmos, ancient and vast, from which we spring."[13] The primordial biotic soup nourished our ancient ancestors as they emerged from that first ocean of life. These memories, according to Sagan, are eternally etched on our evolved psyche.

> The ocean calls. Some part of our being knows this is from where we came. We long to return. These aspirations are not, I think, irreverent, although they may trouble whatever gods may be.[14]

How can anyone know this? Such a belief is nothing more than a hypothesis, and not a very good one at that. This isn't science. It borders on mysticism. Sagan makes it clear that there are no transcendent personal "gods" in his universe, only "accidents"[15] that somehow developed into design and meaning.

At times, however, Sagan muses rhapsodic over a seemingly benign reverence for the cosmos that hints at a deep religious commitment to atheism and elements of paganism. "Our ancestors worshipped the sun," he reflects, "and they were far from foolish. It makes good sense to revere the sun and the stars, because we are their children."[16] But who made the cosmos? How did the cosmos get here? Why is there design, order, and complexity in the cosmos? Sagan never answered these questions. He couldn't as long as the cosmos is all that is ever was or ever will be and he remained a finite creature who had limited knowledge of the universe and access to it.

Conclusion

Defending the biblical worldview means pointing out that all of us argue from a non-neutral starting point. No one is objective. Larry King, host of CNN's "Larry King Live," makes this point with unusual clarity and honesty:

> Mr King... dismisses the idea of objectivity in the news business, putting him at odds with reporters and anchors who

insist their own ideology has nothing to do with their coverage. "All things are subjective," he says, "We are all subjective. The decision as to what ran first on *CBS Evening News* last night was a subjective decision made by [Dan] Rather and others, trying to be objective, saying this is what I think... is the most important thing. As soon as you say the word *I*, that's subjective."[17]

The facts are interpreted in terms of out belief patterns, our presuppositions. The Christian is not given an option of arguing from a supposed neutral starting point. If he does not begin with the assumption that God's Word is true, then he adopts the worldview assumptions of unbelievers.

Notes

1. Greg L. Bahnsen, "The Reformation of Christian Apologetics," *Foundations of Christian Scholarship*, Gary North, ed. (Vallecito, CA: Ross House Books, 1976), 194–95.

2. Jonathan Wells, *Icons of Evolution: Science or Myth? Why So Much of What We Teach About Evolution is Wrong* (Washington, D.C.: Regnery Publishing, 2000), 2–3.

3. C.S. Lewis, "God in the Dock," in *God in the Dock: Essays on Theology and Ethics* (Grand Rapids, MI: Eerdmans, 1970), 244.

4. Rousas J. Rushdoony, *The Mythology of Science* (Nutley, NJ: The Craig Press, 1967), 85.

5. Originally appeared in Isaiah Berlin's *Concepts and Categories* and cited in the London *Daily Telegraph* (November 7, 1977).

6. Quoted in Cornelius Loew, *Modern Rivals to Christian Faith* (Philadelphia, PA: Westminster Press, 1956), 11.

7. Carl Sagan, *Cosmos* (New York: Random House, 1980), 4.

8. Sagan, *Cosmos*, 4.

9. The word *agnostic* was coined by Thomas Henry Huxley (1825–1895). The word is comprised of the prefix *a* which means "without" or "having none" and the Greek word for "knowledge," *gnosis*. An agnostic is someone who is without knowledge on a subject. A religious agnostic claims that he does not have enough knowledge to determine whether God exists. The Bible claims otherwise: "That which is known about God is evident within them; for God made it evident to them. For since the creation of the world His invisible attributes, His eternal power and divine nature, have been clearly seen, being understood through what has been made, so that they are without excuse" (Rom. 1:19–20).

10. Greg Koukl, "You've Got to Believe Something," *The Plain Truth* (January/February 1999), 39.

11. Sagan, *Cosmos*, 257.

12. William R. Fix, *The Bone Peddlers: Selling Evolution* (New York: Macmillan Publishing Co., 1984), xxiv.

13. From the 13-hour long television presentation of *Cosmos* aired in the fall of 1980. Quoted in Richard A. Baer, Jr., "They *Are* Teaching Religion in the Public Schools," *Christianity Today* (February 17, 1984), 12.

14. Sagan, *Cosmos*, 5.

15. Sagan, *Cosmos*, 30.

16. Quoted in Baer, "They *Are* Teaching Religion in the Public Schools," 13.

17. Bob Jones, "It's Good to be King: An Interview with the Master Interviewer," *World* (July 28, 2001), 21.

2

Apologetics in Action

An apology is the defence offered in reply to a specific attack,
accusation or charge. Justin Martyr writes his *1st and 2nd
Apologies* to counter the accusations of immorality that pagans
were passing round against Christians. Origen in his *contra Celsum*
undertakes to repel the charges Celsus had made in writing
against Christianity. In a much later age Bishop Butler in his
Analogy embarks on a famous defence of Christianity against
those who disparaged revelation.[1]

The Bible gives us numerous examples of "apologetics in action,"
from those on the verge of belief to those hostile to the Christian worldview. Jesus defended His divinity by directing the disciples to His own
testimony about Himself and the works He performed: "Believe Me
that I am in the Father, and the Father in Me; otherwise believe on
account of the works themselves" (John 14:11). On another occasion,
Jesus confronted Thomas and his unbelief by presenting Himself alive
and well to the doubting apostle (John 20:24–31). The New Testament
writers show that Jesus was the fulfillment of hundreds of Old Testa-

ment prophecies—from His place of birth in Bethlehem (Micah 5:2) to how He would die (Psalm 22).

Jesus and His disciples were constantly doing battle with opponents who were a lot meaner than today's antagonists. There was more at stake than scoring debating points. Jesus was not passive in the face of hostility and opposition. He met his attackers head on and systematically demolished the arguments they used against Him. Jesus won every argument even though not everyone followed Him (John 6:60–71). He sent the antagonists away mumbling to themselves. When the religious leaders of the day could not defend their worldview, they worked to have Him crucified.

Jesus and the Skeptics

Jesus' defense of the faith against the skeptics, religious leaders, and legal profession had an effect on the people. After hearing Jesus deal with His antagonists, the people began to question the bankrupt ideology of their leaders. First, Jesus' message began to turn the people away from the anti-supernatural worldview of the Sadducees. The Sadducees were the religious skeptics of the day. They didn't believe in the resurrection of the dead, for example. Upon hearing Jesus show the absurdity of the Sadducees' worldview, the people were "astonished at His teaching" (Matt. 22:33).

Next up were leaders from the religious and legal professions: "But when the Pharisees heard that He had put the Sadducees to silence, they gathered themselves together. And one of them, a lawyer, asked Him a question, testing Him" (22:34–35). Jesus again defends the faith against unbelief. Their response? "And no one was able to answer Him a word, nor did anyone dare from that day on to ask Him another question" (22:46).

Something had to be done with this troublemaker. It's no accident that Jesus was taken away to be tried secretly. The people would have turned on their leaders had they known what they had planned for Jesus. Jesus gave the people answers to life's most perplexing questions. Those in power were about to take it all away:

> Then the chief priests and the elders of the people were gathered together in the court of the high priest, named Caiaphas; and they plotted to seize Jesus by stealth, and kill Him. But they were saying, "Not during the festival, lest a riot occur among the people" (Matt. 26:3–5).

Jesus had challenged the perverted worldviews of both the Sadducees and Pharisees, and the people were on the verge of rejecting them, lock, stock, and barrel. In order to keep their public credibility intact and to hide the defects of their worldview, Jesus had to go. His worldview had to be discredited.

Paul and the Skeptics

The Apostle Paul was always ready to defend the faith against anyone who raised a question or an objection. Paul went to the very heart of religious skepticism by confronting the Greek philosophers of Athens with their own ignorance. The Bible says that "his spirit was being provoked within him as he was beholding the city full of idols" (Acts17:16). At this point, Paul went to work defending the faith, "reasoning in the synagogue with the Jews and the God-fearing Gentiles, and in the market place every day with those who happened to be present" (17:17). Even "some of the Epicurean and Stoic philosophers were conversing with him" (17:18). They, however, found that some of his views differed greatly from their own. He was accused of being a "proclaimer of strange demons" (17:18). He was then brought to the Areopagus,[2] a public debating forum more popularly known as Mars Hill, so those in his audience that day could learn more about these new teachings. Here is a summary of Paul's defense in Acts 17:22–33:

Paul and the Men of Mars Hill

1. Paul shows the Greek philosophers that they cannot escape the reality that they are religious, both in theory and practice, pointing out to them their many objects of worship: "And Paul stood in the midst of the Areopagus and said, 'Men of Athens, I observe that you are very religious in all respects'" (17:22).

Application: Every person holds to basic religious commitments. Even atheists are religious. They *believe* there is no God. There is no way an atheist can prove either philosophically, logically, or scientifically that God does not exist. Notice that Paul reminds the Athenians that they are "religious in *all* respects." Their religious ideas give meaning to everything they think and do. But because their religious starting point is distorted, their understanding of the world in which they live is also distorted. A crooked ruler can never be used to draw a straight line.

2. Paul notes that even the Athenians admit that they do not have all the facts, pointing out an altar that they erected "TO AN UNKNOWN GOD" (17:23).

Application: The skeptic wants to be the judge as to whether God exists and what kind of God exists. But how can he ever be sure that the God of His own making exists? Not having all the facts limits the dogmatism of the unbeliever and humbles the believer. Ultimately, since we can never gather all the facts, arguments of a metaphysical nature— the existence of God—come down to a faith-commitment. We are forced, out of necessity, to trust an outside authority which interprets the facts and reveals what we cannot observe. Paul's point is that God is that outside Observer who has revealed Himself to us in His Word and in the person of Jesus Christ.

3. Paul shows the Athenians a way out of their ignorance by describing the only true God as the "Lord of heaven and earth" (17:24).

Application: The Bible never leaves the skeptic in his ignorance. The skeptic is left with nothing helpful if he is only shown that his entire belief system is based upon unknowns or probabilities. He can't be sure of anything within the confines of his own worldview. This much the Athenians admitted. But the Christian's position establishes that because God is "Lord of heaven and earth," the world makes sense. Randomness does not characterize the universe or the way people live. "Christianity provides an explanation even for our ignorance. We may be ignorant because of our finiteness as human beings. Yet, we can be sure that if an answer is to be found it must be done by dependence on the revelation of God."[3] That revelation is reliable because it comes from a God who is "Lord of heaven and earth."

4. Paul shows the Athenians that the true God is in need of nothing, "since he Himself gives to all life and breath and all things" (17:25).

Application: Trusting in the God of the Bible means trusting someone who is able to sustain us in life and death. There is no assurance of this in the skeptic's worldview. The skeptic either depends on himself or he looks to other belief systems to satisfy his spiritual hunger. But there is no guarantee that any of these can supply what he needs, the things that make him human: purpose, love, hope, fulfillment, a sense of meaning and belonging, the relief of guilt, and the assurance of life after death. Only an independent God who is in need of nothing can supply what others cannot supply for themselves. What can an "unknown god" or no god offer? In addition, the atheist uses the breath that God gave him to deny Him.

5. Paul shows the men of Athens that there is no way to escape the presence and government of God since He has "determined their appointed times, and the boundaries of their habitation" (17:26). Neither can they escape the implications of God's sustaining providence.

Application: There is no escaping God. This is what atheists, skeptics, and scoffers do not like. Therefore, any notion of a personal God who sees and judges what man does must be banned from the universe so we can all live independent, autonomous lives, free from all restrictions. The unbeliever hopes to define or rationalize God out of existence. By doing so he destroys any hope of giving meaning to life. When King David was confronted with his sin by the prophet Nathan, David's confession brought him back to reality: God sees and judges all things. There is no escape from the gaze of God: "Against Thee, Thee only, I have sinned, and done what is evil in Thy sight, so that Thou art justified when Thou dost speak, and blameless when Thou dost judge" (Psalm 51:4a). R.C. Sproul comments:

> Here David acknowledges the reality of that guilt and notes two very important factors. First, sin is *ever* before him. It hounds him and pursues him. He sees it wherever he goes. He cannot rid himself of the memory. Like Lady Macbeth, the spot is indelible. Second, he has done evil in the sight of *God*. Thus, David not only sees his sin but he realizes it has not escaped the notice of God.[4]

By acknowleding God and His redemptive work in the person of Jesus Christ, no sinner has to despair.

6. Paul points out that there is a basic difference between God and the universe, between God and man (17:29). Man is a created being who lives in a created world. No man stands independent of God. No man can become a god, because God is *transcendent*.[5]

Application: God tells us very specifically that "my thoughts are not your thoughts, neither are your ways my ways" (Isa. 55:8). Why not? 'For as the heavens are higher than the earth, so are my ways higher than your ways, and my thoughts than your thoughts'" (55:9). Having said this, we should not forget that God is also *immanent*. He is present *with* His creation. While God is not a part of creation as in pantheism, He has not removed Himself from the created order, as in deism. God came to meet with Moses on the mountain, to give him the commandments: "Thus you shall say to the house of Jacob. . . . 'Now then, if you will indeed obey My voice and keep My covenant, then you shall be My own possession among all the peoples of all the earth'" (Ex. 19:3, 5). The Psalmist writes: "Where can I go from Thy Spirit? Or where can I flee from Thy presence? If I ascend to heaven, Thou art there; if I make my bed in Sheol, behold Thou art there. If I take the wings of the dawn, if I dwell in the remotest part of the sea, even there Thy hand will lead me, and Thy right hand will lay hold of me" (Psalm 139:7-10; cf. Jer. 23:23, 24). God is specially present with His people: "For what great nation is there that has a God so near to it as is the Lord our God whenever we call on Him?" (Deut. 4:7). Jesus took on human flesh and "dwelt among us" (John 1:14), promising that He would be with us "always, even to the end of the age" (Matt. 28:20). Of course, the Holy Spirit "came from heaven" to be with us (Acts 2:2). In effect, God is with us—*immanent*—in the Person of the Holy Spirit. God is so near that our words can be heard and our actions judged. Peter accused Ananias of lying to the Holy Spirit (Acts 5:3). He went on to say: "You have not lied to men, but to God" (v. 4).

The transcendence (God is *distinct from us*) and immanence (God is *near to us*) of God are not contradictory concepts.[6] Immanence flows out of God's transcendence, omnipresence, and omnipotence. John Frame writes:

> These two attributes do not conflict with one another. God is close *because* he is Lord. He is Lord, and thus free to make his power felt everywhere we go. He is Lord, and thus able to reveal himself clearly to us, distinguishing himself from all mere creatures. He is Lord, and therefore the most central fact of our experience, the least avoidable, the most verifiable.[7]

7. Paul shows the Athenians that God is no longer overlooking "the times of ignorance." He "is now declaring to men that all everywhere should repent" (17:30), that they must change their *minds* about the God of the Bible, their sin, and Jesus Christ, their Redeemer.

Application: The defense of the faith is not solely about knowledge of the facts but about ethics, that is, how we act. The reason that man seeks to escape from God by rationalizing argumentation is that he has sins to hide from a Judge he doesn't want to face. Most arguments that seek to deny God or the validity of the Christian message are simply smoke screens to obscure the real issue: Man is a sinner who "suppresses the truth in unrighteousness" (Rom. 1:18).

8. Paul demonstrates that God has "fixed a day in which He will judge the world in righteousness through a man He has appointed" (17:31).

Application: The skeptic cannot remain neutral when he is confronted with the gospel. A refusal to decide for Christ with a wait-and-see attitude does not absolve him of his guilt and eventual judgment. Straddling the fence will not save him. Judgment is coming. Even if we do not "win" our argument with the skeptic, we must always warn him of the consequences of unbelief. When the arguments are laid aside, the question still remains: "What do you think of Jesus Christ?" and "What does he think of *you*?"

9. Paul makes it clear that God has furnished proof to all men that this is all true "by raising Him from the dead" (17:31).

Application: The resurrection of Jesus from the dead is only incredible for those who deny God; it is not incredible for those who acknowledge that God is Lord of heaven and earth and supplies to all life, breath, and all things. Why should it surprise us that the God who created the world should recreate a portion of it? This is why Paul could ask his fellow Jews: "Why is it considered incredible among you people if God does raise the dead?" (26:8). The resurrection is a confirmation of God's power and a vindication of His grace. Paul assumes the reality of the resurrection. It proves that Jesus is the final judge. Paul does not argue for the resurrection as a conclusion. He presents it as fact.

"Now when they heard of the resurrection of the dead, some began to sneer, but others said, 'We shall hear you again concerning this'"

(17:32). This is the essence of defending the faith. Some will reject the faith because what you tell them does not fit within the framework of their worldview. Those who rejected the worldview of supernaturalism as presented by Paul did so because their starting point assumed that miracles are impossible. Their worldview was constructed on a foundation of unknowns: unknown gods, unknown forces, unknown random facts, unjustifiable universal laws, and unverified claims to authority. God will no longer tolerate such ignorance. Such a worldview is destined for judgment. It can only lead to skepticism, mysticism, and irrationality. The words to the youthful student Timothy are appropriate advice for any Christian: "O Timothy, guard what has been entrusted to you, avoiding worldly and empty chatter and the opposing arguments of what is falsely called 'knowledge'—which some have professed and thus gone astray from the faith. Grace be with you" (2 Tim. 6:21). Greg Bahnsen sums up the Christian's apologetic task.

> Until the Holy Spirit regenerates the sinner and brings him to repentance, his presuppositions will remain unaltered. And as long as the unbeliever's presuppositions are unchanged, a proper acceptance and understanding of the good news of Christ's historical resurrection will be impossible. The Athenian philosophers had originally asked Paul for an account of his doctrine of resurrection. After his reasoned defense of the hope within him and his challenge to the philosophers' presuppositions, a few were turned around in their thinking. But many refused to correct their presuppositions, so that when Paul concluded with Christ's resurrection they ridiculed and mocked.

> Acceptance of the facts is governed by one's most ultimate assumptions, as Paul was well aware. Paul began his apologetic with God and His revelation. The Athenian philosophers began their dispute with Paul in an attitude of cynical unbelief about Christ's resurrection... .

> Paul knew that the explanation of their hostility to God's revelation (even though they evidenced an inability to escape its

forcefulness) was to be found in their desire to exercise control over God (e.g., v. 29) and to avoid facing up to the fact of their deserved punishment before the judgment seat of God (v. 30). They secretly hoped that ignorance would be bliss, and so preferred darkness to light (John 3:19-20).[8]

Mars Hill Today

Paul's Athenian encounter on Mars Hill is quite modern. All the elements of skepticism, ignorance, and arrogance are present today among those who worship the same ancient idols dressed up with new religious slogans. Just like in Paul's day, the biblical faith is dogmatic. It makes absolute assertions about fundamental concepts: God exists, man was created, sin has infected this world, man is accountable to God, and Jesus Christ is our only hope in life and in death. These declarations are not acceptable to the secular mind-set which does not acknowledge the premise of absolutes that would make man accountable to God.

The goal of the secular worldview is to strip self-proclaimed Christians of their absolute worldview by relegating it to its cloistered domain. If religion does have a part to play in contemporary life, its part is narrowly focused and limited to unscientific areas. Stephen Jay Gould, professor of geology at Harvard and New York University, states that "no factual discovery of science (statements about how nature 'is') can, in principle, lead us to ethical conclusions (how we 'ought' to behave) or to convictions about intrinsic meaning (the 'purpose' of our lives). These last two questions—and what more important inquiries could we make?—lie firmly in the domains of religion, philosophy and humanistic study."[9] Science cannot tell us how to live. Only religion can do that. And since religion is not scientific, we cannot assume that its ethical conclusions are legitimate because they function outside the realm of science.

Gould is involved in a dodge by relegating religion to its own sealed box and then maintaining that religion has the authority to address convictions of purpose and meaning. Of course, the box remains closed. There is no point, Gould insists, where religion and science have *anything* to do with one another. "Science and religion should be equal, mutually respecting partners, each the master of its own domain, and with each domain vital to human life in a different way."[10] And yet, when it comes to the meaning of life and how a person should behave, Gould must turn to religion because he cannot find ethical rules in his evolutionary "scientific" hypothesis. He states that "today, all scientists accept materialism (at least in their workplace), and the philosophically astute realize that it poses no threat to our love for music, subjective insight, and love itself."[11] But if evolution is true— "operating blindly and randomly"[12] as evolutionists insist—there cannot be any scientific justification for morality and meaning because these are outside the realm of science. And since today's scientists are materialists, they cannot account for a "subjective insight" like love. In fact, materialism discounts even "insight." The box labeled religion is to remain closed to the "scientist."

Gould is not alone in this sophisticated form of intellectual schizophrenia. Francis Crick, codiscoverer of the double-helix structure of DNA, sets forth the logical implications of materialism:

> Crick's "astonishing hypothesis" declares that all of our interior states, joys and sorrows, our memories and ambitions, even our personal identity and the cherished notion of free will, are "no more than the behavior of nerve cells."[13]

Crick and Gould use the Christian concepts of love, joy, and sorrow simply as labels to identify the impersonal, purely random "behavior of nerve cells." What's true for "interior states" is also true for morality. Michael Ruse asserts that morality developed in the same way as hands, feet, and teeth—the "ephemeral product of the evolutionary process."[14] According to Ruse, "Morality," like gills in fish and lungs in homo sapiens, "is just an aid to survival and reproduction, and has no being beyond this."[15] In a word, morality is foundationless. The Men of Athens are still with us.

Conclusion

The Apostle Paul confronted the worldviews of his day by understanding them and giving reasoned and biblical answers to their claims and admitted ignorance. The reaction was typical. "Some began to sneer, but others said, 'We shall hear you again concerning this'" (Acts 17:32). We should expect similar reactions today since human nature has not changed. Our apologetic task is no less important in a day of seemingly unrivaled skepticism.

Notes

1. J.K.S. Reid, *Christian Apologetics* (Grand Rapids, MI: Eerdmans, 1970), 10.

2. "The *Council of the Areopagus* was a venerable commission of the ex-magistrates which took its name from the hill where it originally convened. In popular parlance its title was shortened to the 'the Areopagus,' and in the first century it had transferred its location to the Stoa Basileios (or 'Royal Portico') in the city marketplace—where the Platonic dialogues tell us that Euthyphro went to try his father for impiety and where Socrates had been tried for corrupting the youth with foreign deities. Apparently the Council convened on Mar's Hill in Paul's day only for trying cases of homicide. That Paul 'stood in the midst of the Areopagus' (v. 22) and 'went out from their midst' (v. 33) is much easier understood in terms of his appearance before the Council than his standing on the hill (cf. Acts 4:7).... [The commission] exercised jurisdiction over matters of religion and morals." (Greg L. Bahnsen, "The Encounter of Jerusalem with Athens" in *Always Ready: Directions for Defending the Faith* [Texarkana, AR: Covenant Media Foundation, 1996], 16).

3. Richard L. Pratt, Jr., *Every Thought Captive: A Study Manual for the Defense of Christian Truth* (Phillipsburg, NJ: Presbyterian and Reformed, 1979), 87.

4. R.C. Sproul, *The Psychology of Atheism* (Minneapolis, MN: Bethany Fellowship, 1974), 128–29.

5. For a discussion of transcendence and immanence, see Paul G. Hiebert, R. Daniel Shaw, and Tite Tiénou, *Understanding Folk Religion: A Christian Response to Popular Beliefs and Practices* (Grand Rapids, MI: Baker Books, 1999), 47–48.

6. Ray Sutton, *That You May Prosper: Dominion By Covenant* (Tyler, TX: Dominion Press, 1987), chapter 1.

7. John Frame, "God and Biblical Language," *God's Inerrant Word: An International Symposium on the Trustworthiness of Scripture*, ed., John Warwick Montgomery (Minneapolis, MN: Bethany Fellowship, 1974), 173.

8. Bahnsen, *Always Ready*, 270–271.

9. Stephen Jay Gould, "Dorothy, It's Really Oz," *Time* (August 23, 1999), 59.

10. Gould, "Dorothy, It's Really Oz," 59.

11. Stephen Jay Gould, "Darwin's 'Big Book,'" review of *Natural Selection*, by Charles Darwin, R. C. Stauffer, ed. (New York: Cambridge University Press, 1975), in *Science* (May 23, 1975) 188:824–26. Quoted in Henry M. Morris, *That Their Words May be Used Against Them* (Green Forest, AR: Master Books, 1999), 474.

12. Michael D. Lemonick and Andrea Dorfman, "Up From the Apes: Remarkable New Evidence is Filling in the Story of How we Became Human," *Time* (August 23, 1999), 58. For an equally ridiculous hypothesis, see Michael D. Lemonick and Andrea Dorfman, "One Giant Step for Mankind," *Time* (July 23, 2001), 54-61.

13. Daniel Voll, "Soul Searching with Francis Crick," *Omni* (February 1994), 46.

14. Michael Ruse, *The Darwinian Paradigm* (London: Routledge, 1989), 268. Quoted in Paul Copan, *"True for You, Not True For Me": Deflating the Slogans that Leave Christians Speechless* (Minneapolis, MN: Bethany House Publishers, 1998), 46.

15. Ruse, *The Darwinian Paradigm*, 268.

Part Two
Worldview Basics

3

So What's A Worldview?

A worldview is a set of presuppositions (assumptions which may
be true, partially true, or entirely false) which we hold (consciously
or subconsciously, consistently or inconsistently) about the basic
makeup of our world.[1]

On October 30, 1938, America went to war with Mars! On that
Halloween evening, radio listeners were greeted by the music of Ramon
Raquello and his orchestra playing at the Meridian Room in the Hotel
Park Plaza in downtown New York. Then abruptly the music was inter-
rupted by a series of startling news bulletins:

> Ladies and gentlemen, we interrupt our program of dance
> music to bring you a special bulletin from the Intercontinental
> Radio News. At twenty minutes before eight, central time, pro-
> fessor Farrell of the Mount Jennings observatory, Chicago, Illi-
> nois, reports observing several explosions of incandescent gas,
> occurring at regular intervals on the Planet Mars.[2]

News followed that a "huge, flaming object" had fallen to Earth on
a farm in the neighborhood of Grovers Mill, New Jersey. The army was

sent to the scene. Soon a horrified radio audience heard the military personnel being destroyed by an unidentified force. More landings were reported in other parts of the country. Shocked listeners came to the frightening conclusion that Earth was the target of a full-scale invasion from inhabitants of Mars!

The "Invasion by Martians" radio broadcast had been engineered by Orson Welles and the cast of *The Mercury Theater of the Air*. "The program offered fake news reports of a Martian invasion, which a surprisingly large segment of the population took to be the truth, causing widespread panic."[3] The broadcast was so convincing and the panic so great that the "Federal Communications Commission discussed taking disciplinary action, and lawyers for some people who had believed the broadcast threatened to prosecute the Mercury."[4] The effect was so compelling and disturbing, that the FCC established new broadcast guidelines for future radio broadcasts.

War of the Worldviews

The War of the Worlds depicts a clash between *very* alien societies—one planetary world hell-bent on destroying another. The fictionalized Martian attack was relentless. Cobra-like periscopes emitted pulverizing beams of energy that ravaged the countryside. The sleek and deceptively beautiful Martian flying machines destroyed everything in their path.

A similar war rages in our own day. The invasion is not extraterrestrial in the usual sense. Alien worldviews, however, have made their way to planet Earth bringing with them even greater devastation than that depicted in the fictional *War of the Worlds*. Today's real-life battle is between the worldview of biblical Christianity where the infinite and sovereign God of the universe reigns and rules and the worldview of the many varieties of man-centered belief systems where finite and dependent creatures work to rule and reign independent of God.

Man-centered worldviews oppose the biblical worldview at every point. Truth is turned into a lie (Rom. 1:25); good becomes evil, and evil good (Isa. 5:20); darkness is substituted for light, and light for darkness (Matt. 6:23; John 3:19; Isa. 5:20); a "futile" and "depraved mind" (Eph. 4:17; Rom. 1:28) is preferred over a "renewed mind" (Rom. 12:2). "It must be emphasized that it is not just a question of the *mental* rejection of the truth, for what is involved is nothing less than the rebellion of the whole man, man in the totality of his being, mind, emotion, and will, against God. It is the refusal to give God the glory which is his due."[5]

The Bible tells us that those who parade their alien, anti-biblical worldviews "are without excuse. . . . For even though they knew God, they did not honor Him as God, or give thanks" (Rom. 1:20–21). The rejection of the sovereign God of the Bible leads to a downward spiral that begins with perverse thinking and degenerates into corrupt action. What was originally designed to be straight, man has made crooked by suppressing the truth in unrighteousness (Deut. 32:5; Psalm 125:5; Prov. 2:15; 3:32; 14:2; 17:20; 21:8; Phil. 2:15).

Understanding Worldviews

All of us think in terms of worldviews. A worldview is the way each of us looks at and evaluates everything that is seen, experienced, or thought about. Worldviews have been described as a web of beliefs that we carry around in our heads that becomes an "interconnected system of all that we believe. Tied together more or less coherently in this web are all of the beliefs we hold as true. These include the basic beliefs (such as 'I exist' and 'life is worthwhile') and the more trivial ones (such as 'I hope we won't have liver again'). No belief exists in isolation; each belief is connected with all others in one big network."[6]

Every person has a worldview that daily systematizes and organizes tens of thousands of bits of seemingly unrelated pieces of information and varied experiences. In fact, without a coherent worldview, these informational fragments would remain unrelated, disjointed, and ultimately meaningless.

> A person's worldview is the collection of his presuppositions or convictions about reality, which represent his total outlook of life. Nobody is without such fundamental beliefs, and yet many people go through life unaware of their presuppositions. Operating at the unconscious level, their presuppositions remain unidentified and unexamined. The result is that people generally fail to recognize how their world views govern every dimension of their lives: *the intellectual life* (what they believe is true about themselves and their place in history); *the physical* (how they treat or mistreat their bodies by eating, sleeping, and exercising); *the social* (how they interact with friends and enemies, the rich and the poor, the strong and the weak); *the economic* (why they work and how they spend their wages); and *the moral* (what ethical guidelines and obligations direct their thinking about justice and issues such as abortion and euthanasia).[7]

As worldviews develop and mature over time, they sort and interpret familiar information instantaneously. New information is evaluated in terms of what is already known and thought to be true. If some new facts or experiences do not fit within the boundaries of our already established worldview, they are either rejected, ignored,[8] or reinterpreted to make them conform. Someone who understands the finite nature of all creatures, might put aside any unfamiliar findings until additional information can be gathered and evaluated to make sense of the new data in light of what is already known. After some time of thoughtful consideration, adjustments might have to be made to our worldview web to accommodate the new information.

Is Life a Jigsaw Puzzle?

Secularists, humanists, and materialists give the impression that life is a gigantic jigsaw puzzle, and once they find all the necessary pieces, a coherent worldview will come together spontaneously. But there's a catch. Finite creatures can never gather all the facts. And even if they could, what pattern would they follow to put all the pieces in the right places? What are the right places? Religious skeptics tell us that they do not interpret the facts; they only discover them and make them known. The facts, we are told, speak for themselves and that there is no distinguishable predetermined "pattern" to the facts that can be known.

A pattern-less worldview is like expecting that after an hour of shaking a box of jigsaw puzzle pieces, the puzzle will somehow come together into a coherent and discernable whole. But, of course, it can never happen. Someone must show how the pieces fit. That's why a picture is put on the front of the boxes that contain the pieces. An already-established design must be followed in order to make sense of the individual pieces. Those who deny the Christian worldview refuse to believe that there is a prior design to everything that gives the pieces meaning. For example, atheistic evolutionist Richard Dawkins admits that "The world looks as though it had been designed by a master craftsman." In spite of what is obvious even to him, he rejects the assertion that the universe was designed: "We don't need to postulate a designer in order to understand life or anything else in the universe."[9] If Dawkins admits that the universe was designed in any way, he would have to make major adjustments to his worldview that acknowledges a designer.[10] And yet, Dawkins most certainly would expect that those who read his book understand that the thoughts behind the words on the pages were designed by a designer (Dawkins). The book that carries the words of the thoughts of the designer was also designed.

Worldviews Claim to be Internally Consistent

Worldviews consist of specific principles that define them. Theists believe in God, while atheists do not. We should expect to find different worldview principles in each of their belief systems that have *practical* meaning. For example, an atheist should not only have atheistic *beliefs*, but he should also *live* like an atheist. The same is true for advocates of every worldview. One would expect, for example, that those who believe in saving animals and the rain forests also would support protecting the life of unborn human children. If environmentalists believe that a whale or baby seal is important, then we have a right to ask them why they don't also emphasize the protection of defenseless *human* life. The following letter to the editor of *The Atlanta Constitution* makes the point:

> A recent editorial states "an irrational gun lobby . . . regards even sensible restraints as the death knell of private firearms ownership in America" (Bush should go further in crackdown on guns," May 16).
>
> Using this logic, I hope that you would also support the view that an irrational pro-abortion lobby regards even sensible restraints granting protection to the human fetus as the death knell of abortion rights.
>
> The so-called gun lobby and the NRA have supported a plethora of sensible laws, restaints, enforcement of existing laws and consumer education. The pro-abortion lobby gives no ground, no matter how moderate or sensible the legislation may be when it comes to protection of the unborn.[11]

If someone says that everything is relative and subject to change, he will then have to explain the absolutism and the universality of the laws of logic and anything else that does not seem to change. There is no relativist who ever conceptualizes that tomorrow water instead of oxygen might be breathable for humans. If someone says there are no ethical absolutes, he will have to demonstrate why falsifying lab reports in scientific research is forbidden or why cheating on exams is often punishable by expulsion.

Worldviews are Comprehensive

The most self-conscious worldview thinkers work diligently to fit everything into their worldview. In the words of evolutionist Daniel C. Dennett, Darwinism is "a universal solvent" that cuts "right to the heart of everything in sight."[12] Everything, according to Dennett, has meaning only as it is interpreted through an evolutionary grid of assumptions. Dennett believes this so passionately, that he proposes that anyone who holds a theistic worldview should be allowed to live in America, but only in "cultural zoos." But they would not be given freedom to speak openly about their disagreements with the new evolutionary religion enforced by the State. Their views might infect others and disturb the required comprehensiveness of the materialist worldview. If parents are allowed to teach their children that God exists, and the schools are teaching that God does not exist, this creates an intolerable contradiction that a controlled evolutionary society should not tolerate. Dennett writes:

> If you insist on teaching your children falsehoods—that the Earth is flat,[13] that "Man" is not a product of evolution by natural selection—then you must expect, at the very least, that those of us who have freedom of speech will feel free to describe your teachings as the spreading of falsehoods, and will attempt to demonstrate this to your children at our earliest opportunity. Our future well-being—the well-being of all of us on the planet— depends on the education of our descendants.[14]

Not only should the State deny the teaching of creationism in the public schools, Dennett wants the very idea of creationism to be blacklisted as a topic for discussion in public discourse. Dennett wants evolution to be the new enforced State (secular) religion. Those who deny its "divine" status will suffer swift and sure retribution at the hands of the educational establishment and the power of the State. Phillip Johnson writes, "it is not freedom of speech that worries parents, but the power of the atheistic materialists to use public education for indoctrination, while excluding any other view as 'religion.'"[15] Notice that "freedom of speech" only applies to proponents of Dennett's worldview. By "those of us," he means "those of us evolutionists" who will one day control the means of informational dissemination. "Freedom of speech" will only be granted to those who hold the correct opinions. Dennett is being scrupulously honest. If evolution is right, then anti-evolutionary worldviews are wrong, and they should be eliminated by denying their advocates access to constitutional-based forums like the First Amendment to the Constitution.

Worldviews are Exclusive

What follows from the comprehensive nature of worldviews is that they compete against one another for exclusive intellectual domination over every fact. They all work to exclude competitors, because the competitors are in error. This is as it should be. For example, Cardinal Joseph Ratzinger "expressed 'sincere respect' for other religions but attacked 'religious relativism which leads to the belief that one religion is as good as another.'"[16] If different religions hold to radically different theological assumptions about God, man, and the world, they all can't be right. They all could be wrong, but they all can't be right.

Non-Christians understand the exclusive nature of worldviews and work very hard to displace the Christian worldview at every point. If there is no God, then prayer, Bible-based laws, religious holidays, theological training in public schools, religious oaths, chaplains, and mottos like "In God We Trust" are superstitions that should not be tolerated. Arthur C. Clarke, whose various science-fiction works inspired the innovative *2001: A Space Odyssey*, expresses the exclusive nature of the atheistic worldview in non-compromising terms: "Though I am the last person to advocate laws against blasphemy, surely nothing could be more antireligious than to deny the evidence so clearly written in the rocks for all who have eyes to see!"[17] Clarke is so opposed to the notion that God created the world that he describes "creationism" as one of his "pet hates." Clarke believes that a study of the rocks will show to any "objective observer" that all we see has evolved. The Bible tells a different story: "For since the creation of the world His invisible attributes, His eternal power and divine nature, have been clearly seen, being understood through what has been made, so that they are without excuse" (Rom. 1:20). If evolution is right, then all anti-evolutionary worldviews must be wrong. To disagree is to be "antireligious," that is, anti-evolution. To believe in special creation is, in the opinion of Arthur C. Clarke, "blasphemous."

Communism, an uncompromising atheistic worldview, has always had the goal to eradicate every vestige of a theistic worldview from the universe.

> The Communist vision is the vision of Man without God. It is the vision of man's mind displacing God as the creative intelligence of the world. It is the vision of man's liberated mind, by the sole force of his rational intelligence, redirecting man's destiny and reorganizing man's life and the world. It is the vision of man, once more the central figure of the Creation, not because God made man in His image, but because man's mind makes him the most intelligent of the animals. Copernicus and his successors displaced man as the central fact of the universe by proving that the earth was not the central star of the uni-

verse. Communism restores man to his sovereignty by the simple method of denying God.[18]

Non-Christian belief systems cannot afford to allow competition by allowing religion to remain in any form. As long as people believe in a higher law and an absolute sovereign other than the State, then the new ideology can never completely win over the people to the new worldview

In Greenville, Tennessee, some Christian parents who sent their children to the government schools wanted alternative textbooks because of their inaccurate and offensive content. Here's what a syndicated columnist had to say about the parents' request:

> These poor children are being denied the most basic of childhood's freedoms, the right to imagine and learn. Someone should remind their parents the law of this land still requires we educate our children in qualified schools with qualified teachers. That a sound education involves free exploration of ideas and fact. That they may rant and rave against humanism and feminism and any other "ism" on Sunday, but come Monday the children belong in school.[19]

If atheists had their way, the Christian worldview would be relegated to the confines of the church building. A person can hold religious views, but they are to be kept private.

According to a radio editorial, "a man's religion and the strength of his conviction are his own personal matter. Religion should not interfere with politics,"[20] or anything else that is not private. What would this commentator say about the abolition of the slave trade in England and the civil rights movement in the United States? These movements were led by men and women who used religious arguments to defend their views and went public with them. For example, William Wilberforce

(1759–1833), a member of the British Parliament, upon being struck with the injustice inherent in the slave trade, wrote in his diary, "Almighty God has set before me two great objectives: The abolition of the slave trade and the reformation of manners."[21] After much opposition from those who believed that religion should be a private affair, Wilberforce's bill to end the slave trade finally passed in 1807. Had the British government "not been in the hands of Christians there seems little reason to have expected it to mount its massive, expensive, and voluntary campaign against slavery."[22] They put their religious convictions into action to compete with the prevailing worldview that believed that slavery was just.

Of course, the Christian worldview should be working to displace non-Christian worldviews through reasoned arguments and reliance upon the Holy Spirit. A Christian is to destroy "speculations and every lofty thing raised up against the knowledge of God" (2 Cor. 10:5). In principle, there is never any room for compromise. (In practice, however, both a believer and an unbeliever can work together to stop abortion, help the poor, or build a hospital. Why? The unbeliever is working within the Christian's worldview, presupposing that these efforts are worthy of attention even though in principle they contradict the basic assumptions of the unbeliever's worldview.)

Worldviews are Transformational

Worldviews are seen as vehicles for cultural transformation. Many in the entertainment field believe, for example, that they are the nation's conscience and the only guiding light for change. Francis Ford Coppola, best known for the critically acclaimed *Godfather* trilogy, believes that only artists like himself can bring about a transformed world:

> My dream is that the artist class—people who have proven through their work that they are humanists and wish to push

for what Aldous Huxley called the desirable human potentialities of intelligence, creativity and friendliness—will seize the instrument of technology and try to take humanity into a period of history in which we can reach for a utopia. Of course, it is possible for the technology to be misused—we could end up with a Big Brother—but we could also have a balanced society, with an artist class leading the culture toward something approximating a happy family or tribe.

At the moment, the nation is in a fog, and we've got to put our headlights on. Artists—those who rely on their intuition—can be the nation's headlights.[23]

An artist's "intuition" is the presupposed authority for Coppola to bring about this new world. If the film industry is any indication of what we can expect from the artist class, we are in big trouble.

Coppola's transformational optimism, based on the premise that man—either individually or collectively—is the standard, has been tried before. H. G. Wells, the author of numerous popular science fiction thrillers such as *The Time Machine*, *War of the Worlds*, and *The Invisible Man*, described a period of "evolutionary idealism, faith in progress, and complete optimism."[24] He proposed that world leaders should create "a common world religion" that was not linked to Christianity or any other theistic religion.[25] This new man-made world religion would derive its power from a new god, a world government run by world statesmen. "Our true State, this state that is already beginning, this state to which every man owes his utmost political effort, must be now this nascent [beginning] Federal World State to which human necessities point. Our true God now is the God of all men. Nationalism as a God must follow the tribal gods to limbo. Our true nationality is mankind."[26]

But it wasn't long before his optimism turned to despair. Shortly before his death in 1946, Wells wrote *The Mind at the End of Its Tether*, an aptly titled book that was filled with numbing hopelessness: "The

end of everything we call life is close at hand and cannot be evaded. . . .
The writer is convinced that there is no way out or round or through
the impasse. It is the end."[27] Wells had nothing to offer. Bound by his
atheistic presuppositions, he could only conclude that there is "no compelling argument to convince the reader that he should not be cruel or
mean or cowardly."[28] What would fill the void? Wells did not have an
answer. All of his self-appointed gods had failed him.

Worldviews are Distorted

All worldviews are distorted to some degree because of sin and our
inability to know everything in a comprehensive way. Our fallen nature
as well as the fallen world in which we live require that we look to a
fixed standard outside ourselves to put the world of ideas in focus for
us. Sin, with all of its potential for distortion, is not the deathblow to
developing an operating and viable worldview. This point is emphasized by philosopher George Mavrodes:

> Providing a man with a conceptual framework in which he
> can see his whole life as being lived in the presence of God is
> analogous to teaching a man to read a strange script. We can
> give him a key, a sort of Rosetta stone, by telling him the mean-
> ing of one particular inscription. If he believes us he can then
> understand that inscription. But the test of whether he has re-
> ally learned how to read the script, and also the confirmation
> that the translation we gave him was accurate, comes when he
> encounters all the other inscriptions that are scattered through
> this world. If he cannot read them, then he has not yet learned
> that language and is still subject to the doubt that what we gave
> him may not have been the translation at all, but rather a mes-
> sage quite unrelated to what was written. He may even doubt
> that any of the inscriptions are linguistic affairs at all. They may,
> perhaps, consist merely of glacial scratches. But if he finds that

he can read the new inscriptions, if they make sense, if, in fact, he can correspond with those who write that language, and communicate with them, then he has learned that language. And every successful communication increases his grasp of it and also his confidence in it.[29]

The Rosetta Stone analogy is a good way to understand worldviews. The slab of black basalt stone was unearthed by one of Napoleon's officers near the town of Rosetta in northern Egypt in 1799. With its discovery, many of the mysteries of Egyptian society and culture were solved. Carved in Egypt around 200 B.C., the hard marble-like stone includes "a message inscribed in hieroglyphic (at the top), demotic, another lost Egyptian script (in the middle), and Greek (at the bottom). With the aid of the familiar Greek the other two lost Egyptian modes of writing were deciphered."[30]

In a similar way, God has given us a revelatory Rosetta Stone—the Bible—to direct our understanding of Himself, ourselves, the world in which we live, and how we should live in the world He created for us. Without the Bible, we are left to speculate what we *think* is true and right. Such a reading of the world would be like trying to decipher hieroglyphics without a translator.

Conclusion

The construction and exercise of a worldview is inevitable. While the worldview of one person might be developed through study and diverse experiences, and the worldview of another might be undeveloped because of a lack of education and life experiences, they each share a common method of looking at life. They cannot escape evaluating life in terms of their worldview.

Notes

1. James W. Sire, *The Universe Next Door: A Basic World View Catalog*, 3rd ed. (Downers Grove, IL: InterVarsity Press, 1997), 17–18.

2. An account of this famous radio program can be found in Charles Higham, *Orson Welles: The Rise and Fall of an American Genius* (New York: St. Martin's Press, 1985), 123–28. These extraterrestrial villains had earlier debuted in H. G. Wells' classic sci-fi thriller *The War of the Worlds*. A movie version came to the screen in 1958.

3. Scott Siegel and Barbara Siegel, *The Encyclopedia of Hollywood: An A-to-Z of the Heroes, Heroines, and History of American Film* (New York: Facts on File, 1990), 453.

4. Higham, *Orson Welles*, 128.

5. Philip Edgcumbe Hughes, "Crucial Biblical Passages for Christian Apologetics," in *Jerusalem and Athens: Critical Discussions on the Philosophy and Apologetics of Cornelius Van Til*, ed. E.R. Geehan (Nutley, NJ: Presbyterian and Reformed, 1971), 136.

6. Winfried Corduan, *No Doubt About It: The Case for Christianity* (Nashville, TN: Broadman & Holman Publishers, 1997), 66.

7. W. Andrew Hoffecker, "Preface: Perspective and Method in Building a World View," *Building a Christian World View: God, Man, and Knowledge* (Phillipsburg, NJ: Presbyterian and Reformed, 1986), ix–x.

8. For example, Planned Parenthood's purposeful non-response to George Grant's *Grand Illusions: The Legacy of Planned Parenthood*, 4th ed. (Nashville, TN: Cumberland House, 2000), xxvi–xxx.

9. Richard Dawkins, *The Blind Watchmaker: Why the Evidence of Evolution Reveals a Universe Without Design* (New York: W.W. Norton, 1986), 147.

10. William Lane Craig, *Reasonable Faith: Christian Truth and Apologetics*, rev. ed. (Wheaton, IL: Crossway Books, 1994), 170–171.

11. Grant Essex, "Pro-abortion crowd is as irrational as pro-gun lobby," *The Atlanta Constitution* (May 18, 2001), A18. The title given to the writer's letter was added by the paper's editorial staff. The writer was not implying that the "gun lobby" is "irrational" for the simple reason that it *does* support "a plethora of sensible laws," etc.

12. Daniel C. Dennett, *Darwin's Dangerous Idea: Evolution and the Meaning of Life* (New York: Simon and Schuster, 1995), 521.

13. The debate between Christopher Columbus and his critics was not over whether the Earth was flat or round but how big around it was. On this point, Columbus was wrong. There were no flat-Earth advocates of any reputation in the fifteenth century. See Gary DeMar, *America's Christian History: The Untold Story* (Atlanta, GA: American Vision, 1995), 221–34; Gary DeMar and Fred Douglas Young, *To Pledge Allegiance: A New World in View* (Atlanta, GA: American Vision, 1996), 75–82; Jeffrey Burton Russell, *Inventing the Flat Earth: Columbus and Modern Historians* (New York: Praeger, 1991).

14. Dennett, *Darwin's Dangerous Idea*, 519.

15. Quoted in Phillip E. Johnson, "Daniel Dennett's Dangerous Idea," *The New Criterion* (October 1995), 13.

16. Peggy Polk, "Vatican: Other faiths 'defective,'" *Atlanta Constitution* (September 8, 2000), B5.

17. Arthur C. Clarke, Foreword, in James Randi, *An Encyclopedia of Claims, Frauds, and Hoaxes of the Occult and Supernatural* (New York: St. Martin's Press, 1995), xii.

18. Whittaker Chambers, *Witness* (New York: Random House, 1952), 9–10.

19. Rheta Grimsley Johnson, "'People' vs. Fundamentalists," *The Marietta Daily Journal* (September 2, 1986), 4A.

20. A portion of a radio editorial heard over WGST Radio in Atlanta, Georgia, on September 9, 1986.

21. Quoted in Charles Colson, *Kingdoms in Conflict* (Grand Rapids, MI: Zondervan, 1987), 100.

22. Otto J. Scott, *The Secret Six: John Brown and the Abolitionist Movement* (New York: Times Books, 1979), 85.

23. "A Conversation With Francis Coppola," *U.S. News and World Report* (April 5, 1982), 68.

24. Herbert Schlossberg, *Idols for Destruction: Christian Faith and its Confrontation with American Society* (Wheaton, IL: Crossway Books, [1983] 1993), 2.

25. H. G. Wells, *The Outline of History: Being a Plain History of Life and Mankind*, 3rd ed. (New York: The Macmillan Company, 1921), 1093.

26. Wells, *The Outline of History*, 1087.

27. H. G. Wells, *Mind at the End of Its Tether* and *The Happy Turning: A Dream of Life* (New York: Didier, 1946), 1, 4

28. Wells, *The Mind at the End of Its Tether*, 18.

29. George Mavrodes, *Belief in God: A Study in the Epistemology of Religion* (New York: Random House, 1970), 86–87.

30. Charles Adams, *For Good and Evil: The Impact of Taxes on the Course of Civilization* (Lanham, MD: Madison Books, 1993), 17.

4

Worldview Building Blocks

PHILOSOPHY I: (Prerequisite—five hours of sitting around doing nothing). Philosophy I is where you learn how the great thinkers of the past view man's existence, such as Descartes who said, "I think, therefore I am." It turns out he was right because he stopped thinking a while back, and now he no longer is![1]

Many Christians seem to believe that thinking is an act of unbelief. They do not even begin to understand how the Bible might apply, for example, to science, economics, politics, law, or education. They might have *opinions* about these topics but no formulated, thought-out *biblical* worldview. Their opinions are not rooted in any biblical framework of thinking. The same is true when abstract philosophical concepts are brought up for discussion. It just doesn't seem to be "spiritual" to discuss philosophy, even though the word means "the love of wisdom." And as any student of the Bible knows, wisdom is a prized possession (Prov. 2:2; 3:13). The Bible objects to a "philosophy" that is based upon "the traditions of men" (Col. 2:8). The Christian's faith does not rest on "the wisdom of men" (1 Cor. 2:4) or "the appearance of wisdom in self-made religion" (Col. 2:23). There are two types of wisdom: wisdom that is "from above" (James 3:13, 17) and that which is "earthly, natural, and demonic" (3:15). The Christian should develop a biblical philosophy, a love for wisdom that acknowledges that God is the source of all true knowledge.

Engaging the Mind

The mind is like the body. When it isn't pushed into service, it does as little as possible to function. But when concentrated critical thinking is demanded, an untrained, atrophied mind behaves like an out-of-shape body—it falters under the demands of rigorous mental activity. Getting the mind into mental shape is no less difficult than getting the body into top physical condition. Progress is slow and often imperceptible. Incremental change is not very rewarding, but it's the only way to achieve long-term success. Building a "renewed mind" will take time and discipline, but the rewards will be worth it. The best place to start is at the beginning. The Bible tells us that "because of practice" our senses will be "trained to discern good and evil" (Heb. 5:14). Such training will help us to distinguish straight thinking from twisted thinking.

Four Foundation Stones

Worldviews are constructed like houses. A foundation must first be laid before the walls can go up. Four of the most basic foundation stones are principles dealing with material reality (**physics**), questions touching on the different types of things that exist (**metaphysics**), how we attain knowledge (**epistemology**), and ways in which right and wrong are determined (**ethics**). Every worldview, whether theistic or atheistic or any variety of the two, includes these four components. They are necessarily interrelated. Discussions of everything from the origin of man to what happens after death must take place within these four realms.

Physics: Accounting for What's Here

Physics deals with what exists in material form. "The physicist thinks about what exists and how it works; he also seeks to understand reality, from the possibly infinite vastness of the Universe down to the infinitesimal particles that form the substructure of the atom."[2] While many modern physicists dismiss God as the cause of the physical universe, Isaac Newton and Albert Einstein, to name just two examples, "accepted the idea of the existence of God as creator of the Universe." Richard P. Feynman, who was a professor of theoretical physics at the California Institute of Technology, "considers it more likely that the cosmos developed through random physical processes." He assumes that "nature is governed by mathematical rules which must be found by the physicist."[3] Of course, Feynman is not making a *scientific* claim. There is no way to *prove* his assertion. His conclusion about the origin of the universe is based on a series of first-principles—presuppositions—which he has adopted without regard to scientific investigation.

Feynman and others who maintain that the material world is all there is—that physics is everything—have a serious problem. They cannot account for entities like the principles of mathematics because mathematics has no material substance, no physical properties. For example, numbers do not exist as material shapes. They can't be seen or felt. Drawn numbers on a sheet of paper are merely symbols for numerical concepts. Mathematicians can write numeric *symbols* (1, 2, 3, 4, etc.) and formulas ($E=MC^2$), but these aren't the numbers and formulas themselves. How can the physicist *find* "mathematical rules" that govern mathematical axioms in a physics-only world? He can explain the nature of the rules, but the rules themselves do not exist in physical form. Even the explanation of the rules has no material content. All materialists know this, yet they have no problem trusting the trustworthiness of mathematics.

The opposite extreme is to claim, as some eastern religions teach, that what we think we perceive as a material universe is really an illusion ("maya"), a projection of our mind.[4] Both God's revelation—"In the beginning God created the heavens and the earth" (Gen. 1:1)—and everyday experiences inform us that such absurd notions just don't conform to reality. People who claim this world is illusory and transient still walk through open doors and hold their breath when swimming under water.

The Christian's apologetic task is to press those who claim that "physics is all there is" to account for the physical universe and the non-physical entities they use to formulate their worldview. Therefore, a discussion of physical things is an important starting point in a Christian's apologetic task because every worldview must account for what's here.

Metaphysics: Determining Ultimate Reality

Metaphysics is made up of two Greek words *meta* (after) and *physis* (physical). In the simplest terms, metaphysics deals with concepts which are beyond the physical. The word was derived from the naming of a collection of works written by the Greek philosopher Aristotle (384–323 B.C.). In the first century B.C., Andronicus of Rhodes named the books which appeared after Aristotle's works on *Physics*. He simply designated them *Metaphysics* (*meta ta physika*), that is, the works that Aristotle had written "after" he wrote his books that dealt with "physical" properties.

In time, the term has come to mean "beyond" the physical, certainly an appropriate word, since the metaphysician asks questions that are outside the realm where things can be seen, felt, and measured with scientific instruments.[5] Metaphysics asks questions like: What is it to exist and what *sorts* of things exist? Does God exist? What is the relationship between God and the universe? Is the universe eternal? Did an eternal, personal, and omnipotent God create the world? Is the cosmos

physical, spiritual, both, or something else? "Is the universe a self-en-
closed system in the sense that everything that happens is caused by and
thus explained by other events within the system? Or can a supernatural reality (a being beyond nature) act causally within nature? Are miracles
possible?"[6] A person asking metaphysical questions seeks the *ultimate
causes or explanations* for the existence and nature of things. He wants to
understand the limits of possible reality, the modes of existing, and the
interrelationship of existing things.

Epistemology: Determining How and What We Know

Epistemology, the theory of knowledge, from two Greek words
episteme (knowledge) and *logos* (study of), addresses questions of how
we know what we know, including abilities and limitations of the one
seeking knowledge. Is knowledge about the world possible? Can we
trust our senses? What are the proper functions of reason (rationality)
and sense experience (empiricism) in knowledge? Is truth relative, or
must truth be the same for all rational beings? Is knowledge about God
possible? Can God reveal Himself to human beings? These are *epistemological* questions.

Philosophers have debated epistemological questions for centuries.
As one might expect, there are various ways philosophers claim we can
know something. The empiricist asserts that we know through our five
senses, the rationalist through reason, the idealist through the mind or
consciousness, the existentialist through personal experience, the
phenomenologist through perception, the mystic through the inner
being. The agnostic claims that we can't know anything, even though
he seems to know that he can't know.

Epistemology is the most critical aspect of worldview thinking. Logically speaking, epistemology comes before anything else. If we have no
way of being sure what we know is true and foundational, nothing else

can be known. Maybe the world is an illusion after all. Knowing is the key. It is not accidental that the Bible begins with "In the beginning God" (Gen. 1:1), and the Gospel of John opens with "In the beginning was the Word" (John 1:1). God, the world, and those created in His image can only be understood when we *presuppose* that God exists, the Bible is true, and it gives us true knowledge of everything upon which it speaks, and it speaks to everything. God communicates to us through the revelation of His written Word and the revelation of the incarnate Word. This is the true starting point for a sound epistemology.

Ethics: Determining What's Right and Wrong

Ethics is concerned with the question of why any particular action is right or wrong. Are there moral laws that govern human conduct? What are they? Are these moral laws the same for all human beings? Is morality relative? Are moral laws discovered like mathematical formulas, or are they constructed by human beings? Is morality relative to individuals or to cultures or to historical periods? A person's ethical beliefs are based on his epistemological and metaphysical beliefs. Barbara Reynolds, a columnist for *USA Today*, shows that there are ethical implications to one's choice of worldviews. A person's choice of presuppositions will determine how he chooses to live:

> Prohibiting the teaching of creationism in favor of evolution creates an atheistic, belligerent tone that might explain why our kids sometimes perform like Godzilla instead of children made in the image of God.
>
> While evolution teaches that we are accidents or freaks of nature, creationism shows humankind as the offspring of a divine Creator. There are rules to follow which govern not only our time on Earth, but also our afterlife.
>
> * * * * *

If evolution is forced on our kids, we shouldn't be perplexed when they beat on their chests or, worse yet, beat on each other and their teachers.[7]

Reynolds's comments are reminiscent of what C.S. Lewis wrote: "We make men without chests and we expect of them virtue and enterprise. We laugh at honor and we are shocked to find traitors in our midst. We castrate and bid the geldings be fruitful."[8] We strip men and women of the certainty that they are created in the image of God, and we are surprised when they act like the beasts of the field. Of course, the ethical dimension of a person's worldview naturally flows from the metaphysical and epistemological elements. Morality does not rise from a worldview vacuum.

Jeffrey S. Purinton, professor of philosophy at the University of Oklahoma and an admitted atheist, disagrees with the assertion that "if there is no God, there can be no moral truths." He claims that "one has a moral obligation to fulfill one's promises, whether or not God exists."[9] Why? Who says? He never explains how the fulfillment of a moral obligation is required in a world without God. He simply asserts the notion of moral obligation without demonstrating how it's possible or necessary. The professor is engaged in a vicious circular argument: We are morally obligated because we are morally obligated. Purinton assumes to be true what he must *prove* to be true. What's true of moral laws and the justification for their existence is equally true of natural laws and the explanation for their existence and consistency. To say that the world works the way it works because that's the way the world works says nothing meaningful. Why does it work this way? A materialist has no answer that he can formulate that is consistent with his naturalistic assumptions.

Worldview Assumptions

In addition to the foundation stones of all worldviews, it is necessary at this point to discuss the framework of worldviews. This means distinguishing among theories (which are subject to change), operating assumptions (the everyday use of taken-for-granted beliefs about our world), and ultimate presuppositions (essential first-principles that are necessary to make sense of everything).

Theories, Hypotheses, Models, and Laws

Theories are the backbone of the scientific method. Through testing, study, and experimentation scientists determine whether a theory can be validated. Once validated, what started out as a hypothesis becomes a "scientific law," although it can never really be carved into stone. After reaching this status, these tested laws are used for future problem solving. They are treated as necessary starting points in doing further scientific study. Scientists who are engaged in experimental work assume the reliability of the earlier studies. An engineer designing a rocket does not have to run experiments to determine if there are gravitational forces. He works with an already established body of scientific knowledge of what is understood about gravity. The process goes something like this:

> What a scientist does is to examine certain phenomena in the world. He then casts about for an explanation that will make sense of these phenomena. This is the hypothesis. But the hypothesis has to be checked. So a careful checking operation is set up, designed to see if there is, in fact, a correspondence between what has been observed and what has been hypothesized. If it does correspond, a scientist accepts the explanation as correct; if it does not, he rejects it as false and looks for an alternative explanation. Depending on how substantially the statement has been "verified," it becomes accepted as a "law" within science, such as the law of gravity or the second law of thermodynamics.[10]

What is it about our world that assures us that what is true today in regard to a scientific law will be true tomorrow? There must be a set of governing principles that scientists assume to be true that make discovery and formulation of laws possible and reliable. These principles, assumptions about reality that we take for granted and use without thinking, seem always to have been with us. Where do they come from? What makes them reliable? Since they do not exist in tangible form (e.g., there is no actual law of gravity that someone can touch), how can they exist for a materialist who believes that everything that exists has to consist of some material substance in order to be real?

Operating Assumptions

Operating assumptions are, by definition, more fundamental and necessary than theories, models, and scientific laws. Before science can get started in proposing theories, certain assumptions about the way the world works must be assumed to be valid and operationally consistent. Isaac Newton's encounter with a falling apple and the theories that followed did not immediately change the way people lived. Everyone knew the effect of gravity, even though they did not always understand all of its characteristics and functions or give the "scientific law" a name. When people stepped outside, they never considered that they would float away. Rain always fell *down* from a cloud-filled sky, and sailors knew the daily change in the tides. Water was wet, and when it got cold enough, it froze, even if no one knew the freezing point of water.

For millennia, people from around the globe *operated* in terms of these *assumptions* even though they did not always comprehend them theoretically or scientifically. They came to be designated "natural laws," the "laws of nature," or the "laws of Nature's God." These universal laws operated predictably because the majority of people—scientists included—accepted that they were God's laws, established and upheld by Him: "And [Jesus] is the radiance of [God's] glory and the exact representation of His nature, *and upholds all things by the word of His power*" (Heb. 1:3). It is in Jesus, the Bible says, that "*all things hold together*" (Col. 1:17). "It has even been suggested that such a view played a key role in the successful development of science in the Western cultures, and did so because they were influenced by the Judaeo-Christian tradition which fostered faith in the underlying rationality and orderliness of Nature during periods of history when human ideas were inbred by all manner of magical and occult notions."[11]

Life is predictable because God is predictable. Even those who did not embrace a *biblical* worldview knew that they could not develop an ordered world without the shared belief that God was necessary to make it happen.

> That there is a 'natural order' . . . in the world, cleverly and expertly designed by God for the guidance of mankind; that the 'laws' of this natural order may be discovered by human reason; that these laws so discovered furnish a reliable and immutable standard for testing ideas, the conduct, and the institutions of men—these were the accepted premises, the preconceptions, of most eighteenth century thinking, not only in America but also in England and France. They were, as [Thomas] Jefferson says, the 'sentiments of the day, whether expressed in conversation, in letters, printed essays, or the elementary books of public right.' Where Jefferson got his ideas is hardly so much a question as where he could have got away from them.[12]

In cultures where progress was made in mathematics, science, medicine, political theory, and law, people assumed that the world was not an illusion, that truth mattered, and man was a rational being created by a rational God even though at times man behaved irrationally and believed irrational things. Cultures that believed that spirits inhabited trees, rocks, and animals made very little progress culturally and scientifically because they never knew what the spirits might do. There was never a guarantee that what people did one day could be repeated on another day. They were at the mercy of what they believed were impersonal forces controlled by capricious gods who were always changing the rules.

> Pagan religions are typically animistic or pantheistic, treating the natural world either as the abode of the divine or as an emanation of God's own essence. The most familiar form of animism holds that spirits or gods reside in nature. In the words of Harvey Cox, a Baptist theologian, pagan man "lives in an enchanted forest." Glens and groves, rocks and streams are alive with spirits, sprites, demons. Nature teems with sun gods, river goddesses, astral deities.[13]

These false operational assumptions meant that the world could not be studied in a reliable and systematic way. "As long as nature commands religious worship, dissecting her is judged impious. As long as the world is charged with divine beings and powers, the only appropriate response is to supplicate them or ward them off."[14] As a result, technological, medical, scientific, and moral progress came to a standstill in cultures where people could not agree on basic operating assumptions of how and why things work the way they do.

The Ultimate Presupposition

In the Christian worldview, there is a reason why scientific laws, theories, and operational assumptions like the "laws of nature" function with reliability. Behind them we find a network of fundamental first principles established and governed by God. "This God is not a fact of the universe, or the mere force behind the universe. He is not something whose existence may be questioned or denied while we yet come to true conclusions about the facts of the universe. The God of the Bible is necessary to the existence of all the facts of the universe. He created them and only in Him can they have their true meaning."[15] The world works the way it does because God established it that way.

Conclusion

All worldviews share the same elementary building blocks. They differ only in the content. Every worldview must be explained in terms of how to account for the world in which we live, the fundamental principles of reality, how we know what we know, and how we live. Accounting for these building blocks is a necessary first step in the development of any worldview and the eventual defense of the Christian worldview.

Notes

1. From the comic strip "Funky Winkerbean" by Tom Batiuk, Field Enterprises, 1980.

2. Jefferson Hane Weaver, *The World of Physics: A Small Library of the Literature of Physics from Antiquity to the Present*, 3 vols. (New York: Simon and Schuster, 1987), 1:29.

3. Weaver, *The World of Physics*, 34. Feynman's "random physical processes" are explained as "something like a great chess game being played by the gods." (Feynman, "Basic Physics," in *The Feynman Lectures on Physics* [Reading, MA: Addison-Wesley, 1963], 2:2. Quoted in Weaver, *The World of Physics*, 37).

4. See Charles S. Braden, "Maya," *Encyclopedia of Religion*, ed. Vergilius Ferm (New York: Philosophical Library, 1945), 477; Josh McDowell and Don Stewart, *Handbook of Today's Religions* (San Bernardino, CA: Here's Life Publishers, 1983), 288–289.

5. "Metaphysics is thus distinguished from physics by its generality; whereas the assertion 'Heat causes expansion of gases' refers to particular facts, which can be tested, the assertion 'Every event has a cause' is part of Metaphysics for it is supposed to be true of absolutely every event." (Keith Ward, *Fifty Key Words in Philosophy* [Richmond, VA: John Knox Press, 1968], 44).

6. Ronald H. Nash, *Life's Ultimate Questions: An Introduction to Philosophy* (Grand Rapids, MI: Zondervan, 1999), 15.

7. Barbara Reynolds, "If your kids go ape in school, you'll know why," *USA Today* (August 27, 1993), 11A.

8. C. S. Lewis, *The Abolition of Man* (New York: Macmillan, [1947] 1972), 35.

9. Jeffrey S. Purinton, "Letters to the Editor," *U.S. News & World Report* (November 13, 2000), BC-55.

10. Francis A. Schaeffer, *Whatever Happened to the Human Race?* in *The Complete Works of Francis Schaeffer: A Christian Worldview*, 5 vols. (Westchester, IL: Crossway Books, 1984), 5:359. For further discussion of this topic, see Charles E. Hummel, *The Galileo Connection: Resolving Conflicts between Science and the Bible* (Downers Grove, IL: InterVarsity Press, 1986), 179–197.

11. John D. Barrow, *The World Within the World* (Oxford, England: Clarendon Press, 1988), 23.

12. Carl Becker, *The Declaration of Independence: A Study in the History of Political Ideas* (New York: Alford A. Knopf, 1951), 26–27.

13. Nancy R. Pearcey and Charles B. Thaxton, *The Soul of Science: Christian Faith and Natural Philosophy* (Wheaton, IL: Crossway Books, 1994), 23–24.

14. Pearcey and Thaxton, *The Soul of Science*, 24.

15. Alan Cairns, "Presuppositionalism," *Dictionary of Theological Terms* (Greenville, SC: Emerald House Group, Inc., 1998), 275.

5

Worldviews in Conflict

It is sadly ironic that the basic features of the naturalistic worldview, which so many people in the formerly Marxist nations are now
rejecting, remain attractive to great numbers of educated people
in the West. One major reason for this, I am convinced, is that few
Americans have been taught to think in terms of worldviews. They do
not know what a worldview is; they could not spell out the content of
their own worldview if their lives depended upon it; they are unaware
of how various aspects of conflicting worldviews clash logically.[1]

The foundation of a proper study of God, the universe, and man is God and His revelation, not man and his ideas about God. There are all types of descriptions of "god" floating around—from Aristotle's Prime Mover to the New Age belief that god is a part of all of us and we are a part of god, a jazzed up version of pantheism, the belief that all (*pan*) is god (*theos*). Our move into this third millennium has prompted some to "work together to find a new image of God." Desmond Tutu, former archbishop of South Africa and Nobel Peace Prize winner, asserts that "No religion can claim to have the whole truth about the mystery of faith."[2] What standard will these god-makers use to fashion their new deity? Our description of God, therefore, must go beyond the mere belief in *a* god; we must base our appeals to truth on the one *true* God. This true knowledge comes from the Bible. Scripture defines God for us.

A pluralist does not like the idea that there is an exclusive God with an exclusive law and an exclusive way of salvation. If we're going to have religion, the pluralist asserts, then all gods and religions should be equal. Logically, of course, this is nonsense. R. Albert Mohler, Jr., exposes the irrationality of those who allege that Christians are wrong to bring the gospel message of salvation in Jesus Christ to Jews and other people of different faiths:

> Abraham Foxman, national director of the Anti-Defamation League, argues that it is "pure arrogance" for any religion to claim to know "the truth." But most religions, in one way or another, make this claim: It is the nature of religious belief, which stands precisely against today's cultural relativism. It is certainly at the heart of Christian belief. After all, we are followers of the one Who said: "I am the Way, the Truth, and the Life" [John 14:6].[3]

Following the logic of the pluralist, should we also insist that all views of mathematics, science, geology, ethics, and everything else for that matter, should be regarded as equal statements of belief and practice even when their stated principles contradict one another? Would a religious pluralist in need of a heart transplant accept the contradictory views of four heart surgeons who each claim that one procedure is just as good as any other? I doubt it. And yet, a high percentage of people are willing to live with religious contradictions even though they rarely if ever practice them in their daily lives.

Avoiding the Dilemma

The naturalist avoids the pluralist dilemma by maintaining that there are no gods. This is hardly a solution. By claiming to reject all gods, the self-proclaimed atheist makes himself, some principle, or the cosmos itself a new god. For example, the worldview of naturalism[4] teaches that nature is the whole of reality. Technically, what is studied by the techniques of natural science is all that there is, so there is no need for exploration that goes beyond the observable universe. Everything has its origin in matter and thus has no real existence apart from it and should not be explained in any other terms. There is no "mind," for example. Thought is reduced to chemical reactions of brain tissue. Values are culturally determined and are therefore always in flux. Religion and the idea of God are the projections of people who want to believe in something beyond what they can see.

A worldview that is synonymous with naturalism is secularism. A secularist is someone who "is completely time-bound, totally a child of his age, a creature of history, with no vision of eternity. Unable to see anything in the perspective of eternity, he cannot believe God exists or acts in human affairs."[5] The English word "secular" is derived from *saeculum*, a Latin term that "refers to this world's temporal dimension, the 'now' of the 'here and now' (*hic et nunc*),"[6] and only the here and now.

This one-dimensional view of life is not a new phenomenon. The secularists of biblical times expressed it this way: "For there is nothing good for a man under the sun except to eat and to drink and to be merry" (Eccl. 8:15; cf. 10:19; Luke 12:19). If there is nothing beyond the grave, then "let us eat and drink, for tomorrow we die" (1 Cor. 15:32; cf. Isa. 22:13; 56:12). The Christian worldview does not reject this world or the things of this world as evil. All that God created is good (Gen. 1:31). All that we do should be evaluated in terms of God's Word. "Whether, then, you eat or drink *or whatever you do*, do all to the glory of God" (1 Cor. 10:31). Since there is no afterlife and no authority greater than the individual for the naturalist, worldly pleasure without the threat of consequences in either this life or the next are man's only reasonable pursuits.

For secularism, all life, every human value, every human activity must be understood in light of this present time. The secularist either flatly denies or remains utterly skeptical about the eternal. He either says there is no eternal or if there is we can know nothing about it. What matters is *now* and only *now*. All access to the above and beyond is *blocked*. There is no exit from the confines of this present world. The secular is all that we have. We must make our decisions, live our lives, make our plans, all within the closed arena of this time—the here and now.[7]

The following proposition is fundamental to the naturalistic or secular worldview: "As non-theists, we begin with humans, not God, nature not deity. Nature may indeed be broader and deeper than we now know; and new discoveries, however, will but enlarge our knowledge of the natural."[8] A significant question remains: How does the naturalist *know* for a certainty that any of what he believes is true since he is finite and fallible, and he is never sure that what's true today will be true tomorrow? The following ten presuppostions demonstrate the futility of embracing the worldview of natural with any type of consistency and intellectual integrity.

I. The universe is self-existent and solitary

There are various theories about the origin of the physical universe. One theory proposes that the cosmos "originated in a single cataclysmic explosion some ten or twenty billion years ago."[9] A super dense "cosmic egg" exploded and expanded its matter into what we call the cosmos. One day in the far distant future, the stuff of the universe will collapse in on itself and repeat the process. Others disagree, concluding that "the universe has existed for an infinite time—without beginning or end."[10] In either case, the universe just is. Scientists can only study it in its present form. There is no "why" in a scientific study of the cosmos.

Naturalists have no way to account for the existence of the universe, and their assumptions about its origin must be taken on faith. While the universe can be studied in present time, only guesses can be made concerning its origin. For example, Eric J. Lerner, who believes the universe is infinite, admits that "it is not possible to *prove* scientifically that the universe is infinite. But it is quite possible to claim we have no observational evidence that it is finite."[11] Lerner presuppositionally limits "observational evidence" to his own definitional framework. God is not "observational evidence" in Lerner's way of thinking. On the contrary, "that which is known about God is evident with them; for God made it evident to them. For since the creation of the world His invisible attributes, His eternal power and divine nature, have been clearly seen, being understood through what has been made, so that they are without excuse" (Rom. 1:19–20).

The biblical view is that the universe was created by God at a point in time, "in the beginning" (Gen. 1:1). The writer of Hebrews tells us that "by faith we understand that the worlds were prepared by the word of God, so that what is seen was not made of things which are visible" (Heb. 11:3). Any study of the universe and its parts reflects the attributes and purpose of God as the Creator. This means that the created order is rational, explainable, predictable, useful, and intelligible, but only the Christian can explain why. "Non believers may hear all the notes of science, but without the theistic context and perspective they will not hear the song."[12]

2. Matter is all there is

Since there is no personal God beyond, in, or over the universe, then matter is the whole ball of wax. There is no spirit, soul, or mind. With the advent of the computer, materialists believe they have found the perfect scientific mechanism to demonstrate that the notion of a mind has been concocted out of primitive religious assumptions. Since religion is mythological, so is the mind. "The machinists' model of consciousness is the computer; they see the brain as a superior model, somewhat more versatile than the industrial-strength Cray super-computer."[13] The machinists' computer analogy is faulty, however. The machine is nothing without the program. The program is nothing without the programmer. Where did the programmer come up with the ability to put together a program? Who designed and built the computer?

Philosopher Daniel Dennett presupposes that "the mind is somehow nothing but a physical phenomenon. In short, the mind is the brain."[14] "The brain," insists MIT's Marvin Minsky, in equally presuppositional fashion, is just "hundreds of different machines . . . connected to each other by bundles of nerve fibers, but not everything is connected to everything else. There isn't a 'you.'"[15] To these pure naturalists, humans are nothing more than organic machines.

On the contrary, man is inescapably related to God in a way that separates him from the rest of the created order. Man is more valuable than the "birds of the air" (Matt. 6:26) and the "lilies of the field" (6:28–30). Man is a special creation, not because he has a mind, but rather, man has a mind because he is a special creation. Man has been made "a little lower than God" (Psalm 8:5). Such a ranking puts man in a position of rulership over the rest of the created order, including, but not limited to, "all sheep and oxen, and also the beasts of the field, the birds of the heavens, and the fish of the sea, whatever passes through the paths of the seas" (Prov. 8:7–8).

Animals react to and are motivated by rewards and punishments instead of by reasoned arguments: "A whip is for the horse, a bridle for the donkey" (Prov. 26:3a). God never says to the animals, "Come, let us reason together" (Isa. 1:18). Image bearers of God are instructed not to "be as the horse or as the mule *which have no understanding*, whose trappings include bit and bridle to hold them in check" (Psalm 32:9).

3. The universe is evolving with no predictable pattern

What we see today may not act in the same way tomorrow. Chance "dictates" the direction the universe will take. Man may not be the highest of evolved animals in one hundred thousand years. A *Planet of the Apes* scenario is a real possibility within the naturalistic worldview.[16] Here's how one naturalist explains it:

> The human species has inhabited this planet for only 250,000 years or so—roughly .0015 percent of the history of life, the last inch of the cosmic mile. The world fared perfectly well without us for all but the last moment of earthly time— and this makes our appearance look like an accidental after- thought than the culmination of a prefigured plan. Moreover, the pathways that have led to our evolution are quirky, improb- able, unrepeatable and utterly unpredictable. Human evolution is not random; it makes sense and can be explained after the fact. But wind back life's tape to the dawn of time and let it play again—and you will never get humans a second time.
>
> We are here because one odd group of fishes had a peculiar fin anatomy that could transform into legs for terrestrial crea- tures; because the earth never froze entirely during an ice age; because a small and tenuous species, arising in Africa a quarter of a million years ago, has managed, so far, to survive by hook and by crook. We may yearn for a "higher" answer—but none exists. This explanation, though superficially troubling, if not terrifying, is ultimately liberating and exhilarating. We cannot read the meaning of life passively in the facts of nature. We must construct these answers ourselves—from our own wisdom and ethical sense. There is no other way.[17]

Since a "higher answer" does not exist for the naturalist, then all things are possible and permissible, including theft, slavery, rape,[18] murder, and genocide. And there is nothing in an evolving worldview to tell us that these things are evil. "In the words of sociobiology's founder, E.O. Wilson, 'the basis of ethics does not lie in God's will'; instead, ethics 'is an illusion fobbed off on us by our genes' because of its survival values."[19] At the same time, to be consistent with one's presuppositions, there is no way to do science within the circle of the naturalistic worldview because the scientific method requires predictability and consistency.

4. The end of man is extinction

Since there is no God, there can be no judgment, no heaven, no hell. John Lennon's *Imagine* is the credo of the naturalistic worldview.

> Imagine there's no heaven
> It's easy if you try
> No hell below us
> Above us only sky.
> Imagine all the people
> living for today. . . .[20]

Life after death, while it may be a possibility for the naturalist, is still left to chance and ignorance. No one can know within the parameters of naturalism. The best naturalism can offer is extinction and scant reports of "bright lights" as people near death's door and return with stories of "peacefulness" and "tranquility." Of course, with naturalism, why does it matter? Man is nothing more than physical substance: a conglomeration of randomly put together atoms.

5. There can be no certainty

The naturalist can never be certain that what he believes is true. Given the fact (as naturalism teaches) that everything is evolving, "truth" is an every-changing concept. What is "true" today may be "false" tomorrow. "One could well ask: 'If the mind, like all else in nature, is still evolving, how can we be sure that its present structure and operation guarantee any truth?' For example, did the Law of Contradiction, which is necessary for truth, evolve like the rest of the body? How can we be sure that there's not some new mental law, now struggling to be born, a law which will enable us to get even closer to the truth about reality? Would this new law confirm or contradict evolution and naturalism?"[21] With naturalism, we can never know. Charles Darwin understood the implications of his own evolutionary theory: "With me the horrid doubt always arises whether the convictions of man's mind, which has been developed from the mind of the lower animals, are of any value or at all trustworthy. Would anyone trust in the convictions of a monkey's mind, if there are any convictions in such a mind?"[22] The naturalist has to go back further than the "monkey mind" to the amoeba and the pre-biotic soup of swirling chemicals.

6. Naturalism is committed to its own kind of miracles

The naturalist would have us believe that "Everything came from nothing. Order came from chaos. Harmony came from discord. Life came from nonlife. Reason came from irrationality. Personality came from nonpersonality. Morality came from amorality."[23] This is truly a miraculous worldview. The naturalist ridicules the belief system of Christianity because it teaches that God created the world and ordered its design. Science can never consider the religious or the miraculous since these realms fall outside the investigative domain of science. And yet, the naturalist wants us to believe that an intricately designed universe developed without a designer. But when trying to illustrate the process of evolution, naturalists turn to examples of design. Tim Berra, an evolutionist, uses the "evolution of the Corvette" as an example of how biological evolution takes place. "The point is that the Corvette evolved through a selection process acting on variations that resulted in a series of transitional forms and an endpoint rather distinct from the starting point. A similar process shapes the evolution of organisms."[24] Of course, each and every design change came about through the conscious decision of design engineers who put their ideas on paper (or more probably on a computer that was also designed and built by a designer). Each element of the design had to be constructed by tool and die specialists to manufacture the parts and then assembled by highly trained workmen. Some evolutionists want us to believe that the universe only *seems* to be designed.[25]

7. Life's purpose is self-actualization

Pleasure may often be the only goal of the naturalist, since for him man is nothing more than an animal. Nerve endings—receptors of either pain or pleasure—are the naturalist's guide. If it feels good, do it. Ethical norms have no role to play. For years we've been teaching young people that they are nothing more than highly evolved animals. Why are we surprised when they act according to their nature? Then there is the constant refrain from the sexual revolutionaries that "It's my body and I can do what I want with it." Everything from abortion and sexual promiscuity to drug taking and teen suicide can now be justified.

8. Salvation is based on human effort

Man "saves" himself through education, law, science, technology, and politics. Naturalistic "salvation" has nothing to do with the forgiveness of sins and a new life in Christ. Rather, "salvation" is solely in terms of personal and (sometimes) social betterment. One of the doctrinal pillars of the *Humanist Manifesto II* is, "No deity will save us; we must save ourselves."[26] And how does the naturalist propose that man will save other men?: "Using technology wisely, we can control our environment, conquer poverty, markedly reduce disease, extend our life-span, significantly modify our behavior, alter the course of human evolution and cultural development, unlock vast new powers, and provide humankind with unparalleled opportunity for achieving an abundant and meaningful life."[27] But why?

9. Values are relative and subjective

What type of ethical norms should we expect from a self-existent universe, an evolving order, and a biological component called man? Values evolve along with man and his world. Ethical considerations are tied to whatever works for maximizing the pleasure of the greatest number. Joseph Fletcher sums up naturalistic ethics with this declaration: "I think there are no normative moral principles whatsoever which are intrinsically valid or universally obliging."[28] Following his premise consistently, "In a godless universe, what one 'animal' does to another 'animal' is ethically irrelevant, and there is no moral basis for anger or outrage against anything. Whatever happens happens, and that is all there is to it."[29]

10. Human life is expendable if the cause is good enough

Who defines "good enough"? We kill animals for food. Man is only a highly evolved animal. Therefore man can be killed for any number of "socially acceptable reasons": over-population, high medical costs for the terminally ill, and the inconveniences of too many children. After a debate on the abortion issue, one of the participants had the opportunity to speak with some of the students in attendance: "[M]ost of the students already recognized that the unborn child is a human life. Nevertheless, certain social reasons are considered 'high enough' to justify ending that life. According to some of the women, examples of 'high enough' reasons include protecting pregnant teenagers from the psychological distress of bearing a child, helping poor women who aren't able to care adequately for a child, and preventing children from coming into the world 'unwanted.' Many charged that pro-life philosophies are not 'socially accept-able' because they fail to deal realistically with these problems."[30]

Communism's horrors are often justified with the infamous quip made by communist admirers of the failed Soviet utopian experiment Sidney and Beatrice Webb, "You can't make an omelet without breaking eggs." How many eggs were actually broken to make this omelet? The authors of *The Black Book of Communism*[31] estimate that as many as 100 million people died over a span of 80 years from the implementation of the communist ideology. Stalinist apologists often dismissed the horrors of the "purge" because it was all for a good cause—the liberation of the masses![32]

11. All lifestyles are normative

Once ethical norms become arbitrary, we can expect the dismantling of long-standing Christian familial relationships like marriage and heterosexuality. Radical feminist Gloria Steinem once described marriage as an institution that destroys relationships. "I don't think marriage has a good name," she wrote in 1987. "Legally speaking, it was designed for a person and a half. You become a semi-non-person when you get married."[33] So is Gloria a semi-non-person now that she is married? Social relationships have to evolve along with nature. For example, in Marxist theory, which is nothing more than the political side of philosophical naturalism, the family is viewed as an institution in evolutionary process that will pass away in time. Engels remarked that "human society arose out of a troupe of tree-climbing monkeys."[34] It should not surprise us, therefore, that biblical marriage is coming under attack. Homosexual couples are going to Vermont to "bless" their "unions" under the guise of legal respectability by civil decree.

12. Civil government is the creation and savior of man

As with the origin of the family, civil government is also a creature of the evolutionary process. The individual is of no consequence. Those with the greatest power control everything. All totalitarian regimes begin with the fallacies of naturalism and become perpetrators of unspeakable atrocities as they follow its ethical implications. Nazi Germany is a modern-day example: "It is thus necessary that the individual should finally come to realize that his own ego is of no importance in comparison with the existence of his nation; that the position of the individual ego is conditioned solely by the interests of the nation as a whole ...that above all the unity of a nation's spirit and will are worth far more than the freedom of the spirit and will of an individual."[35]

13. Human rights are subjective and created by the State

Why should we expect the protection of fundamental rights when man is nothing more than an animal? Why should the weak be protected from the strong? With naturalism there is no reason.

All talk about human rights comes from those nations that have had a Christian base. The most familiar philosophy of human rights is found in the Declaration of Independence (1776). "All men," it states, "are endowed by their Creator with certain inalienable Rights, that among these are Life, Liberty and the pursuit of Happiness."

The philosophy of rights is intimately tied to the reality of the Creator who alone grants rights. No God, no rights. The Declaration makes it clear that these inalienable rights are not granted by governments; rather, they are an endowment, a gift, of the Creator of the universe. On the other hand, there is the French Declaration of the Rights of Man (1789) and the more recent United Nations' Declaration of Human Rights (1948), which are indicative of governments as the grantors of rights. If governments can give rights, they can just as easily revoke them. "The State giveth. The State taketh away. Blessed be the name of the State."

Some institution takes on the divine attributes, usually civil government, the State. The State then acts as a tyrannical and capricious god:

controlling lives, confiscating property, closing the borders of the country in order to keep its "subjects" from going to what the State perceives to be another god. Conde Pallen's utopian novel *Crucible Island* depicts what happens when the true God is rejected. Man looks for a substitute provider so that "the individual should have no thought, desire, or object other than the public welfare, of which the State is the creator and the inviolable guardian. As soon as the child is capable of learning, he is taught the Socialist catechism, whose first questions run as follows:

> *Q. By whom were you begotten?*
> A. By the sovereign State.
> *Q. Why were you begotten?*
> A. That I might know, love, and serve the Sovereign State always.
> *Q. What is the sovereign State?*
> A. The sovereign State is humanity in composite and perfect being.
> *Q. Why is the State supreme?*
> A. The State is supreme because it is my Creator and Conserver in which I am and move and have my being and without which I am nothing.
> *Q. What is the individual?*
> A. The individual is only a part of the whole, and made for the whole, and finds his complete and perfect expression in the sovereign State. Individuals are made for cooperation only, like feet, like hands, like eyelids, like the rows of the upper and lower teeth.[36]

A biblical worldiew understands the state to be a servant of God (Rom. 13:1–4) that has only a limited *civil* role.[37]

14. Man's environment accounts for all the "evil" in the world

Of course, there really is no ethical evil for the naturalist. "Good" and "evil" are nothing more than subjective categories of what people like and dislike at any given time. For the naturalist, evil (unpleasant acts) must have a physical cause. Man's environment, the world in which he lives, is at fault. Famine, death, and man's cruelty to others can all be explained environmentally. Change a person's environment and the person will change. Give the thief enough food to eat, and he will stop stealing. For the environmentalist[38] "salvation is escape from an evil environment to a good one. In the good environment, man will develop his physical and mental abilities in all directions."[39] In a naturalistic worldview there can be no other explanation for "evil" except the world. Sin never enters the picture. The Christian should be reminded that Adam and Eve sinned while living in a paradise. They enjoyed perfect health and unparalleled living conditions. Jesus avoided temptation while fasting in a wilderness. If a person's environment is the cause of either good or bad behavior, then Adam and Eve should never have sinned.

15. Everything is relative

End of discussion. Nothing you say can make any difference because your opponent does not believe in absolutes. (Of course, maintaining that everything is relative is an absolute statement.) Most of America's youth have been raised on the relativism doctrine.

> There is one thing a professor can be absolutely certain of:
> almost every student entering the university believes, or says he
> believes, that truth is relative . . . . The students' backgrounds
> are as various as America can provide. Some are religious, some
> atheists; some are to the Left, some to the Right; some intend to
> be scientists, some humanists or professionals or businessmen;
> some are poor, some rich. They are unified only in their relativ-
> ism and their allegiance to equality.[40]

Relativism is the offspring of naturalism. The relativistic worldview postulates that absolutes are impossible. What is wrong today can be right tomorrow. In principle, fixed standards do not exist in a relativistic world. Of course, once naturalism wins the day through getting everybody to adopt a relativistic philosophy, relativism is discarded because it would allow critics to question the new status quo brought on by relativism. Relativism is only used to dethrone worldviews that maintain ethical absolutes based on the sovereignty of a Creator. Once the old worldview is disposed of (in this case, the Christian worldview), the advocates of the new worldview do not allow others to tamper with the new order. All things are indeed relative, except the doctrine of relativism once the relativists gain power. This is best demonstrated in the writings of counter-culture icon Herbert Marcuse:

> Marcuse was a fashionable radical intellectual of the 1960s who believed that tolerance and free speech mostly serve the interests of the powerful. So he called frankly for "intolerance against movements from the right, and toleration of movements from the left." To restore the balance between oppressors and oppressed, he argued, indoctrination of students and "deeply pervasive" censorship of oppressors would be necessary, starting in college.
>
> By the late 1980s, many of the double standards Marcuse called for were in place.[41]

Free speech is only for those who are "right." This is why relativism is the handmaiden of naturalism. Once a person begins with the premise that the universe is ethically standardless, relativism takes over by making all worldview options legitimate. Any challenge to the newly established relativistic worldview is met with repression. In the worldview of relativism, all beliefs and values are equally true. "As are all religions, all 'sexual orientations,' all values, and all beliefs . . . even though they may be contradictory. (The exceptions, of course, are any religions, values, beliefs, etc., that proclaim the existence of objective truth)."[42]

Conclusion

In order to deal with conflicting worldviews, the Christian must presuppose distinctions, absolutes, and logical discourse. Because of the advent of bizarre assumptions about reality, it is becoming more difficult to make a case for absolutes. The Christian apologist must force, in logical terms, opposing worldview advocates to live consistently with their presuppositions.

Notes

1. Ronald H. Nash, *Worldviews in Conflict: Choosing Christianity in a World of Ideas* (Grand Rapids, MI: Zondervan, 1992), 9.

2. "New image of God urged by Tutu, others," *Atlanta Journal/Constitution* (February 13, 2000), A4.

3. R. Albert Mohler, Jr., "Conversion Controversy," *Wall Street Journal* (September 17, 1999), W15. Also see Gary DeMar, "Trapped in His Own Rhetoric," *The Biblical Worldview* (August 1999), 2. It's ironic that the New Testament records a stubborn reluctance by the Jews to take the gospel to the Gentiles. Peter had to see a vision from God before he would believe that the gospel was also for Gentiles (Acts 10).

4. *Naturalism* as a philosophical worldview should not be confused with "naturalism" as a study of wildlife and the environment.

5. James Hitchcock, *What is Secular Humanism?* (Ann Arbor, MI: Servant Publications, 1982), 10–11.

6. R. C. Sproul, *The Consequences of Ideas: Understanding the Concepts that Shaped Our World* (Wheaton, IL: Crossway Books, 2000), 148.

7. R. C. Sproul, *Lifeviews: Understanding the Ideas that Shape Society and Today* (Old Tappan, NJ: Revell, 1986), 35.

8. Paul Kurtz, ed., *The Humanist Manifesto I and II* (Buffalo, NY: Prometheus Books, 1973), 16.

9. Eric J. Lerner, *The Big Bang Never Happened: A Startling Refutation of the Dominant Theory of the Origin of the Universe* (London: Simon & Schuster, 1992), 4.

10. Lerner, *The Big Bang Never Happened*, 4.

11. Lerner, *The Big Bang Never Happened*, 388, note.

12. Del Ratzsch, *Science and Its Limits: The Natural Sciences in Christian Perspective*, 2nd ed. (Downers Grove, IL: InterVarsity Press, 2000), 159.

13. David Gelman, et al. "Is the Mind an Illusion?," *Newsweek* (April 20, 1992), 71. The Cray computer, named after its founder Seymour Cray, is made up of numerous parallel computers that contain thousands of microprocessor chips designed to work on a single problem at once by dividing the task among the individual computers. By comparison, traditional computers, such as the Cray-3, contain one or a handful of processors.

14. Quoted in Gelman, "Is the Mind an Illusion?," 71.

15. Quoted in Gelman, "Is the Mind an Illusion?," 72.

16. Pierre Boulle, *Planet of the Apes*, trans. Xan Fielding (New York: Vanguard Press, 1963). The two movie versions are very different from the book. It is in the movies that evolution predominates.

17. Stephen Jay Gould, "The Meaning of Life," *Life Magazine* (December 1988), 84.

18. Randy Thornhill and Craig T. Palmer, *A Natural History of Rape: Biological Basis for Sexual Coercion* (Cambridge, MA: MIT Press, 2000).

19. Nancy Pearcey, "Darwin's dirty secret," *World* (March 25, 2000), 15.

20. Lennon also wrote: "Imagine no possessions/I wonder if you can/No need for greed or hunger/a brotherhood of man/Imagine all the people/Sharing all the world." When Lennon

was murdered in 1980, he left "a staggering monetary legacy estimated at $275 million—not bad for one who referred to himself as an 'instinctive socialist,' for one who believed in the abolition of 'all money, police, and government.'" (David A. Noebel, *The Legacy of John Lennon: Charming or Harming a Generation?* [Nashville, TN: Thomas Nelson, 1982], 11).

21. Arlie J. Hoover, *Dear Agnos: A Defense of Christianity* (Grand Rapids, MI: Baker Book House, 1976), 106.

22. *Life and Letters of Charles Darwin*, ed. Frances Darwin (New York: Johnson Reprint), 1:285. Quoted in Hoover, *Dear Agnos*, 106–107.

23. Robert A. Morey, *Death and the Afterlife* (Minneapolis, MN: Bethany House, 1984), 191.

24. Tim Berra, *Evolution and the Myth of Creationism: A Basic Guide to the Facts in the Evolution Debate* (Stanford, CA: Stanford University Press, 1990), 118. Quoted in Phillip E. Johnson, *An Easy-to-Understand Guide for Defeating Darwinism by Opening Minds* (Downers Grove, InterVarsity Press, 1997), 62.

25. Richard Dawkins, *The Blind Watchmaker: Why the Evidence of Evolution Reveals a Universe Without a Design* (New York: W.W. Norton, 1986). For a refutation, see Michael Behe, *Darwin's Black Box: The Biochemical Challenge to Evolution* (New York: The Free Press, 1996).

26. Kurtz, ed., *Humanist Manifesto I and II*, 16.

27. Kurtz, ed., *Humanist Manifesto I and II*, 14.

28. Joseph Fletcher and John Warwick Montgomery, *Situation Ethics: True or False?: A Dialogue Between Joseph Fletcher and John Warwick Montgomery* (Minneapolis, MN: Bethany Fellowship, 1972), 15.

29. John Blanchard, *Does God Believe in Atheists?* (Auburn, MA: Evangelical Press, 2000), 521.

30. "Students Defend Abortion For 'High' Social Reasons," *The Rutherford Institute*, 1:2 (January/February 1984), 8.

31. Stephane Courtois, Nicolas Werth, Jean-Louis Panne, Adrzej Paczkowski, Karel Bartooek, and Jean-Louis Margolin, *The Black Book of Communism: Crimes, Terror, Repression*, trans. Jonathan Murphy and Mark Kramer (Cambridge, MA: Harvard University Press, 1999).

32. S.J. Taylor, *Stalin's Apologist—Walter Duranty: The New York Times's Man in Moscow* (New York: Oxford University Press, 1990).

33. Quoted in "Once anti-marriage, Steinem takes vows at 66," *Atlanta Constitution* (September 7, 2000), D1.

34. Friedrich Engels, *Anti-Duhring* (1934). Quoted in Francis Nigel Lee, *Communist Eschatology: A Christian Philosophical Analysis of the Post-Capitalistic Views of Marx, Engels and Lenin* (Nutley, NJ: The Craig Press, 1974), 322.

35. Adolf Hitler at Buckenburg, October 7, 1933, in *The Speeches of Adolf Hitler, 1929–39*, N. H.Baynes, ed., 2 vols. (Oxford, 1942), 1:871–72. Quoted in Leonard Peikoff, *The Ominous Parallels: The End of Freedom in America* (New York: Stein and Day, 1982), 3.

36. Conde Pallen, *Crucible Island: A Romance, an Adventure and an Experiment* (New York: The Manhattanville Press, 1919), 109–10.

37. See Gary DeMar, *God and Government*, 3 vols. (Powder Springs, GA: American Vision, 2001).

38. This use should not be confused with the one referring to care for the environment.

39. Rousas J. Rushdoony, *Salvation and Godly Rule* (Vallecito, CA: Ross House Books, 1983), 66.

40. Allan Bloom, *The Closing of the American Mind: How Higher Education Has Failed Democracy and Impoverished the Souls of Today's Students* (New York: Simon & Schuster, 1987), 25.

41. John Leo, "When rules don't count: Double standards are no accident; they arise from a theory," *U.S. News & World Report* (August 7, 2000), 14. For further discussion on Marcuse, see Alan Charles Kors and Harvey A. Silvergate, *The Shadow University: The Betrayal of Liberty on America's Campuses* (New York: The Free Press, 1998), chap. 4.

42. Josh McDowell and Bob Hostetler, *The New Tolerance* (Wheaton, IL: Tyndale House Publishers, 1998), 72.

Part Three
Defensive Strategies

6

Establishing the Starting Point

At the center of every world view is what might be called the
"touchstone proposition" of that world view, a proposition that is
held to be *the* fundamental truth about reality and serves as a
criterion to determine which other propositions may or may not
count as candidates for belief.[1]

Christian apologetics begins by establishing an authoritative starting
point. Like Archimedes (287?–212 B.C.), who once boasted that given
the proper lever and a place to stand, he could "move the earth," the
Christian apologist seeks to base his defense on a secure foundation to
move the hearts and minds of sinners to embrace the eternal hope found
in the gospel of Jesus Christ. But upon what would Archimedes stand
to "move the earth"? He couldn't stand on the earth to move the earth.
Archimedes needed a place to stand (*pou sto*) *outside* the earth, a solid
place *independent* of the earth he wanted to move. His lever also needed
a fulcrum. This, too, had to rest on something other than the earth.

Atlas had a similar problem when he was condemned by Zeus to
stand eternally at the western end of the earth to hold up the sky. (In
artistic renderings, Atlas is depicted as holding up the world.) But what

is Atlas standing upon? And what is what he's standing upon standing upon? (You can see where this is going!)

> An often told story has a modern philosopher lecturing on the solar system. An old lady in the audience avers: Earth rests upon a large turtle. "What does this turtle stand on?" the speaker needles. "A far larger turtle." As the scholar persists, his challenger retorts: "You are very clever but it is no use, young man. It's turtles all the way down."[2]

"Turtles all the way down" is the atheist's dilemma. Instead of turtles, it's finite humans all the way down. No matter what the worldview, there comes a point in time when a resting point must be admitted. Anyone involved in debate over any topic must deal with the issue of a sound and fixed starting point. It is fundamental. All debate will finally come to rest on a starting point that has no other place to go for a foundation. It's the bedrock of worldview support.

In the final analysis, the Christian's starting point is the Word of God which rests upon God Himself. "[M]en need an *epistemological* 'Archimedean point of reference' to understand their cosmos and themselves; but only a revelation from One transcendentally outside of the cosmos can provide the *pou sto* essential to knowledge, since man can never break out of his finite cosmic perspective."[3] God is the One who stands outside the universe. In order for us to know how the world works, we must turn to Him. God is our "Archimedean point of reference."

"Here I Stand"

When the sixteenth-century German Reformer Martin Luther "was called to defend his rejection of indulgences before the church and before the emperor, Luther, alone and in peril of his life, appealed to the authority of the Word of God. 'Here I stand,' he said; 'I can do no other.'"[4] There was no appeal to tradition, the expert testimony of church scholars, scientists, or even the precisely fashioned creeds. It's not that these aren't helpful; they simply are not *ultimate* authoritative starting points.

In Matthew 7:24–27, Jesus points out that "the strength of a foundation determines whether a house will withstand heavy rains and strong winds. If a man builds his house on sand, it will fall; but if he builds his dwelling on solid rock, it will stand secure even in a fierce storm."[5] If the foundation upon which the apologist uses to build his worldview is compromised in any way, then it will eventually collapse when challenged. Therefore, the starting point in any defense of the truthfulness of the Christian worldview is all-important. Will it be a foundation of sand or one of solid rock?

Establishing the Touchstone

It is upon a final standard—a standard to which no greater appeal is made—that all worldviews rest.[6] What we are looking for in our apologetic task is a reliable gauge of truth that does not depend on the fallible, finite, and fallen character of man for validation. What we need is an authoritative *touchstone* by which all other claims to ultimate authority can be tested:

> In the days of the gold rush men used a touchstone, a fine grained dark stone, such as jasper, to determine the quality of the gold which they had discovered. Today a Geiger counter is used to locate uranium and other precious metals. In baseball the umpire makes the decisions in the contest between the pitcher and the batter. In the courtroom the judge decides questions of law. In their respective fields the touchstone, the Geiger counter, the umpire and the judge speak with authority.[7]

But even these are not *ultimate* authorities. More fundamental principles and guidelines stand behind these measuring devices. The umpire is bound by a rule book. A group of men determine the rules that are finally published in the book. But the very idea that there are objective rules is fundamental to the entire process. Where do the concepts of value, right and wrong, rules, and the principle of judgment come from? Where do these precepts find their validity so that people generally follow them with little or no argument? How does one account for such abstractions in a materialistic universe? Are they made up? Do they change from generation to generation? When it comes to the most important questions about life and death...

- Who am I?
- What am I?
- Why am I here?
- Does God exist?
- If God does exist, how can I know him?
- What happens to me after death?
- How should I live my life?
- Are there moral absolutes?
- Does life have meaning?

... we want and need reliable and authoritative answers. To answer these questions (and many others like them) with certainty and authority, an ultimate and reliable standard must be found. For centuries, philosophers have embarked on such a quest. How successful have they been? If the history of philosophy is any indicator, the results are at best mixed. From platonism to post-modernism, from Aristotle to Zoroaster, each view of the world seemingly contradicts every other view.

Don't Always Trust the Experts

All argumentation will inevitably be taken back to a single philosophical starting point from which the person arguing will appeal for ultimate authority to support his worldview. Numerous starting-points are put forward as the foundational basis for thinking straight:

- rationalism: reason rules
- mysticism: unknown forces rule
- hedonism: pleasure rules
- relativism: we get to make up our own rules
- post-modernism: there are no rules
- pragmatism: it's a rule only if it works
- materialism: only matter matters
- monism: all is one so there is nothing to argue about

And if specific philosophical systems are not enough to establish an authoritative starting point, then there is the appeal to any number of self-proclaimed or institutionally sanctioned experts: a brilliant college professor, the writings of a Zen Master, the directives of a cult leader, the latest scientific studies, the writings or revelations of self-appointed religious leaders, statistical analysis, opinion polls, the Constitution of the United States, psychics, fortune tellers, frequently quoted philosophers, newspaper and magazine editors, judges, television news anchors, Oprah, the high-minded opinions of Hollywood actors, or even alien life forms. Even some atheists hope against hope that someone (other than a personal God) is "out there" to give meaning to the cosmos.

So-called experts, no matter what their field of study or how much information they gather, are finite in knowledge and fallible in practice. Put simply, they don't know everything, and they make mistakes. For every group of experts that claims to know something, there are always other groups of experts who claim they can dispute the findings of the first group of experts. The Bible describes it this way: "The first to plead his case seems just, until another comes and examines him" (Prov. 18:17).

Christopher Cerf and Victor Navasky, after compiling thousands of expert opinions and declarations about innumerable subjects over thousands of years, summarize their findings:

> Our research has yielded (and we have systematically cata-
> logued and footnoted for the first time) thousands of examples
> of expert misinformation, disinformation, misunderstanding,
> miscalculation, egregious prognostication, boo-boos, and occa-
> sional just plain lies. And based on our preliminary findings we
> can say with some confidence that the experts are wrong with-
> out regard to race, creed, color, sex discipline, specialty, country,
> culture, or century. They are wrong about facts, and they are
> wrong about theories, they are wrong about dates, they are wrong
> about geography, they are wrong about the future, they are wrong
> about the past, and at best they are misleading about the present,
> not to mention next week.[8]

In brief, "Just because most of the authorities in a field are shouting in unison that they know the truth, it ain't necessarily so."[9] An expert's opinion is only as good as the starting point being used to evaluate the facts.

Every decision that man has made and will make is determined by the place he decides to take his stand. Where does man stand when he makes a decision about the rightness or wrongness of certain behavior? Prior to the Fall, Adam "gladly acknowledged the fact of God's sovereignty over him and the fact of his own creaturehood. God was his *pou sto* for knowledge, his final reference point for every human predication. It was God who determined for him right and wrong, and he willingly thought God's thoughts after Him."[10] It was Adam's decision to shift his *pou sto* that made the Fall a fall. He no longer stood on the solid foundation of God's Word, but instead chose to view his own opinion as a reliable place to stand. After the Fall, it became man's nature "to suppress God's revelation to him, both general and special. He found the most successful means of doing this to be a preoccupation with his own ideals and purposes on the one hand, and increasing sin and immorality on the other."[11]

Christians will never win the war against triumphalistic man-centered worldviews until they challenge the place where the critics stand and force them to live consistently with it. This cannot be done if the Bible is never brought into the discussion.

The Standard of Truth

The Bible is the standard of truth. The Bible presents a specific view of the world, of man, of God, and of authority. Anything that is not consistent with the biblical worldview is not true. The Bible is also the Christian's ethical standard. It teaches us to distinguish between right and wrong, and the commandments of God present us with our ethical duty. If we "walk in the law of the LORD," our ways will be "blameless" (Psalm 119:1).

Second Timothy 3:16-17 is one of the places where Scripture talks about itself as the final authority, the place where we are to take our stand. Paul tells his young protégé, Timothy, to

> continue in the things you have learned and become convinced of, knowing from whom you have learned them; and that from childhood you have known the sacred writings which are able to give you wisdom that leads to salvation through faith which is in Christ Jesus. All Scripture is inspired of God and profitable for teaching, for reproof, for correction, for training in righteousness; that the man of God may be adequate, equipped for every good work (2 Tim. 3:14-17).

Several things should be noted from this passage of Scripture. First, Paul says that *all* Scripture is profitable. When he wrote this, there was no written New Testament. The "sacred writings" Paul had in mind were the Old Testament. Christians shouldn't read only the New Testament. We shouldn't think that only the New Testament is helpful to us as Christians. Paul says that *all* Scripture is profitable. We should therefore make every effort to become thoroughly acquainted with the whole Bible, not just with our favorite books. In fact, it is impossible to understand and apply the teaching of the New Testament without understanding the content and context of the Old Testament (Luke 24:27, 44–45).

What profit do we gain from knowing Scripture? Paul mentions several: wisdom that leads to salvation, training in righteousness, correction, reproof, and rebuke. Scripture confronts our sin, and leads us to Christ. Scripture reveals God's character to us. This must always be the center of our interest when we study Scripture: to know God.[12] Scripture is first of all God's means of giving us new life in Him.

Second, Paul gives the reason why Scripture is profitable; it is the highest possible reason. Scripture is profitable because it is "inspired of God." Actually, the Greek word here really means "expired of God," or "God-breathed." Scripture, the written Bible, is the product of God's breath. God breathed the very words of the Bible.

Elsewhere, of course, we learn that God used *men* to write the Bible, and these men had different gifts, temperaments, writing styles, and emphases. The Bible didn't fall from the sky. But these men were "carried" by the Holy Spirit of God, so that the words that they wrote were the very words of God (2 Peter 1:21).

What Paul is saying here is quite amazing. He's saying that God's own words are recorded on the pages of the Bible! Do you want to know what God says? We can know what God, the Creator of heaven and earth, says, by reading the Bible! How ungrateful, then, are those who refuse to listen to the voice of their Creator, who speaks to us out of pure mercy and grace.

Finally, Paul says that the Bible equips the Christian "for every good work." The Bible gives us God's opinion and direction in *every area of life*! The Bible is not just a book about worship. It tells a lot about worship, to be sure. In fact, worship is one of the most important things in the Bible. But that is not all the Bible teaches us. The Bible is not just a book to tell us how to run a church.

Paul says that the Bible guides us in every area of life. It not only *teaches* us, but actually *equips* us for every good work. It teaches about how to make a lasting and godly marriage. It teaches us how to raise our children. It tells us how to treat our neighbor. It tells us how we should spend our money. It teaches us what laws are best. It teaches us what kind of crimes the civil government should punish, and what punishments are best. It teaches us basic truths that can be applied in every area of study: history, medicine, law, sociology, economics, literature and art, and every other area.

Since the Bible is our ultimate standard, there is nothing more important in apologetics than a thorough knowledge of the Bible. The apologist must know what he's defending before he can defend it effectively. Thus, the most important part of our preparation is to read, study, and meditate on the Scriptures.

Defending the Authority of Scripture

The Bible must be used in the defense of the faith for a variety of reasons. First, we must always argue with the understanding that the Bible is true. We can never accept the unbeliever's standards of truth, since they are foolish. Even when we are not actually citing Scripture, we should be operating within a biblical worldview.

Most unbeliever's will raise an immediate objection when we appeal to Scripture as our standard of truth. "How do we know that the Bible is true?" they will ask. Apologists have given many different answers to this question. Some point out that the Bible has always been confirmed by archeological and historical evidence. Others say that the biblical view of the world is true to our experience of the world. Others point out that the biblical writers were either insane, evil, or they were telling the truth. Given the evidence we have, it is more plausible to conclude that they were telling the truth. All these arguments have their place. But we want to fit these arguments into a technique that does justice to the methodology outlined in the Bible.

Circular Reasoning

The Bible claims to be God's Word. This is our starting point. Of course, just because a book says it's God's Word does not make it so. But if a book is God's Word, it would certainly claim to be God's Word. If a book is God's Word, then what it said would be true. It may seem odd that we would cite the Bible to prove that the Bible is God's Word. This is what philosophers call a "circular argument." When we prove the authority of the Bible by citing the Bible, we have assumed from the beginning that the Bible is authoritative. Is this just a vicious circle of reasoning that won't get us anywhere? It may seem that we need to prove the truth of the Bible by some other outside "neutral" standard. Of course, if we did that, we would have to ask what makes this outside standard authoritative? We would have only created another circle that needed defending.

There are problems with some kinds of circular arguments. But you might be surprised to know that you can't help arguing in a circle. At some point, everyone has to argue in a circle. Why? Because everyone, as we have seen, has certain assumptions. No one is neutral. When someone challenges your assumptions or belief patterns, you either have to use a circular argument, or you have to change your presuppositions, which will also lead to a circular argument.

> [A] rationalist [for whom reason has final authority] can prove the primacy of reason only by using a rational argument. An empiricist [for whom experience has final authority] can prove the primacy of sense-experience only by some kind of appeal to sense-experience. A Muslim can prove the primacy of the Koran only by appealing to the Koran. But if all systems are circular in that way, then such circularity can hardly be urged against Christianity. The critic will inevitably be just as "guilty" of circularity as the Christian is.[13]

Of course, not all circular arguments are reasonable or valid. For a person to claim that he should be worshiped because he is god, based on his own assertion that he is god, is not the type of circular argument that is being examined. "Circularity in a system is properly justified *only* at one point: in an argument for the *ultimate* criterion of the system."[14]

But what happens when two circular arguments—each claiming ultimate authority for their worldview—don't agree? Each worldview must be "put to the test," working out the logical implications of the stated presuppositions. Which one best fits with reality? For example, the Bible contains thousands of prophecies about numerous events spanning thousands of years. The Bible sets the standard for determining how to evaluate prophecies: They must always come to pass; there can be no mistakes (Deut. 18:18–22). The Bible can be easily tested by its own standards (see chapter 17).

Scripture and Presuppositions

How can we use circular reasoning in apologetics? First, as we have seen, Scripture provides the basic framework of our world view. When we answer an unbeliever's objections to Christianity, we must ultimately refer him to Scripture. This does not mean that we need to cite proof texts for everything. It does mean, however, that we should let the unbeliever know that Scripture is our ultimate authority. We never accept the unbeliever's standard of authority, or pretend to be neutral.

Second, it may be helpful to show the unbeliever that he too has some ultimate standard of truth, some final authority. He therefore uses circular reasoning as well. His final authority may be his own mind, his experience, or the opinions of others whose convictions are based on some undisclosed ultimate standard. But he has some final authority to which he appeals. If we press him for an answer, he will ultimately fall into a circular argument. As was claimed earlier, the rationalist can defend himself only by a rational argument.

Third, having shown the skeptic that he has presuppositions, we can show that Scripture is superior to his authority. If his final authority is his own reason, for example, we can point out that he has no reason to trust in reason if we live in an erratic universe that can randomly change tomorrow. How could reason ever be trusted in the context of a worldview that is always in flux? A person who claims reason is the final arbiter of truth must first presuppose that reason is the ultimate standard. He will use reason to justify reason's status as authoritative.

Evolutionary thought is especially vulnerable to circularity since it teaches that the human mind (actually, the brain) is the result of a series of chance modifications that took place over great spans of time by unseen random forces. Why trust the evolved brain of an advanced ape? What kind of confidence can be placed in the random firing of "neurochemical reactions" in a substance of soft tissue that supposedly evolved by chance over aeons of time? No one has made this point better than Christian apologist C. S. Lewis:

If minds are wholly dependent on brains, and brains on bio-chemistry, and bio-chemistry (in the long run) on the meaningless flux of atoms, I cannot understand how the thought of those minds should have any significance than the sound of the wind in the trees. . . . Christian theology can fit in science, art, morality, and the sub-Christian religions. The scientific point of view cannot fit any of these things, not even science itself.[15]

There is no accounting for the significance of man and the world, between dreaming and waking, rationality and irrationalism, illusion and reality if the rationalistic materialists are right. The Darwinian perspective "provides no room for geniuses, big and small, or even the existence of reason."[16]

What is the source and justification for morality? Former atheist and Marxist Gene Genovese confesses that he "'had long been troubled by the lack of a moral foundation in Marxism. . . . It wasn't clear to me that you could have that foundation without a belief in God. I mean, you can be an atheist and live a perfectly moral life, but what is it grounded in?'"[17]

Pure rationalists cannot account for moral principles using their atheistic starting point. To put it simply, rationalists have to be inconsistent in order to function in a world that they maintain is random, unpredictable, and impersonal. They assume an ordered, rational, and personal universe even though they cannot account for it. To be consistent within the confines of their random worldview would lead them to despair and hopelessness. Life would be consistently meaningless.

Scripture, on the other hand, is God's Word to man. As God's Word, it is our final authority. God is the Lord. He knows everything exhaustively. He has all power and authority. It makes sense, when we look at things biblically, to trust Scripture as the standard of truth and error, right and wrong.

Borrowed Capital

If religious skeptics have forsaken biblical presuppositions, why is it that they are able to think rationally, work in terms of the scientific method, and develop concepts of morality? The answer is quite simple. Anti-Christians are philosophically schizophrenic. They are rarely consistent with the assumptions of their atheistic worldview. "The success of modern science has been due to its 'borrowed capital,' because modern science is like the prodigal son. He left his father's house and is rich, but the substance he expends is his father's wealth."[18] Those who deny God and assert that the world and all of its consequences came into being randomly have no way to account for their worldview. "[N]atural man does have knowledge, but it is borrowed knowledge, stolen from the Christian-theistic pasture or range, yet natural man has no knowledge, because in terms of his principle the ultimacy of his thinking, he can have none, and the knowledge he possesses is not truly his own. . . . The natural man has valid knowledge only as a thief possesses goods."[19] Robert Bork makes a similar point:

> Some few years ago friends whose judgment I greatly respect argued that religion constitutes the only reliable basis for morality and that when religion loses its hold on a society, standards of morality will gradually crumble. I objected that there were many moral people who are not at all religious; my friends replied that such people are living on the moral capital left by generations that believed there is a God and that He makes demands on us. The prospect, they said, was that the remaining capital would dwindle and our society become less moral. The course of society and culture has been as they predicted, which certainly does not prove their point but does provide evidence for it.[20]

Anti-Christian worldviews are held together by adhesives stolen from the Christian worldview. The Bible tells us that in Christ all things are held together (Heb. 1:3). The skeptic cannot account for the cohesion of the world from within his own system. If left to itself, the man-centered worldview of modern skepticism would, like the overturned war machines of Wells' *War of the Worlds*, lay ruined upon Earth's landscape, made inactive by its own inherent self-destructive worldview. "God is a necessary presupposition of all possible knowledge. That is to say, in order to justify knowledge, one must assume the existence of God. If this is true, then obviously atheism cannot be rationally affirmed."[21]

Conclusion

If a traveler decides to take a journey, and he has all the necessary equipment for the task, but he heads off in the wrong direction, all his skill and efforts will be in vain because he will not reach his planned destination. The same is true for the person who has a sharp and informed mind who takes his stand on the slippery slope of skepticism. His efforts, while marked with erudite arguments, will be without merit because his first step was in the wrong direction.

Notes

1. William H. Halverson, *A Concise Introduction to Philosophy*, 4th ed. (New York: Random House, 1981), 414.

2. Charles W. Petit, "Life and Culture: Cosmology," *U.S. News & World Report* (August 16/23, 1999), 74.

3. Robert L. Reymond, *The Justification of Knowledge* (Phillipsburg, NJ: Presbyterian and Reformed, 1976), 30n.

4. Gene Edward Veith, "Millennium on our Mind," *World* (August 7, 1999), 27.

5. Richard L. Pratt, Jr., *Every Thought Captive: A Study Manual for the Defense of Christian Truth* (Phillipsburg, NJ: Presbyterian and Reformed, 1979), 1.

6. Greg L. Bahnsen, *Always Ready: Directions for Defending the Faith* (Texarkana, AR: Covenant Media Foundation, 1996), 70–75.

7. George M. Marston, *The Voice of Authority* (Nutley, NJ: Presbyterian and Reformed, 1960), xv.

8. Christopher Cerf and Victor Navasky, "Introduction to the Original (1984) Version," *The Experts Speak: The Definitive Compendium of Authoritative Misinformation*, rev. ed. (New York: Villard, [1984] 1998), xxvii.

9. William R. Fix, *The Bone Peddlers: Selling Evolution* (New York: Macmillan, 1984), xix.

10. Reymond, *Justification of Knowledge*, 85.

11. Reymond, *Justification of Knowledge*, 86.

12. J. I. Packer, *Knowing God* (Downers Grove, IL: InterVarsity Press, 1973).

13. John M. Frame, *Doctrine of the Knowledge of God: A Theology of Lordship* (Phillipsburg, NJ: Presbyterian and Reformed, 1987), 130.

14. Frame, *Doctrine of the Knowledge of God*, 130.

15. C.S. Lewis, "Is Theology Poetry?" Delivered at the Oxford Socratic Club, 1944, published in *They Asked for a Paper* (London: Geoffrey Bles, 1962), 164–65.

16. Stanley L. Jaki, *The Savior of Science* (Washington, D.C.: Regnery Gateway, 1988), 25.

17. Quoted in Michael Skube, "A Change of Heart," *Atlanta Journal/Constitution* (August 1, 1999), M3.

18. Rousas J. Rushdoony, *The Mythology of Science* (Nutley, NJ: Craig Press, 1967), 87.

19. Rousas J. Rushdoony, *By What Standard?: An Analysis of the Philosophy of Cornelius Van Til* (Tyler, TX: Thoburn Press, [1958] 1983), 24.

20. Robert H. Bork, "Preface," Herbert Schlossberg, *Idols for Destruction: Christian Faith and Its Confrontation with American Society* (Wheaton, IL: Crossway Books, [1983] 1993), xviii.

21. Francis J. Beckwith and Stephen E. Parrish, *See the Gods Fall: Four Rivals to Christianity* (Joplin, MO: College Press, 1997), 151.

7

Building on First Principles

A "presupposition" is not just any assumption in an argument, but
a personal commitment that is held at the most basic level of
one's network of beliefs. Presuppositions form a wide-ranging,
foundational *perspective* (or starting point) in terms of which
everything else is interpreted and evaluated. As such, presuppositions have the greatest authority in one's thinking, being treated as
one's least negotiable beliefs and being granted the highest
immunity to revision.[1]

Have you ever gotten into an argument with someone over a political, ethical, or religious question and found that you just could not
come to an agreement? Maybe you saw a movie together and could not
concur on what it was all about. You saw the same movie but "saw" it
differently. Why the disagreement? First, the difference could be one of
perspective. Everyone sees things in a unique way because of unique
experiences and interests. One of you might have watched the movie
with an eye on the symbolic elements. Another might have watched
looking for philosophical ideas. Someone might have evaluated it in

terms of its story line and character development. These are differences of perspective. There is nothing wrong with having different perspectives. At this level, every perspective would make up a part of the whole. They could all be correct. A discussion would help you see different dimensions of the movie and enrich your understanding of it.

Second, your disagreement could be more fundamental. Your disagreement about the movie could be a dispute over presuppositions, those fundamental standards that we use to interpret life. Disagreements about issues often result from a more fundamental disagreement about the evaluating principles each person uses to evaluate the facts. The same facts are there for everyone to examine and appraise. So what keeps people from holding similar opinions when the same facts are common to all? At one level we know it's a spiritual problem. In some cases God blinds their eyes (John 12:40) or hardens their heart (Ex. 4:21) so they will not understand (Matt. 13:13). In other instances, God gives "them over to a depraved mind" (Rom. 1:28). They couldn't see the truth even if it bit them, because their reasoning processes are so distorted by sin.

In addition to what God does to those seeking to be their own god, there is also a pro-active side whereby individuals make the claim that they are autonomous and "objective" truth seekers when in reality they are biased truth concealers. They purposely "suppress the truth in unrighteousness" (Rom. 1:18) and set their mind "on the flesh" (8:6). They know the truth, but they cover it up so they won't have to confront a righteous God.

Finally, there are those who have been taken "captive through philosophy and empty deception, according to the tradition of men, according to the elementary principles of the world, rather than according to Christ" (Col. 2:8). Instead of turning to God for the construction of their worldview, they turn instead to other creatures like themselves who have the same creaturely limitations and distortions. In effect, they build their worldview out of inferior building materials.

The Beginning of Knowledge

The Bible states, "The fear of the LORD is the *beginning* of knowledge" (Prov. 1:7). True knowledge does not take place unless one begins with the presupposition that God exists and His Word is supreme. If the starting point is something other than God and His Word, then that other thing becomes the ultimate governing presupposition. "If the Word required something more certain than itself to give it validity, it would no longer be *God's* Word."[2] This means that at one level the facts do not speak for themselves. They are always interpreted in terms of a person's adopted worldview that is constructed from a network of presuppositions. Objectivity and neutrality, as they relate to worldviews, are myths.

> Beware of the man who tells you that he will explain—fully explain—any complex human action or event by resort to "coldly objective," "empirically verifiable," "statistical data." He is deceiving himself, and perhaps seeking to deceive you.
>
> For in the first place we do not all see the same event in exactly the same way, let alone interpret it the same way—not even events which do not involve the complicating factor of human purpose.[3]

Presuppositions are the deciding factor in determining how facts are interpreted and combined to give particular content to a worldview. "A presupposition is something assumed or supposed in advance. . . . One could say that to 'presuppose' is to conclude something before the investigation is commenced."[4] A presupposition is not proved by anything else more ultimate. For purposes of reaching answers to fundamental questions, a presupposition is "a belief over which no other takes precedence."[5]

A person who asserts that all things must be tested by the standard of reason has assumed—ultimately presupposed—that reason is the test for truth. If he appeals to some other principle to verify that reason is ultimate, then that new principle becomes ultimate. When there is no other principle upon which to appeal, an ultimate presupposition has been established. Ultimately, how does a person *know* that reason— or anything else, for that matter—is the standard? Greg L. Bahnsen describes it this way:

> All argumentation about ultimate issues eventually *comes to rest* at the level of the disputant's presuppositions. If a man has come to the conclusion, and is committed to the truth of a certain view P, when he is challenged as to P, he will offer supporting argumentation for it, Q and R. But of course, as his opponent will be quick to point out, this simply shifts the argument to Q and R. Why accept them? The proponent of P is now called upon to offer S, T, U, and V as arguments for Q and R. And on and on the process goes. The process is complicated by the fact that *both* the believer and unbeliever will be involved in such chains of argumentation. But all argument chains must come to an *end* somewhere. One's conclusions could never be demonstrated if they were dependent upon an infinite regress of argumentative justifications, for under those circumstances the demonstration could never be completed. And an incomplete demonstration demonstrates nothing at all.
>
> Eventually all argumentation terminates in some logically primitive starting point, a view or premise held as unquestionable. Apologetics traces back to such ultimate starting points or *pre*suppositions. In the nature of the case these presuppositions are held to be *self-evidencing*: they are the ultimate authority of one's viewpoint, an authority for which no greater authorization can be given.[6]

Either finite, fallible, and fallen man is the measure of all things or the infinite, infallible, and perfect God of the Bible is the measure of all things. "Non-Christians substitute something else—another god, themselves, pleasure, money, rationality, or whatever—as that to which they are ultimately committed and that which governs all of life."[7]

So then, the Christian, the pagan, the agnostic, and the atheist interpret the world by an appeal to certain essential presuppositions that at their foundational level are religious. ("Religious" is here being defined as "ultimately foundational," not simply belief in a god.)[8] "This means that many people may rightly call themselves atheists meaning that they do not believe there are any gods ('a-theist' means literally 'no-god'), but they will still have a religious belief if they regard anything whatever as the self-existent on which all else depends."[9] Those beliefs "on which all else depends" are presuppositions, and everyone has them, from the astronomer to the bushman. "There can be no philosophy, and, indeed, no quest for truth in any field, without presuppositions. Mathematics has its axioms; science rests on the assumption of the orderliness of nature which makes possible a formulation of its laws. Presuppositions in any field determine the nature of the procedures that are followed in it."[10]

When is a Fact a Fact?

Presuppositions determine whether a fact is truly a fact for someone's chosen worldview. For example, a person holding anti-supernatural presuppositions will ignore, reinterpret, or even discard evidence that does not support his worldview in order to ensure that his worldview is not invalidated. Throughout this process the claim is made by anti-supernaturalists that they are being neutral and objective, that they don't hold presuppositions that influence the way they evaluate evidence. As one skeptic of scientific objectivity observes, "How good *was* the evolutionary evidence? Perhaps in addition to those 100 million facts that proved evolution, there were another 100 million facts they had chosen to ignore that proved something else."[11] Presuppositions determined the reality of a fact.

The history of battles between Christians and non-Christians, super-naturalists and anti-supernaturalists, and creationists and evolutionists, will show that adherents on both sides come to every piece of evidence with presuppositions in hand. No one is truly impartial. "On the question of God's existence neither Darwin nor Newton were 'objective' or value-free."[12] In fact, no matter what the intellectual enterprise, presuppositions always lead the way. Not even science is an objective enterprise.

> Sealed off in their working enclaves, scientists routinely try to explain away any anomalies that their research might turn up. Only when forced by mounting evidence to confront these anomalies will some scientists—they are always rare—make a sudden mental shift which permits them to break with normal science. This is how scientific revolutions occur.[13]

History is filled with examples of so-called objective scientific experts rejecting new evidence that would supplant an unworkable theory to explain reality. Many prominent scientists rejected Louis Pasteur's (1822–1895) contention that microscopic organisms caused certain diseases despite the overwhelming evidence he put forth. While "spontaneous generation"[14] was discredited by experiments performed by Francesco Redi in his detailed *Experiments on the Generation of Insects* in 1688, the theory "was too deep-rooted to die."[15] Long-held presuppositions governed the interpretation of the facts.

Biologists were still supporting "spontaneous generation" theories in the nineteenth century. Through a series of carefully formulated experiments, Pasteur showed that micro-organisms—germs—were responsible for food spoilage and infection. Was everyone convinced after the presentation of Pasteur's evidence? Objections to Pasteur's experiments remained. In 1872, Henry Bastian, professor of pathological anatomy at University College, London, "published his *Beginnings of Life*, in which he emphatically supported the old idea that life could be produced from non-living matter."[16] The facts alone could not convince Bastian because his well-guarded presuppositions would not let him "see" the new facts.

In the late 1790s, the Académie Française was involved in a public debate over the reality and nature of meteorites. While there were meteor showers in the eighteenth century, no member of the Académie had actually seen the bits of rock and iron that survive the fiery descent through earth's atmosphere. Peasants and countryfolk had come across the extraterrestrial projectiles, but the scientists did not believe the witnesses. They believed that the streaks of light they saw in the sky were atmospheric phenomena similar to lightening. For these scientists, it was illogical and absurd to believe that rocks could fall from the sky.

> Once this explanation had been arrived at, the Académie was impervious to further testimony. It simply didn't matter what evidence was produced or how well it was attested. On July 24, 1790, a widely witnessed shower of meteorites fell in southwest France. Samples of these meteorites and three hundred statements by witnesses were sent to the Académie. But the scientists "knew" rocks could not fall from the sky. It was "a physically impossible phenomenon," and they, after all, were the most respected authorities of the time. Accordingly, the Academicians ridiculed the rock samples and the statements by the witnesses and sent them back.
>
> The greatest impediment to the advancement of science is not lack of evidence but lack of perspective.[17]

A false theory of reality discounted the validity of any new evidence, because the evidence did not fit the theory. A similar type of argument is used to explain the existence of the world and man's place in it. "The existence and the design of the world points to a Creator," says the theist. "Not so," says the atheist. "Matter is self-existing, and over time evolved into the universe that we now see." The theist and the atheist are looking at the same evidence and yet come to different conclusions as to what the evidence means. In a similar fashion, the theist looks at the intricate makeup of man himself and concludes that this evidence supports a belief in a designer. The atheist looks at what he considers to be evidence for his position and concludes that it supports a belief in the marvels of natural selection.[18]

But evidences do not have the ability to "speak." The fossil record, looked at by evolutionists as incontrovertible proof that their position is true, must be interpreted. "Unfortunately, fossils do not come with labels reading, 'I am an ancestor of man,' 'I am the ancestor of the chimpanzee,' or 'My line became extinct.'"[19] The evolutionist and the creationist are interpreting the facts in terms of an established belief system. Ultimately, then, this question remains: What standard is being used to interpret the evidence and how reliable is that standard?

Even after being confronted with a preponderance of evidence, history shows us that people holding contrary opinions will not always change their views because they do not like the alternative. In effect, they will believe a hypothesis even though there is little or no evidence to support it. Consider the following:

> D.M.S. Watson, known to the public for his B.B.C. talks popularizing the Darwinian notion that human beings descended from primates, declared in an address to his fellow biologists at a Cape Town conference: "Evolution itself is accepted by zoologists not because it has been observed to occur or... can be proved by logically coherent evidence to be true, but because the only alternative, special creation, is clearly incredible."[20]

C. S. Lewis was astounded at Watson's frank admission. Lewis responded: "Has it come to that? Does the whole vast structure of modern naturalism depend not on positive evidence but simply on an *a priori* metaphysical prejudice? Was it devised not to get in facts but to keep out God?"[21] Since believing in God did not suit Watson, he decided to believe in a worldview that could not be supported by the facts. Evidences do not speak for themselves as Lewis wants to maintain. There is always a prior commitment to some belief system that interprets the facts. At least Watson was honest enough to admit it.

Are Evidences Unimportant?

Worldviews aim to make the facts of experience fit together into a cogent system. New ideas often disturb established worldviews. Factual claims that do not fit a person's adopted worldview are often discarded as non-facts or determined to be irrelevant to the argument. For example, when Jesus was raised from the dead, the chief priests hoped they could explain the event away by claiming that the whole story was fabricated by Jesus' disciples. The soldiers who reported the resurrection were given large sums of money to say, "His disciples came by night and stole Him away while we were asleep" (Matt. 28:13). The priests and the soldiers knew that this was not true. Even so, they presented it as an established fact.

What about those who knew the truth about the resurrection? Did they become believers in light of the resurrection evidence? Not all of them. Many were content to dismiss the obvious testimony of eyewitnesses to keep their anti-supernatural worldview intact. No amount of evidence which can be presented will convince someone who does not like the implications of the evidence:

> This is true of even the most "convincing" Christian argument—a cogent case for the historicity of the resurrection. Upon hearing such an argument, one listener may reply, "Aha, this *is* ultimately a chance universe in which even the most unexpected of things can happen once. A man rising from the dead, can you

imagine that?" Or another may say, "Erik Von Daniken must be right. Jesus must have been one of those men from outer space, evidently from a planet where men are so constituted that they come back to life after dying." In neither case has the data been seen to confirm that claim which it was intended to confirm—that Jesus is divine, the Son of God.[22]

How can this be? Why doesn't evidence always convince? In the case of evidence relating to Jesus Christ, once a person acknowledges that He is indeed the Son of God, a change of heart and mind results. Repentance from sin and trusting in Jesus' finished work on the cross are the necessary responses in light of the evidence. In order to avoid submission to Christ as God, many people go out of their way to dismiss the facts or reinterpret them to be absolved of having to face the risen Christ. The naturalist must find ways to explain away the apparently *super*natural. When an explanation is not readily available, he asks for more evidence (that he interprets in terms of his worldview) rather than abandon his naturalism as a philosophy. The Bible describes this as "suppressing the truth in unrighteousness" (Rom. 1:18).

Conclusion

Getting a skeptic to admit that he believes in terms of presuppositions and not on the basis of facts alone is sometimes a difficult task. But it is necessary when trying to establish the point that facts are often what we make them. Even the admission by a skeptic that he thinks and believes in terms of presuppositions does not necessarily mean that he will abandon his anti-supernatural worldview and embrace the Christian worldview. Many people saw Jesus heal the sick and raise the dead. Not all of them believed.

Notes

1. Greg L. Bahnsen, *Van Til's Apologetic: Readings and Analysis* (Phillipsburg, NJ: Presbyterian and Reformed, 1998), 2, note 4.

2. Edward John Carnell, *An Introduction to Christian Apologetics* (Grand Rapids, MI: Eerdmans, 1948), 66. Emphasis in original.

3. Silvester Petro, *The Kingsport Strike* (New Rochelle, NY: Arlington House, 1967), 27–28.

4. Josh McDowell, *The New Evidence that Demands a Verdict* (Nashville, TN: Thomas Nelson, 1999), 351

5. John M. Frame, *The Doctrine of the Knowledge of God* (Phillipsburg, NJ: Presbyterian and Reformed, 1987), 45, 125.

6. Greg L. Bahnsen, *Always Ready: Directions for Defending the Faith* (Texarkana, AR: Covenant Media Foundation, 1996), 71–72. Also see Richard Purtill, *Reason to Believe* (Grand Rapids, MI: Eerdmans, 1974), 83–84.

7. John M. Frame, *Cornelius Van Til: An Analysis of His Thought* (Phillipsburg, NJ: Presbyterian and Reformed, 1995), 136.

8. Philosopher Gordon Allport comments: "Every man, whether he is religiously inclined or not, has his own ultimate presuppositions. He finds he cannot live his life without them, and for him they are true. Such presuppositions, whether they be called ideologies, philosophies, notions, or merely hunches about life, exert creative pressure upon all conduct." (Cited in James L. Christian, *Philosophy: An Introduction to the Art of Wondering* [New York: Holt, Rinehart, and Wilson, 1977], 13).

9. Roy A. Clouser, *The Myth of Religious Neutrality: An Essay on the Hidden Role of Religious Belief in Theories* (Notre Dame, IN: University of Notre Dame Press, 1991), 26–27.

10. Georgia Harkness, *Mysticism: Its Meaning and Message* (Nashville, TN: Abingdon Press, 1973), 56.

11. William R. Fix, *The Bone Peddlers: Selling Evolution* (New York: Macmillan, 1984), xix.

12. Joyce Appleby, Lynn Hunt, and Margaret Jacob, *Telling the Truth About History* (New York: W.W. Norton and Co., 1994), 164.

13. Appleby, Hunt, and Jacob, *Telling the Truth About History*, 164.

14. Abiogenesis: the origin (*genesis*) of life from non (*a*) life (*bio*).

15. Colin A. Ronan, *Science: Its History and Development Among the World's Cultures* (New York: Facts on File Publications, 1982), 431.

16. Ronan, *Science*, 432.

17. Fix, *The Bone Peddlers*, xviii.

18. These two approaches are contrasted in Michael J. Behe, *Darwin's Black Box: The Biochemical Challenge to Evolution* (New York: The Free Press, 1996) and Richard Dawkins, *The Blind Watchmaker: Why the Evidence of Evolution Reveals A Universe Without Design* (New York: W.W. Norton, 1986).

19. Fix, *The Bone Peddlers*, 4.

20. Quoted in Herbert Schlossberg, *Idols for Destruction: Christian Faith and Its Confrontation with American Society* (Wheaton, IL: Crossway, [1983] 1993), 144-45.

21. C.S. Lewis, *They Asked for a Paper* (London: Geoffrey Bles, 1962), 163.

22. Thomas V. Morris, *Francis Schaeffer's Apologetics: A Critique* (Chicago, IL: Moody Press, 1976), 108n.

8

Putting Reason in Perspective

In everyday language rationalism has come to mean the attempt to judge everything in the light of reason. Bound up with this is the assumption that, when this is done, reason will have completely disposed of the supernatural, and that we will be left with nothing but nature and hard facts.[1]

Some philosophers hold that what we ultimately know is formulated solely by our ability to reason independent of any outside authority. In its most blatant form, such a view is "thinking that operates independently of God."[2] For some, reason becomes the standard by which all other standards must be tested. Using reason in this way is called *rationalism*. A person who believes that reason is the ultimate standard is called a *rationalist*.

The rationalists developed various phrases and slogans that expressed the supremacy of reason. All ideas must be "in accord with reason." They must be "tried before the bar of reason." Any idea that does not "satisfy the demands of reason" must be rejected. All ideas must "justify themselves before reason." Philosophy begins and ends with the "first principles of reason."[3]

In the final analysis, the rationalist says, "If it's not reasonable, then it cannot be true." That's just the point. There is no universal "standard of reasonableness" that everyone agrees on. Two or more very "reasonable" people can and do disagree on any number of subjects, and yet each believes that he is being the most rational. Even with agreed upon laws of logic, philosophers often come to different conclusions on any number of subjects. A rationalist might defend his rationalist approach by claiming that it's the *principles* of reason that are ultimate not the failed attempts of people who use reason. Fair enough. But this still doesn't account for why the principles of reason are ultimately reasonable.

The Enlightenment philosophers of the eighteenth century rejected special revelation (the Bible) as the ultimate standard of authority and declared reason to be supreme. "In their view miracles and other phenomena not explained by natural laws and reason were mere superstitions."[4] Reason was elevated to god-like status. "Europe disintegrated because the goddess of Reason, whom the French revolutionaries placed, in the shape of a Parisian streetwalker, upon the altar of Notre Dame,"[5] became France's new authority. She was "carried shoulder-high into the cathedral by men dressed in Roman costumes."[6] The church of Notre Dame was reconsecrated to the "Cult of Reason." Reason, not revelation, ruled. While these philosophers were not atheists, even so, they reasoned as if God did not exist. Their worldview was deistic. A deist believes that God created the universe "and instilled within it natural laws to ensure its orderly operation." Consequently, "the world runs according to God's precise initial design without any need for His intrusion. . . . Because deism rejects divine intervention in the affairs of the created world, the only means available for man to know God is through what has been made—the creation itself. Verbal revelation in the Bible, the deity of Christ, and miracles are all discarded as possibilities."[7] For the deist, reason is a law unto itself, as though man's mind were self-sufficient, not in need of divine revelation. This attitude commonly leads people to think that they are in a position to think independently, to govern their own lives, and to judge the credibility of God's word based on their own insight and authority.[8]

In time, theistic rationalism, which rejected even the possibility of special revelation, turned into atheistic rationalism with the publication of Charles Darwin's *On the Origin of Species* (1859). The doctrine of evolution destroyed belief in God because its starting point is self-consciously atheistic. In 1862, Charles Hodge concluded that Darwinism "is Atheism." Hodge went on to write, "This does not mean, as before said, that Mr. Darwin himself and all who adopt his views are atheists; but it means that his theory is atheistic, that the exclusion of design from nature is . . . tantamount to atheism."[9]

The secular religionists had put their trust in technology and the Darwinian worldview of promised evolutionary advancement. Survival of the fittest had become the new ethical standard. The American industrialist Andrew Carnegie embraced the social implications of Darwin's theories and applied them to the world of business. "That light came in as a flood and all was clear. Not only had I got rid of theology and the supernatural, but I found the truth of evolution."[10] John D. Rockefeller, using Darwinian logic, believed that "The growth of a large business is merely the survival of the fittest."[11]

Darwin's theory had swept the universe clean of any need for a deity. Soon after the publication of *On the Origin of Species*, everything was up for grabs. Darwin had created a spiritual ozone hole, a chance and impersonal universe that became a metaphysical dead end. The depletion of the canopy of God's grace and moral order over our world soon increased the incidence of spiritual cancer. Could a cure be found? A purely rationalistic, materialistic, and impersonal explanation for the existence of man and his world proved to be inadequate and unacceptable for many. As much as the materialists wanted to deny it, man is a spiritual creature, and he needs spiritual nurturing.

Man was becoming less than human through the entire supposed scientific process outlined by Darwin and the followers of his new naturalistic and scientific religion. The atrocities of Josef Stalin and Adolf Hitler revealed in stark detail how despotic and cruel the impersonal worldview of naturalism could be. It is no accident that Communism and Nazism claimed Darwin as their patron saint. Darwin's approach to origins found an enthusiastic adherent in Karl Marx and his communist successors. Marx wrote to Friedrich Engels in 1866 that Darwin's *Origin of Species* "is the book which contains the basis in natural history for our view."[12] There are no absolutes, man is nothing, and the State is everything. For Communism, the advancement of the State is the march of god on earth. Communism insures this through raw power, the Gulag, and the "necessary" extinction of millions to bring the "ideals" of Communism to the masses.[13]

It is significant to note that "after 1949 when the communists took control of China, the first new text introduced to all the schools was neither Marxist or Leninist, but Darwinian."[14] With Darwin, all things are permissible. For a fleeting moment, Communism was seen as the new god that would save us. But even here, disillusionment set in. It, too, was a materialist god that had failed to deliver on its promises.[15]

No Foundation for Reason

Of course, if there is no God, there is no word from God. Man is left on his own to formulate his own worldview and system of morals. But if evolution is true, then there can be no assurance of the reliability of anything, even reason. For example, Richard Dawkins, who dismisses any notion of design in the cosmos is left with a staggering dilemma. "Dawkins ceaselessly urges us to be rational, but he does so in the name of a philosophy that implies that no such thing as rationality exists, for our thoughts are at the mercy of our genes and memes."[16]

An atheistic rationalist creates a closed system of his own making. Only those things within his worldview are real. Of course, he defines the nature of reality. Those things that do not fit his rationalistic world-view do not exist. As a result, the consistent rationalist will reject the reality of God, the soul, angels, special revelation, miracles, providence, immortality, sin, and the need for salvation. For the atheistic rational-ist, "'Good' and 'bad' as ideas are rooted in bodily tissue as realities."[17] Only those things that can be seen, handled, and analyzed are real and verifiable. "Good" and "bad," whether conduct or opinions, are subjec-tive terms that are defined for the moment.

> In rejecting God, the atheist still has to face evil in the world
> and explain where it came from. Can he? I doubt it. But the
> atheist also has to explain where good comes from. If there is no
> God, it's hard to make any sense out of either of those concepts.
> If there is no God, then there is nothing that is evil or good. You
> have to have a standard of good and evil that stands outside of
> us to define what evil and good actually are.[18]

The definition of what's good and bad can change tomorrow in the random worldview of the rationalist since he defines the parameters of his own worldview. If he wants to include a new behavior and declare it to be moral, he only has to redraw the lines of his worldview. When a group of high level Nazi officers were conferring on how to rid Ger-many and Europe of the "Jewish Problem," the issue of law arose. One of the participants maintained that the law as written did not permit them to disenfranchise the Jews. Seizing an opportunity, another re-sponded matter-of-factly, "We make the laws we need."[19]

Reason is a Tool

The biblical understanding of reason and the use of the mind in pursuing rational lines of arguments is quite different from that of the rationalist. "The Christian is not hostile to reason as reason, but to Reason as god. The Christian does not believe in reason [as an ultimate authority]; he believes in God and he uses reason under God."[20] We were created to use our minds. "Do not be as the horse or as the mule which have no understanding" (Proverbs 32:9a). The Christian who does not think in terms of God's Word is described as "senseless and ignorant," like the "beast" (Psalm 73:22). They act "like unreasoning animals" (2 Peter 2:12). Reasoning is required of the Christian and non-Christian, but on God's terms. In this way, "reason can be thought of as a *tool*—man's intellectual or mental capacity. Taken in this sense, reason is a gift of God to man, indeed part of the divine image. When God bids His people 'Come let us reason together' (Isa. 1:18), we see that, like God, we are capable of rational thought and communication. God has given us our mental abilities to serve and glorify Him. It is part of the greatest commandment of the law that we should"[21] love God with our mind (Matt. 22:37).

The Bible tells us that the world is a rational place in which to live. The world runs by fixed and predictable laws. This is why it can be studied, investigated, and analyzed with the assurance that what's true today will be true tomorrow. Is it any wonder that science, music, and the arts, to name just three areas of study, had their greatest advances in the Christian West where an environment for inquiry and experimentation was cultivated?[22] Loren Eiseley writes in *Darwin's Century* that "it is the Christian world which finally gave birth in a clear, articulate fashion to the experimental method of science itself.... *[T]he sheer act of faith that the universe possessed order and could be interpreted by rational minds....* It is surely one of the curious paradoxes of history that science, which professionally has little to do with faith, owes its origins to an act of faith that the universe can be rationally interpreted, and that science today is sustained by that assumption."[23]

Understanding Reason's Limitations

But like any tool, reason can be misused—like trying to cut glass with a hammer or studying the stars with a microscope. In a similar way, the limited and autonomous (Greek: *auto*=self and *nomos*=law) mind, unaided by special revelation (the Bible), is incapable of making dogmatic and final assertions about eternal truths. Like the hammer that's not designed to cut glass or the microscope that's powerless to search out the stars, the mind is limited in its capacity to judge truths that are beyond its capacity. The Bible declares:

> "For My thoughts are not your thoughts, neither are your ways My ways," declares the LORD. "For as the heavens are higher than the earth, so are My ways higher than your ways, and My thoughts than your thoughts" (Isa. 55:8–9)

Does this mean that the only things that we truly know come from special revelation? Not at all. As Cornelius Van Til writes, "It is true of theology that it gets its facts about God almost exclusively from the Bible. We say almost exclusively, because we also learn about God from nature. . . . We do not limit ourselves entirely to the Bible when we study anything else."[24] This is why God created us with eyes to see, ears to hear, noses to smell, and hands to feel. "The hearing ear and the seeing eye, the LORD has made both of them" (Prov. 20:12).

> The earliest scientist was very likely to be a believer who did not think scientific inquiry and religious devotion incompatible. On the contrary, his motivation for studying the wonders of nature was a religious impulse to glorify the God who had created them. Indeed, though he studied the physical creation, he was unlikely to be a scientist per se (the term "scientist" was not coined until 1834) but a churchman. Especially in the English countryside, the parson-naturalist was a common figure.[25]

Even so, all that we learn from experience and observation must be interpreted by some standard. "For the Christian all interpretation of any fact of 'nature' even by 'reason' should be performed self-consciously as an act of re-interpretation of God's revelation."[26]

The Law of Non-Contradiction

It seems that nearly anything can be believed today, even obvious contradictory worldviews. Some people are willing to live with inherent contradictions because they have been told that pluralism, diversity, and tolerance demand it. We are informed by the religious pluralists, "It doesn't matter what you believe about God, as long as you're sincere in your beliefs." We are assured that there are many ways to God. But what if one set of religious beliefs *contradicts* another set of religious beliefs? In the worldview of religious diversity, all religions are equal *even if they're contradictory*. No single religious tradition is any more true than any other religious tradition. While this makes for happy harmony on paper, in the real world, it just doesn't work. Try asserting diversity in the following areas:

- "It doesn't matter what you believe about *mathematics*, as long as you're sincere in your beliefs."
- "It doesn't matter what you believe about *electricity*, as long as you're sincere in your beliefs."
- "It doesn't matter what you believe about *Nazism*, as long as you're sincere in your beliefs."
- "It doesn't matter what you believe about *slavery*, as long as you're sincere in your beliefs."
- "It doesn't matter what you believe about *medicine*, as long as you're sincere in your beliefs."

Few people would tolerate such nonsense, but many are very comfortable with the concept that all religions are valid even when they are contradictory. This is not a new idea. "The early church was surrounded by religious pluralism and syncretism.... Celsus, a pagan who attacked Christianity [in the second century], wrote, 'It makes no difference if one invokes the highest God or Zeus or Adonai or Sabaoth or Amoun, as the Egyptians do, or Papaios, as the Scythians do.'"[27] It's not much different today when the Salem Religious Association, of Salem, Massachusetts, admitted a new member—a witch of the Rosarian Order of Wicca, a pagan faith involving worship of the forces of nature. "It just means that we're recognizing it as a valid faith tradition," said Rev. Randy Wilkerson of St. Peter's Episcopal Church.[28] No matter that Wicca and Christianity are contradictory faiths!

The Law at Work

Tolerating conflicting claims to truth arises when the law of non-contradiction is abandoned, a law that finds its validity in God's character. It's no surprise, therefore, that we see a growing acceptance of contradictory belief systems in a time when atheism seems to be the official religion of the modern world.

What is the law of non-contradiction, and why is it important in the Christian's apologetic task? This logical law states that something cannot be one thing (A) and another thing (non-A) at the same time and in the same sense. An object cannot be round and square at the same time in the same sense. A square block of wood could be put on a lathe and turned into a ball. In this case the block would now be a ball, but it would not be a square block and a ball *at the same time*. An object might have attributes of squareness and roundness (an octagon), but it could not be said that it is either a circle or a square.

The Bible assumes the validity of the law of non-contradiction when it states,

- "No one can serve two masters; for either he will hate the one and love the other, or he will hold to one and despise the other. You cannot serve God and mammon" (Matt. 6:24).
- "He who is not with Me is against Me; and he who does not gather with Me scatters" (Matt. 12:30).
- "A good tree cannot produce bad fruit, nor can a rotten tree produce good fruit" (Matt. 7:18).
- "Any kingdom divided against itself is laid waste, and a house divided against itself falls" (Luke 11:17).

Can something be true and false at the same time and in the same way? Can God exist and not exist? The law of non-contradiction says no. All who reason, even those who deny the law's validity, assume its soundness *before they begin to reason, and as they argue to defend their position.*

> Strictly speaking, the law of noncontradiction cannot be proved. The reason is simple. Any argument offered as proof for the law of noncontradiction would of necessity have to assume the law as part of the proof. Hence, any direct proof of the law would end up being circular. It would beg the question.[29]

While at the theoretical level some people try to dismiss the law of non-contradiction, at the practical level, it's impossible. A person who asserts that the law is not valid must assume the law's validity in order to argue for its dismissal. For example, the claim that "no one can know anything" assumes that at least one thing can be known. In practical terms, a person who denies the law of non-contradiction must still live with its consequences in the real world. Ronald H. Nash shows how absurd seemingly profound and open philosophical systems are ultimately absurd and impractical when it comes to the real world:

I once heard of a young man who was called into his local office of the Internal Revenue Service for an audit. The reason for his trouble was his failure over several years to file a tax return. When asked by the IRS agent why he had failed to file, the youth replied that in college he had learned that the law of non-contradiction is an optional, nonnecessary principle. Once he had learned that there is no difference between *B* and non-*B*, it was only a matter of time before he realized that no difference exists between filing a tax return and not filing a tax return. "That's very interesting," said the tax agent. "I've never heard that one before. Since you believe that no difference exists between *B* and non-*B*, I'm sure you also believe that there is no difference between being in jail and not being in jail!"[30]

Some college professors are notorious for presenting absurd assumptions all in the name of openness, pluralism, diversity, and tolerance even though they don't work in the real world and they don't run their classrooms in terms of their promoted relativism.

Pluralism acts as a wedge to destroy the notion that there are absolutes. Pluralism thrives in an environment where contradictions are accepted as normative. With the leveling of religion comes the leveling of morality. All lifestyles are permitted in the name of diversity and pluralism. In nearly every case, Christians are the losers.

Pluralism is the bait for Christians to embrace a distinctiveless Christianity. We are to "trust" secular and religious advocates of pluralism since we all supposedly share common concerns and values. Christians are encouraged to set aside only a few of the distinct doctrines of the Christian faith so as not to offend anyone. Once these are discarded, Christians are free to speak on any subject as long as biblical absolutes are left out of the discussion.

The call for Christians to adopt pluralism is just another way of diluting the truth. Pluralism becomes a club to pound out the theological bumps that makes Christianity unique among all the religions of the world. And what is the fruit of the new and improved pluralist worldview?

> As soon as the words "Our pluralistic society will not per-
> mit . . ." are uttered, Nativity scenes are dismantled, Christmas
> vacation becomes Winter Holiday, and a moment of silence in
> public schools is no longer merely a vain illusion but a prohib-
> ited sin against pluralism. But say "Our pluralistic society re-
> quires…" and homosexual activists receive affirmative action
> support for job demands, parents need not be notified of a mi-
> nor daughter's intention to abort their grandchild, and Rotary
> Clubs and saunas are [turned into] unisex [establishments].
> Whether or not one endorses pluralism seems to be a litmus test
> for whether one is *persona grata* in the modern world.[31]

The pluralists, in their desire to be heard, have abandoned the very thing that will make a fundamental difference in the world: Jesus Christ and the uniqueness of God's written revelation.

Is pluralism biblically defensible? Should the Christian back off, giving a supposed equal opportunity to other competing minority or majority positions in the name of pluralism when those positions advocate unbiblical and anti-Christian lifestyles? Do we allow abortion for competing systems when they claim the "pluralist" model in defense of their position? Should the State allow "homosexual" marriages? Would the Mormon be permitted to practice polygamy?[32] Should Satanists be permitted to worship according to the "dictates of their own conscience"? Denying the law of non-contradiction makes it all possible.

Borrowed Capital

How is it possible that people who deny the law of non-contradiction function reasonably well in the real world? For example, an atheist can have no true understanding of anything if he presupposes that God does not exist, and yet most atheists act fairly rational and moral.

But how can the atheist trust his thinking processes in a world where randomness rules? Within the atheist's worldview there is no way to account for rational thought, cause and effect, the law of non-contradiction, and laws of logic, all necessary tools for thinking straight. What's logical today may be illogical tomorrow, according to consistent atheistic accidentalism. Who can ever know what tomorrow will bring? *Que sera, sera*—"Whatever will be, will be"—is the only possible standard for the atheist.

If this is true, then how can the atheist think rationally when his own worldview will not support the concept of rationality? How can chance bring about order? The atheist, in order to think logically and enjoy the results of rational thought, must jettison his chance-based presuppositions and adopt the design-based presuppositions of the biblical worldview: Man can think rationally because God is rational; man can think logically because God is logical; the law of non-contradiction operates because there are no contradictions in God. Why is reason reasonable? Why is logic logical? Why is the law of non-contradiction non-contradictory? Rationality, logic, and the law of non-contradiction do not operate independent of God. They operate consistently and dependably because they are enjoined to God's character. Without God these laws that govern thinking would not exist. The atheist, therefore, must be *inconsistent* with his chance-based worldview and borrow presuppositions from the Christian worldview in order to validate his invalid worldview.

Conclusion

Tolerance, diversity, and inclusion are the philosophical watchwords of our day. In order to acknowledge cultural differences, we are being told that we must abandon the notion of distinctions at the worldview level. All worldviews are acceptable except any worldview that maintains that not all worldviews are acceptable. Even though contradictions exist, they are to be embraced in the name of diversity and good will.

Notes

1. Colin Brown, *Christianity and Western Thought: A History of Philosophers, Ideas, and Movements* (Downers Grove, IL: InterVarsity Press, 1990), 173.

2. David K. Clark, *Dialogical Apologetics: A Person-Centered Approach to Christian Defense* (Grand Rapids, MI: Baker Books, 1993), 13.

3. Robert A. Morey, *Battle of the Gods: The Gathering Storm in Modern Evangelicalism* (Southbridge, MA: Crown Publications, 1989), 124.

4. Richard Cobb, gen. ed., *Voices of the French Revolution* (Topsfield, MA: Salem House Publishers, 1988), 25.

5. Richard Hertz, *Chance and Symbol* (Chicago, IL: The University of Chicago Press, 1948), 100.

6. Francis A. Schaeffer, *How Should We Then Live?* (1976) in *The Complete Works of Francis A. Schaeffer: A Christian Worldview*, 5 vols. (Wheaton, IL: Crossway Books, 1984), 5:122.

7. W. Gary Phillips and William E. Brown, *Making Sense of Your World from a Biblical Viewpoint* (Chicago, IL: Moody Press, 1991), 79.

8. Greg L. Bahnsen, *Always Ready: Directions for Defending the Faith* (Texarkana, AR: Covenant Media Foundation, 1996), 113.

9. Charles Hodge, *What Is Darwinism? And Other Writings on Science and Religion* (Grand Rapids, MI: Baker, 1995), 156–57. For a contemporary discussion of the design issue in the discussion of origins, see William A. Dembski, *Intelligent Design: The Bridge Between Science and Theology* (Downers, Grove, IL: InterVarsity Press, 1999).

10. Quoted in John W. Whitehead, *The End of Man* (Westchester, IL: Crossway Books, 1986), 53.

11. James Burke, *The Day the Universe Changed* (Boston, MA: Little, Brown and Company, 1985), 271.

12. R. L. Meek, ed., *Marx and Engels on Malthus* (New York: International Publishers, 1954), 171. Quoted in Michael Pitman, *Adam and Evolution* (London, England: Rider & Company, 1984), 24.

13. Mark Kramer, ed., *The Black Book of Communism: Crimes, Terror, Repression*, trans. Jonathan Murphy and Mark Kramer (Cambridge, MA: Harvard University Press, 1999); Robert Conquest, *The Great Terror: A Reassessment* (New York: Oxford University Press, 1990); and Lloyd Billingsly, *The Generation that Knew Not Josef: A Critique of Marxism and the Religious Left* (Portland, OR: Multnomah Press, 1985).

14. Pitman, *Adam and Evolution*, 24.

15. Richard H. Crossman, *The God that Failed* (Chicago, IL: Regnery Gateway, [1949] 1983).

16. Phillip E. Johnson, "A Summary Critique: The Robot Rebellion of Richard Dawkins," *Christian Research Journal*, 22:1 (1999), 56. A "meme" (pronounced "meem") is a replication of a belief pattern, an idea passed on and adopted by others. It's analogous to a gene, but it has no physical substance. It's the evolutionist's way of accounting for the non-material side of thought, that is, the mind.

17. Lionel Tiger, *The Manufacture of Evil: Ethics, Evolution and the Industrial System* (New York: Harper & Row, 1987), 17.

18. Greg Koukl, "You've Got to Believe Something," *The Plain Truth* (January/February 1999), 39.

19. From the HBO Special, *Conspiracy* (2001).

20. Rousas John Rushdoony, *The Word of Flux: Modern Man and the Problem of Knowledge* (Fairfax, VA: Thoburn Press, 1975), 36.

21. Bahnsen *Always Ready*, 113.

22. "From the beginning of the thirteenth century onward we see a persistent effort to integrate Aristotelian natural philosophy with Christian theology, a goal that was not achieved without soul-searching and struggle. In the end, Christianity took its basic categories of thought and much of its metaphysics and cosmology from Aristotle. . ." (David C. Lindberg and Ronald L. Numbers, "Introduction," *God and Nature: Historical Essays on the Encounter between Christianity and Science* [Berkeley, CA: University of California Press, 1986], 10). For example, Copernicus's sun-centered hypothesis was a rejection of Aristotelian physics.

23. Loren Eiseley, *Darwin's Century* (Garden City, NJ: Doubleday Anchor Books, 1958), 62. Emphasis in original.

24. Cornelius Van Til, *An Introduction to Systematic Theology*, Volume 5 of the series *In Defense of the Faith* (Philadelphia, PA: Presbyterian and Reformed, 1974), 15.

25. Nancy R. Pearcey and Charles B. Thaxton, *The Soul of Science: Christian Faith and Natural Philosophy* (Wheaton, IL: Crossway Books, 1994), 19.

26. Van Til, *An Introduction to Systematic Theology*, 15.

27. Paul Copan, *"True For You, but Not True For Me": Deflating the Slogans that Leave Christians Speechless* (Minneapolis, MN: Bethany House Publishers, 1998), 73.

28. "Diversity," *USA Today* (July 19, 1993), 3A.

29. Ronald H. Nash, *Worldviews in Conflict: Choosing Christianity in a World of Ideas* (Grand Rapids, MI: Zondervan, 1992), 82.

30. Ronald H. Nash, *Life's Ultimate Questions: An Introduction to Philosophy* (Grand Rapids, MI: Zondervan, 1999), 195.

31. Harold O. J. Brown, "Pluralism in Miniature," *Chronicles* (May 1988), 13.

32. In the nineteenth century, the Supreme Court declared that polygamy was out of accord with the basic tenets of Christianity: "It is contrary to the spirit of Christianity and the civilization which Christianity has produced in the Western world." *Late Corporation of the Church of Jesus Christ of Latter Day Saints v. United States*, 136 U.S. 1 (1890). Earlier the Court declared that "Bigamy and polygamy are crimes by the laws of all civilized and Christian countries.... To call their advocacy a tenet of religion is to offend the common sense of mankind." (*Davis v. Beason*, 133 U.S. 333, 341-342 [1890]).

Part Four
Real World Apologetics

9

Leaping into the Void

Because of the prestige of science as a source of power, and
because of the general neglect of philosophy, the popular [world-
and-life view] of our times contains a large element of what may
be called "nothing-but" thinking. Human beings, it is more or less
tacitly assumed, are nothing but bodies, animals, even machines....
Values are nothing but illusions that somehow got themselves
mixed up with our experience of the world.[1]

"Is God Dead?" With a black background and bright red lettering,
Time magazine's April 8, 1966 cover dared to question the existence of
God in a nation where "In God We Trust" is its motto. Screenwriter
Edward Anhalt, quoted in the *Time* issue, sums up the God-is-dead
worldview: "God is an infantile fantasy, which was necessary when men
did not understand what lightning was. God is a cop-out."[2] The materialists tell us that God is dead because we no longer need Him to explain our world and the way it works. The God-is-dead theologians
claim that "*God is Man*. Or God is the Universe."[3] The results are the
same: With the death of God, man becomes God. There's nothing new
under the sun (Gen. 3:5).

The editors at *Time* were not the first to question the existence of God. The "death of God" movement has a long history. According to the naturalists and materialists, God died a long time ago. Those who want to hold onto theistic notions are only in denial.[4] For example, when Napoleon asked French astronomer Pierre-Simon Laplace (1749–1827) why his multi-volume *Celestial Mechanics* made no mention of "the author of the universe," he answered: "Sire, I have no need of that hypothesis."[5]

Taking their lead from the work of Isaac Newton,[6] scientists like Laplace proposed that the workings of the cosmos could be explained with the cold precision of mathematics without the need of the "God hypothesis." Of course, almost no one dared to ask the origin of the mathematical principles that were used to rid us of God. Anyway, mathematics can only explain so much.

> But for all of its power, mathematics, even armed with the power of calculus, has failed to fully answer the problem of complexity. The universe is far messier and more unpredictable than any equation can capture. Mathematics, as the language of physics, enables science to describe the movement of bodies in space, but what it cannot do is describe the full complexity of those bodies in anything but equations as complex as the subject itself. No equation can capture the essence of a fly, much less explain how the whole universe was created from a point of singularity.[7]

The Bible comes to the point when it attacks the absurdity of the no-God hypothesis: "The fool has said in his heart, 'There is no god'" (Psalm 14:1; 53:1). Without an omniscient and omnipotent God, nothing makes sense. Joseph-Louis Lagrange, who worked with Laplace on *Celestial Mechanics*, when he heard of Laplace's remark to Napoleon, "is said to have shaken his head at his colleague's skepticism, commenting, 'But it is a beautiful hypothesis just the same. It explains so many things.'"[8]

God Returns

Within three years of asking "Is God Dead?," a new question was put forth in appropriate psychedelic colors, this one appearing on the cover of the December 26, 1969 issue of *Time*: "Is God Coming Back to Life?" The answer was a resounding yes! But in what form? God was about to be resurrected in numerous incarnations in hopes of restoring meaning to an impersonal cosmos. That pursuit continues even today by parents who "still want to make sure their kids grow up with God."[9] Rabbi David Wolpe writes that "People want to feel they're more than DNA-decided robots and that life is more than a roulette wheel of genes."[10] Well said, but in many cases the new deities are an amalgamation, a multi-faceted set of gods and goddesses created in man's own image to fit current needs. The revival of "spirituality" comes by way of "religious shortcuts"[11]:

> Millions turned to personal reflection, seeking awareness and growth in the human potential movement, employing a smorgasbord of approaches: Arica training, astral projection, biofeedback, EST, Gestalt, Hare Krishna, humanistic psychology, massage, psycho-cybernetics, primal therapy, rolfing, Scientology, sensitivity training, Sufism, T'ai Chi, transcendental meditation, yoga, Zen. Sufi saying: "The one who knows his self knows God." And many found their God, as the decade eventually became a time of religious awakening, when individuals en masse were "born again."[12]

The new gods of the new religions were radically different from the personal and redemptive God of biblical Christianity. Sin and the need for reconciliation are dismissed as man's ultimate cosmic problems. Raising one's consciousness to embrace god-like principles make up the creeds of the new religions. In every new religious substitute, man is at the center. Man is god!

"Beep, Beep, Beep. . . "

It's no accident that the desire for renewed cosmic meaning grew out of the uneasy Cold War decade of the 1950s and the Counter Culture 1960s among young people who were trying to "find themselves" in an unpredictable world filled with moral uncertainty.

Technological man had created a weapon of mass destruction that was used to kill thousands of civilians at Hiroshima and Nagasaki. While atomic power in the form of a weapon brought an end to the war, it left people troubled. Many from the post-World War II generation "were shaken and sobered by 'free' societies that had exhumed the specters of barbarism—the Nazi concentration camps, the allied bombing of Cologne and Dresden, the holocaust of Hiroshima—and were settling down uncomfortably to the bleak prospects of a continuing Cold War."[13] There was no longer any place to hide from the effects of a nuclear explosion.[14]

How could we live comfortably when America's military policy in dealing with the Soviet Union was called MAD, Mutual Assured Destruction?[15] America's modern wars were fought, to use the title of a World-War-I-era song, "over there." But now an atomic weapon could be delivered by long-range bombers with almost pin-point accuracy to any spot on the globe. No one was safe. With the Soviet Union's launch of Sputnik 1 on October 4, 1957, a more troubling threat emerged: Intercontinental Ballistic Missiles (ICBM). Sputnik-anxiety is portrayed in the movie *October Sky* based on the book *Rocket Boys* by Homer Hickam, Jr.[16] This heightened anxiety intensified the race to space and eventually filled our missile silos. Pundits called the launch of the first man-made satellite a "bloodless Pearl Harbor." The incessant "beep, beep, beep" that could be picked up on any radio fascinated and troubled the nation. The anxiety had become so great that some families built fallout shelters in their backyards. Here's how one person recalled the era:

> We might not remember Hiroshima, but we recall fallout
> shelters. Civil Defense. Air raid sirens. We hid beneath school
> desks, stored contingency rations. We set our dials on Conelrad
> [CONtrol of ELectromagnetic RADiation]. We lived in the back-
> wash of nuclear holocaust without thinking such a condition
> absurd…. A nightmare was eternity spent underground, in a
> concrete bunker, alone.[17]

The paranoia was satirized in the movie *Blast from the Past* (1999)
where a family enters its shelter in 1962 and doesn't resurface for 35
years. At the time, there was nothing funny about the prospects of a
possible nuclear strike. Signs were posted around cities marking where
fallout shelters were located in case of a Soviet first-strike. If the explosion didn't kill you, the radiation would. Air raid drills were practiced
along with the traditional fire drills in public schools.

As part of the CONELRAD system, it was obligatory for all radios
sold after 1953 to have the AM frequencies 640 and 1240 kHz marked
with small triangles on the dial. The triangles were referred to as CD
marks, for Civil Defense, to make finding the frequencies easy. This
requirement was dropped when the CONELRAD system was replaced
by the Emergency Broadcast System in 1963.

Bomb anxiety spawned a number of popular end-of-the-world
novels (*Canticle for Leibowitz* and *Alas, Babylon*),[18] films (*On the Beach*,
Fail-Safe, and *Dr. Strangelove*),[19] television shows (a few "Twilight
Zone" episodes, *The Day After*, and *Testament*), songs (Barry McGuire's
"Eve of Destruction"), and numerous non-fiction warnings about
"nuclear winter."

While science brought a near end to polio, eradicated smallpox,
made life easier with technological advances in every field of endeavor,
advanced agricultural development so as to almost eliminate famine,
and removed much of the drudgery in the home with a glut of electrical appliances, the post-World War II generation and beyond began

to question the dark side of technology and its potential for spiritual bankruptcy.

> Post-Hiroshima letters-to-the-editor in the nation's news-
> papers... reflected praise and fear of science in about equal pro-
> portions. "Science a Menace" and "Science Moving Too Fast"
> were typical captions. A letter in the *Portland Oregonian* called
> the bomb "the idiot child of science and the machine age." A
> *Louisville Courier-Journal* reader urged a moratorium on research
> until scientists became more "morally adept." Give science a rest
> until we spiritually catch up, agreed a *Boston Globe* subscriber.[20]

The editor of *Scientific American* summed up the ambivalence over science when he wrote, "To the average civilized man of 1950, science no longer means primarily the promise of a more abundant life; it means the atomic bomb."[21] A popular protest sign reads "Science=Death."

The Great Atomic Tribulation

While editorial writers, ethicists, and the general public were de-bating the morality of the bomb and the future of science, biblical Christians, for the most part, added to the shroud of doom by claiming that the bomb was the prelude to a prophetic inevitable Armageddon of atomic origin. "Down to 1945, prophecy interpreters typically envi-sioned this 'burning day' in naturalistic terms—earthquakes, comets, volcanic eruptions—or as an eschatological event beyond human un-derstanding.... With the coming of the atomic bomb, everything changed: it seemed that man himself, in the throes of war, stumbled on the means of his own promised doom."[22] Christians were told that they should welcome such a scenario "and pray for its nearness."[23]

According to modern prophecy writers, Christians will not suffer from a nuclear conflagration because they will be "raptured" from the "great atomic tribulation." This unbiblical idea became just another form of escape from a troubled world.[24] Decade after decade of failed predictions about an always near "rapture" or second coming of Christ turned people away from the church's worldview message.[25] The Bible seemed only to be a book about escape from a troubled world. Young people were looking for answers on how to live in the here and now. Many would reject religion altogether, while others pursued other forms of spiritual fulfillment.

The Beat Goes On

The first ripple of discontent that became a movement was expressed by members of the Beat Generation, "the authentic religious voice of the Atomic Age."[26] The 1950s writings of Jack Kerouac, Allen Ginsberg, Neal Cassady, and William S. Burroughs, laid the foundation for the Counter Culture 1960s and beyond. The 1950s are often thought of as the "Happy Days Era" or "The Good Old Days." Television shows like *Leave It To Beaver*, which premiered on October 4, 1957, the day the Soviet Union launched Sputnik, *Father Knows Best*, *The Donna Read Show*, and *Ozzie and Harriet* depicted more of what families had lost than what was really happening in post-war America. *Leave It To Beaver* "only began to gain mass popularity as that family model, and the era it represented, disappeared and the nation longed for both it and the stability it represented."[27] These shows were not realistic, and not one of them dealt with religion, social issues, and the generational unrest that was quaking below the surface. "Audiences tuned in because television simply reflected what most people thought—or hoped—was real: there was an American Way. Everyone was the same, living in suburbs, married, and happy."[28]

The film *Rebel Without a Cause* (1955) was an attempt to portray an undercurrent of youth restlessness, generational separation, and familial disruption in what was becoming a depersonalized and fractured society. Nearly all the families in *Rebel* are dysfunctional. The fathers are either disengaged or overbearing. In reaction, the teenagers create their own family structure: Jim (James Dean) and Judy (Natalie Wood) take on the role of surrogate parents to the "orphan" John ("Plato"), played by Sal Mineo. In *Leave It To Beaver*, June Cleaver wears a dress, high heels, and pearls, even when she cooks and washes the dishes. Ward is always ready with just the right word of fatherly advice and measured discipline that is perfect for every situation. On the other hand, Jim Backus, who plays James Dean's father in *Rebel*, is spineless, permissive, indecisive, and henpecked. He wears an apron around the house. He is no *Father Knows Best*. But even in this teen-angst movie of alienation, normalcy is the nuclear family and an ordered society.[29]

The American Way of life was about to be challenged from all sides. Real generational estrangement would take place. Every traditional value would be called into question. The post-war generation, the baby boomers, were directionless. In their minds, there was no turning back the clock. The generation gap was born.

> Not knowing precisely where they were going, they defined themselves by what they were for and against. They were against soul-numbing materialism ('Moneytheism'); for imagination, self-expression, Zen. Against society's approved depressives (al-cohol, barbiturates); for outlawed stimulants like marijuana, amphetamines, and mescaline. Against rationalism, repression, racism; for poetry, free sex, jazz.[30]

Materialism was out, spiritual things were in, and it really did not matter what form the spirits came in. "Inwardly, these excesses are made to serve a spiritual purpose, the purpose of an affirmation sill unfocused, still to be defined, unsystematic."[31] For some, mind-altering drugs be-came a form of spiritual experimentation. For others, "drugs were an escape from the reality of their lack of talent."[32] In the first article about the "Beat Generation," John Clellon Holmes wrote, "unlike the Lost Generation [after World War I], which was occupied with the loss of faith, the Beat Generation is becoming more and more occupied with the need for it. As such, it is a disturbing illustration of Voltaire's reliable old joke: 'If there were no God, it would be necessary to invent him.' Not content to bemoan his absence, they are busily and haphazardly inventing totems for him on all sides. . . . [There is an] almost exaggerated will to believe in something, if only in themselves. It is a will to believe, even in the face of an inability to do so in conventional terms. And that is bound to lead to excesses in one direction or another."[33]

While not everyone was "lost" or "beat"[34] in the first half of the twentieth century, enough of the worldview of the Beat Generation leaders trickled down to influence a new generation of intellectuals and social activists who wanted to make changes and to believe in something of their own making. Idealistic professors adopted the worldview of the Beat Generation renegades and assigned their books and poetry to students. Jack Kerouac's *On the Road* (1957), which has been described as "the testament" of the Beat Generation,[35] and *Dharma Bums* (1958), were two of the most influential. Their impact created a monumental worldview shift among students and young people in the 1960s.[36]

> When the hippies made their appearance on the scene in the mid-'60s, it was widely supposed that they had come from nowhere and had no ancestors. They were, however, the direct descendants of the Beats, like most everything else that followed in the turmoil of the '60s. The Beats were of considerable social importance in the 1950s. They were regarded as a threat to the established order—this was the dreaded McCarthy era—as they questioned the conservative corporate and suburban values that were so widely and publicly extolled. Jack Kerouac, with the publicity that followed the publication of *On the Road*, mainstreamed the Beats. And from 1957 on, the writings and acerbic musings of the Beats were beginning to fall on the right ears—college kids. And if you had gone out and asked who the Beats were on any college campus in 1958, for example, you prob-

ably would've heard the same . . . names mentioned over and over. Kerouac and Allen Ginsberg would have topped the lists.[37]

Remnants of the Beat Generation can be seen in the television sit-com *The Many Loves of Doby Gillis* (1959) where Bob Denver, best known for his role as "Gilligan" of *Gilligan's Island*, starred as Maynard G. Krebs. Maynard was a goatee-wearing and unwashed Beatnik carica-ture who was adverse even to the word "work." Other popular shows portrayed "Beatnik" themes as a part of America's underground culture: *Peter Gunn, Alfred Hitchcock Presents*, and *Mr. Lucky*.[38] The caricature came to life during the 1960s among a sizeable number of disenchanted intellectuals on college campuses from coast to coast. The Beats became Hippies, described by Ronald Reagan as those who "Dress like Tarzan, have long hair like Jane, and smell like Cheetah."[39]

Do Not Bend, Fold, Spindle, or Mutilate

After so many years of having a naturalistic worldview dominate our culture, the results have been, ironically, just the opposite of what the rationalists expected. The rebellion of students on college campuses in the 1960s was a revolt against the impersonalism of the modern university and its self-conscious matter-only worldview. An anonymous letter published in a 1966 issue of the *Freedom of Speech Newsletter* ex-pressed the sentiments of impersonalism that had arisen at the Univer-sity of California at Berkeley. The author's outlook was probably typical of many students:

> It is something we see everywhere on campus but find hard to define. Perhaps it was best expressed by the sign one boy pinned to his chest: "I am a UC student. Please don't bend, fold, spindle, or mutilate me."[40] The source of our strength is, very simply, the fact that we are human beings and so cannot forever be treated as raw materials—to be processed.

Students were thought of and treated as "numbers," nothing more than a punch-card, an electronic entry in a dispassionate machine run by nameless and faceless bureaucrats, a perfect picture of what our world had become with the technocrats in charge. The counter culture's depiction of reality as plastic and impersonal was an accurate one. The movie *The Graduate* (1967) portrays this impersonalism early in the movie when Ben Braddock, played by Dustin Hoffman, a recent college graduate, is told to pursue a career in plastics, "a scene that brutally exemplifies the cultural decay of the old order. . . . Ben doesn't know what he wants out of life, but he is certain he doesn't want" what they are offering if it means living like them.[41] Other movies of the era depicted an anti-technology bent. *Planet of the Apes* (1968), starring Charlton Heston, depicts a nearly barren Earth that got that way because the "maniacs" misused technology and "blew it up." Distopian movies like the *Mad Max* trilogy, *Terminator*, *Bladerunner*, and *The Omega Man* recount similar themes.

A rationalistic and materialist-centered universe ruled solely by impersonal and non-purposed physical forces does not generate feeling, purpose, compassion, moral authority, or virtue. Without God, everything human succumbs to the random control of impersonal forces in a mechanistic cosmos manipulated by technocrats. This is poignantly depicted in the first *Star Wars* (1977) movie where Darth Vader, "Dark Father," is described as "more machine than man." The technological Empire creates a desert world wherever it rules. In the sequel, *The Empire Strikes Back* (1980), Luke gains spiritual power on a planet that teems with life, a primordial Garden of Eden. George Lucas, a child of the 1960s and the alter ego of Luke Skywalker, tries to recapture what has been lost by restoring spirituality to the cosmos. But he can manage only an impersonal Force that "surrounds us and penetrates us." The Force is benign and can be used for either good or evil. For Lucas, one religion is just as good as any other as long as it is "spiritual."[42]

The disenchanted, disillusioned, and spiritually demoralized were calling on god—any god—to return to reclaim a world that had dismissed Him as an illusion fit only for children and those who turned to religion as a crutch. But what form would the new deity take?

Young people began to find ingenious ways to "rage against the machine" and to fill the void left by the materialists with spiritual alternatives to the religiously antiseptic worldview of naturalism. "The discovery that reason alone will not do, that the vast technological and social changes taking place on our society leave us with few clear guidelines, leads us to feel that we are, indeed, in a universe that resembles the Buddhist principle of the 'Great Void.'"[43]

Conclusion

Nature abhors a vacuum, and so do worldviews. The rejection of one worldview only means that another takes its place. The hope was that if God was dismissed from the universe, our free and rational minds could go on without Him in the new materialist utopia where science was the new god. It was not long before the void was filled with all kinds of spiritual substitutes.

Notes

1. Aldous Huxley, *Science, Liberty, and Peace* (New York: Harper, 1946), 291.

2. Quoted in "Toward a Hidden God," *Time* (April 8, 1966), 83.

3. William Braden, *The Private Sea: LSD and the Search for God* (London: Pall Mall Press, 1967), 17. Emphasis in original. For a helpful discussion of what the God-is-dead movement meant by the phrase, see the chapter "The Death of God" in *The Private Sea.*

4. Michael Harrington, *The Politics at God's Funeral: The Spiritual Crisis of Western Civilization* (New York: Holt, Rinehart and Winston, 1983).

5. Quoted in Clifton Fadiman, *The Little, Brown Book of Anecdotes* (Boston, MA: Little, Brown and Company, 1985), 343.

6. While Newton was a theist, "he essentially studied a mechanistic universe, disregarding the teleology [purpose] of God's design." (David L. Larsen, *The Company of the Creative: A Christian Reader's Guide to Great Literature and Its Themes* [Grand Rapids, MI: Kregel Publications, 1999], 105). Also see Russell Kirk, *The Roots of the American Order*, 3rd ed. (Washington, DC: Regnery Gateway, 1991), 338 and Charles B. Thaxton, "A Dialogue with 'Prof' on Christianity and Science," *God and Culture: Essays in Honor of Carl F. H. Henry*, eds. D. A. Carson and John D. Woodbridge (Grand Rapids, MI: Eerdmans, 1993), 292–298.

7. Michael S. Malone, "God, Stephen Wolfram, and Everything Else," *Forbes ASAP* (November 27, 2000). This article can be found at www.forbes.com/asap/2000/1127/162_4.html

8. Quoted in Fadiman, *The Little, Brown Book of Anecdotes*, 343.

9. Barbara Kantrowitz, "Raising Spiritual Children," *Newsweek* (December 7, 1998), 62.

10. Kantrowitz, "Raising Spiritual Children," 63.

11. Mark Oppenheimer, "'Cheap grace' sought by consumers who want religion without any effort," *Atlanta Constitution* (October 25, 2000), A15.

12. Terry H. Anderson, *The Movement and the Sixties: Protest in America from Greensboro to Wounded Knee* (New York: Oxford University Press, 1995), 409.

13. Os Guinness, *The Dust of Death: The Sixties Counterculture and How It Changed America Forever* (Wheaton, IL: Crossway Books, 1994), 89–90.

14. Seymour Melman, *No Place to Hide: Fallout Shelters—Fact and Fiction* (New York: Grove Press, 1962).

15. The MAD hypothesis went something like this: America has enough nuclear weapons to blow up the Soviet Union, and the Soviet Union has enough atomic weapons to blow up America and her allies. Since both countries know this, neither one will start a war because such a war would result in mutual assured destruction.

16. Homer A. Hickam, Jr., *Rocket Boys: A Memoir* (New York: Delacorte, 1998).

17. Quoted in Anderson, *The Movement and the Sixties*, 24. Here's how a 1950's Civil Defense publication described the situation: "At the first indication of enemy bombers approaching the United States, all television and FM radio stations will go off the air. All standard (AM) stations will likewise go silent. The CONELRAD stations, 640 and 1240, are your surest and fastest means of getting emergency information and instructions. Mark those numbers on your radio set, now!"

18. For a thorough study of how fiction writers dealt with the nuclear threat, see Paul Brians, *Nuclear Holocausts: Atomic War in Fiction, 1895–1984* (Kent, OH: The Kent State University Press, 1987).

19. Margot A. Hendriksen, *Dr. Strangelove's America: Society and Culture in the Atomic Age* (Berkeley, CA: University of California Press, 1997).

20. Paul Boyer, *By The Bomb's Early Light: American Thought and Culture at the Dawn of the Atomic Age* (New York: Pantheon Books, 1985), 269.

21. Quoted in Boyer, *By The Bomb's Early Light,* 274.

22. Paul Boyer, *When Time Shall Be No More: Prophecy Belief in Modern American Culture* (Cambridge, MA: The Belknap Press of Harvard University Press, 1992), 116.

23. Robert Glenn Gromacki, *Are These the Last Days?* (Old Tappan, NJ: Fleming H. Revell, 1970), 152.

24. For an assessment of these doctrines, see Gary DeMar, *Last Days Madness: Obsession of the Modern Church,* 4th ed. (Powder Springs, GA: American Vision, 1999) and *End Times Fiction: A Biblical Consideration of the Left Behind theology*(Nashville, TN: Thomas Nelson, 2001).

25. Francis X. Gumerlock, *The Day and the Hour: Christianity's Perennial Fascination with Predicting the End of the World* (Powder Springs, GA: American Vision, 2000).

26. Ian MacDonald, *Revolution in the Head: The Beatles' Records and the Sixties* (New York: Henry Holt and Co., 1994), 5–6.

27. Steven D. Stark, *Glued to the Set: The 60 Television Shows and Events that Made Us Who We Are Today* (New York: The Free Press, 1997), 83–84.

28. Anderson, *The Movement and the Sixties,* 22.

29. Peter Biskind, *Seeing is Believing: How Hollywood Taught Us to Stop Worrying and Love the Fifties* (New York: Owl Books, 2000), 207–210.

30. MacDonald, *Revolution in the Head,* 6.

31. Gilbert Millstein, "Books of the Times," *The New York Times* (September 5, 1957), ii. Article reproduced in the 40th anniversary edition of Jack Kerouac's *On the Road* (New York: Viking, [1957] 1997).

32. Jon Margolis, *The Last Innocent Year: America in 1964 [The Beginning of the "Sixties"]* (New York: William Morrow, 1999), 110.

33. John Clellon Holmes, "This Is The Beat Generation," *New York Times Magazine* (November 16, 1952).

34. "Beat" means to be spent; to have a feeling of emptiness. "Beatnik" (Beat + Sputnik) and "dead beat" are derogatory terms used to describe those who adopted the worldview and lifestyle of Beat writers. Writing in 1948, Kerouac had said, "'The Word "beat" originally meant poor, down and out, deadbeat, on the bum, sleeping in subways.'" But by 1954 he was reinterpreting it as 'beatific,' born of a vision in which he saw prophetically 'the rumblings of a new soul.'" (Quoted in Guinness, *The Dust of Death,* 91). For a history of the period, see Bruce Cook, *The Beat Generation: The Tumultuous '50s Movement and Its Impact on Today* (New York: Charles Scribner's Sons, 1971).

35. Millstein, "Books of the Times," ii. "The original 1951 manuscript for Jack Kerouac's classic Beat Generation novel *On the Road* was sold for $2.2 million at Christie's auction house

Tuesday [May 22, 2001], the highest price ever paid for a literary manuscript at auction. The buyer: Jim Irsay, owner of the Indianapolis Colts football team. Irsay says he wants to put the 120-foot-long, single-spaced, typewritten scroll 'on display alongside the Lombardi Trophy, emblematic of victory in the Super Bowl.' Kerouac died a penniless alcoholic at age 47." ("'On the Road' scores auction touchdown," *USA Today* [May 23, 2001], 1D).

36. Anderson, *The Movement and the Sixties*, 38.

37. John W. Whitehead, "Gregory Corso: Poet and Revolutionary," The Gadfly Buzz (June 25–29, 2001). <www.gadfly.org>

38. Jack Mingo, ed., *The Whole Pop Catalog: The Berkeley Pop Culture Project* (New York: Avon Books, 1991), 83.

39. Another version has it: "A hippie is someone who looks like Tarzan, walks like Jane and smells like Cheeta."(Nat Shapiro, ed., *Whatever It Is, I'm Against It* [New York: Simon & Schuster, 1984], 119).

40. Prior to the advances made in the computer industry related to data storage, data entry was done by rectangular-shaped cards that were fed into computing machines. Each card had small rectangular holes punched to represent bits of information on every student: name, birthdate, Social Security number, etc. When fed through an optical or mechanical reader, only the punched holes were read. The collected data were stored on large reels of magnetic tape. The cards carried this warning: "Do not bend, fold, spindle, or mutilate." A spoiled card could not be read by the machines.

41. David Brooks, *Bobos in Paradise: The New Upper Class and How they Got There* (New York: Simon and Schuster, 2000), 32. Bobos are "Bourgeois Bohemians," a mix of yuppie and counterculture values.

42. Bill Moyers and George Lucas, "Of Myth and Men," *Time* (April 26, 1999). Lucas is a fan of Joseph Campbell's religious worldview. See Tom Snyder, *Myth Conceptions: Joseph Campbell and the New Age* (Grand Rapids, MI: Baker Books, 1995).

43. John H. Garabedian and Orde Coombs, *Eastern Religions in the Electric Age* (New York: Tempo Books, 1969), 8.

10

Filling the Spiritual Vacuum

"[Y]oung people are turning to the East for new religions, for
a cosmic consciousness, for new ways of thinking to help
them make sense of the confusion and brutality in their
country, to free their minds from thought conditioning,
thought control and robotization."[1]

In the grandest of ironies, while American planes were bombing military targets in Southeast Asia, and an ideological war was raging with other Asian nations, young people in America were looking to the East for spiritual wisdom. This contradiction is a microcosm of what has been going on religiously in America for decades. Spiritual seekers were willing to embrace the paradoxical, even the irrational, if it meant peace of mind and the renewal of both personal and cosmic meaning. "The marijuana high gave many young people a taste of the Eastern approach to experience: intuitive and aesthetic rather than logical, mystical rather than scientific, contemplative rather than active."[2]

It's been said that when people stop believing in God, they don't believe in nothing, they believe in anything, no matter how absurd.[3]

With the apparent death of rationalism and the questioning of how science and technology are used, the worldview of the irrational was born. "Twentieth-century rationalism has stumbled, its wings severely clipped by psychoanalysis and modern philosophy. The door to the nonrational, the irrational, and super-rational is wide open."[4] By the irrational we mean the abandonment of logic, reason-based arguments, and the law of non-contradiction. The irrational has manifested itself through astrology, the *Ouija* board, Tarot, ESP, psychics,[5] crystals, paganism, Wicca, goddess worship, nature worship, and any number of crackpot expressions of "spirituality," all in the name of finding cosmic meaning.[6] Expectations run high that there is meaning "out there" or "in here," that is, within our own being. The new spirituality is an explicit rejection of the impersonalism generated by those who insist that matter is the only thing that matters.

This return to spirituality and the questioning of a matter-only worldview, while commendable, has not always turned out to be a good thing. Not all spirits are created equal. Just as there are all types of food for the body, there is "spiritual food" for the soul (1 Cor. 10:3). Not all foods meet the nutritional demands required by our spiritual nature. Just as there is "junk food" that can rob the body of essential nutrients and can turn a healthy body into an anemic one, there are all types of spiritual junk food that can wreck spiritual health. This says nothing about spiritual poisons (Rev. 16:13).

It's fashionable to have an open mind. But like an open sewer, you never know what will drain there. Our society has moved from a religious absolutism found in the Bible to an undiscerning spiritual openness. Only those who insist that there is only one way are open to criticism. "Openness—and the relativism that makes it the only plausible stance in the face of various claims to truth and various ways of life and kinds of human beings—is the great insight of our times. The true believer is the real danger."[7]

The Rebirth of Gods and Goddesses

The religious seeker with an uncritical open mind will find himself swept away by "every wind of doctrine" (Eph. 4:14), every appealing opinion (2 Tim. 4:3), and every spiritual counterfeit to fill the spiritual void (1 Tim. 4:1). Pluralism is the new common spirituality.

> Pluralism refers to a diversity of religions, worldviews, and ideologies existing at one time in the same society. We are socially heterogeneous. One religion or philosophy doesn't command and control the culture. Instead, many viewpoints exist. We have Buddhists and Baptists, Christian Reformed and Christian Scientist—all on the same block, or at least in the same city. This can have a leveling effect on religious faith.[8]

All religions and lifestyles are permitted, as long as the believer is sincere, even if he is sincerely wrong. The only view that is not tolerated is the view that does not tolerate all views. Christianity came on the scene with Jesus saying, "I am *the* way and *the* truth and *the* life; *no one comes to the Father but by Me*" (John 14:6). How intolerant of Him to exclude Mayan spirits, the Buddha, Mohammed, and just plain decent folk who happen to believe in astrology and Tarot cards! Once a person has given up the belief in distinctions, differences, and contradictions, then anything and everything can be believed at the same time and with equal conviction. Such a belief is a direct assault on the Christian worldview with its ethical distinctions. "We are faced, as it were, by the accumulation of long centuries of Christian ethical strain. Good, bad—salvation, damnation—success, failure—wealth, poverty; all humanity is twisted, strained and torn apart between those conflicts, between trying to go from the negative to the positive."[9] But if these distinctions can be eliminated from the start, then all such striving disappears. There can no longer be just one way, one savior, one god. All is one without distinction.

Modern pluralism presents one prevailing opinion about Jesus Christ. Like all great religious leaders, he is special but not unique; and he is certainly not exclusive. That would be closed- and narrow-minded. He is classed with the multitude of mas- ters, grouped with the gurus, but not exalted as supreme. He is tucked into a comfortable corner of the religious pantheon so as to disturb no one.

The assumption is that Jesus just couldn't have claimed to be the only way; that's undemocratic! So instead of facing Christ's challenge as it stands, the whole idea is dismissed as anti-plural- istic, and closed-minded.[10]

Pluralism teaches that there can be no true religion over against all false religions. Christianity is *a* religion but not *the* religion, says the pluralist. The Bible can *sometimes* be taught as literature like Shakespeare, but it cannot be taught as the Word of God. Such an exclusive religious view would offend Moslems, Buddhists, Mormons, and most certainly agnostics and atheists. The unsuspecting are then open to any and all philosophical gurus who are ready, willing, and seemingly able to lead the way to a new vision of reality, even if the way is absurd. Of course, "religious relativism which leads to the belief that one religion is as good as another,"[11] even when they teach different things about God and salvation, is illogical and contradictory, but not in a world where irrationalism becomes rational.

The Sound of One Hand Clapping

It is the illogic and contradiction that makes such belief systems so meaningful for the new religious seekers. The depreciation of rational thought and "western logic" are considered the essence of enlighten- ment. "The sound of one hand clapping" is supposed to be profound *because* it's a contradiction. Of course, the notion of one hand clapping is nonsense if the law of non-contradiction is valid.

In a "Rockford Files" episode, Jim Rockford, played by James Garner, tries to have a rational conversation with a young woman who has been snared and influenced by a cult that champions irrationalism as enlightenment. They're sitting in a restaurant when the woman spouts off some nonsense that she has found enlightenment. "It's like the sound of one hand clapping," she tells Rockford. Frustrated, Rockford slaps her across the face and says, "That's the sound of one hand clapping."

Harvey Cox, professor at Harvard Divinity School and some-time dabbler in eastern philosophy, describes his attempt to meditate on the supposed profundity of "the sound of one hand clapping." He finally gave up: "I began to marvel at the absurdity of the whole principle. . . . Finally, after several weeks of mounting fury and anxiety, I quit." He admitted that he had been "had" by the lure of eastern irrationalism.[12]

The idea that "all is one," technically known as a *monistic* (*mono*=one) worldview, is supposedly a more enlightened way to look at the world rather than to dwell on a worldview that deals in distinctions. The Beatles popularized monism with their "I Am the Walrus" (1967) with its "all is one" refrain: "I am he as you are he as you are me and we are all together." If all is one, then there are no distinctions. With no distinctions, comparisons and evaluations cannot be made. There is no right or wrong, up or down, in or out, rational or irrational, sane and insane. Logical thought cannot take place without distinctions. Such is the worldview of mystics.[13] But in the end, even mystics use reasoned arguments and distinctions in an attempt to refute reasoned arguments and distinctions which are used to refute mysticism.

Even so, pluralists continue to tell us that we are now free to choose our own religion, even invent a new one if it suits us. The popularity of the new spirituality is simply the revival of ancient pagan religious philosophies dressed up in modern garb. Norman Geisler and David Clark write:

In the first century, Saint Paul debated two groups of Greek philosophers at a place called Mars Hill [Acts 17:22–34]. Paul's antagonists were the Epicureans and the Stoics. Like Paul, Christians in the West today are locked in debate with both Epicureans and Stoics.

When the American Atheists met in Denver recently, Madalyn Murray O'Hair declared that there is no God. Shirley MacLaine soon came to town to pronounce that she and all her listeners are gods. Shortly thereafter, in a Denver crusade, Billy Graham preached that Jesus alone is God. These well-known champions of three world views have rekindled that ancient Mars Hill debate.[14]

Atheism and paganism have certainly been around for a long time, and the Bible deals with both of them in short order. The Old Testament speaks directly to the atheist when it declares, "The fool has said in his heart, 'There is no God'" (Psalm 14:1). But atheism was not a big problem in biblical times. It was the multiplicity of gods that had to be confronted and the methods spiritual seekers used to contact them. God's special revelation became just one revelation among so many others.

The Medium is the Message

Mediums and spiritualists were commonplace in Israel. Keep in mind that generations of Israelites lived under the sway of Egyptian polytheism: the Nile River, the Sun, and the Pharaoh himself were thought to be gods. The ten plagues attacked ten gods of Egypt. The Egyptian worldview was carried out of Egypt during the Exodus and seduced a number of Israelites (Ex. 32:1–5). Remnants of the rival polytheistic religion remained until the time of Israel's monarchy. Action was taken by King Saul to purge the land of rival religions: "And Saul had removed from the land those who were mediums and spiritists" (1 Sam. 28:3). Unfortunately, the king did not complete the task. In spite of God's repeated warnings, Saul sought a woman who was a "medium" (1 Sam. 28:7), someone who claimed that communicating with the dead and learning the mysteries of the universe were possible through a gifted few. There is no neutrality. It is either God's revelation or the pursuit of revelation from some other source . Notice that Saul did not consult the devil or demons. He chose a former prophet in Israel— Samuel. How could this be wrong?

In the midst of Israel's theocracy, false religions, in the form of channeling, spiritism, and demonism, were practiced. God gave Israel a number of laws prior to her entry into the promised land to keep the people from deception and judgment (Ex. 22:18; Lev. 19:31; 20:6; Deut. 18:10–11). We should not be surprised, therefore, when we read about similar pagan practices in our own officially religiously pluralistic nation.

With the death of Solomon, the slide into a counterfeit spirituality continued with the apostate king Ahaziah. After falling ill after an accident, the king issued this command to his servants: "Go, inquire of Baal-zebub, the god of Ekron, whether I shall recover from this illness" (2 Kings 1:3). Any attempt to pursue other gods, to give them any form of legitimacy is condemned. "Thus says the LORD, 'Is it because there is no God in Israel that you are sending to inquire of Baal-zebub, the god of Ekron?'" (2 Kings 1:6).

These early dabblings with a new spirituality were attempts to get around God's revelation. The adherents of polytheism sought other voices by which to live their lives. Again, none of this should surprise us. Man's first sin was succumbing to a temptation to evaluate all of life in terms of a standard other than the Word of God (Gen. 3:1). Little has changed since the days of Saul, Ahaziah, and the philosophers of Paul's day. Today, polytheism goes by the more modern and acceptable "religious pluralism."

If One is All then All is One

Like so many in Israel, millions of Americans believe that there is no king in America. They believe that there is no single sovereign authority by which we must direct our lives. As a result, every man does what he believes is right in his own eyes (Judges 17:6). Today's religious pluralism is a modern expression of ancient polytheism that has been revived by the death-of-God theology and promoted by a cadre of self-appointed religious practitioners.

A multiplicity of gods means a multiplicity of opinions about everything. Jeff Nutall describes the rise of the new polytheism this way: If "one-is-all-and-all-is-one-so-what-the-hell."[15] Everyone is free to create his own gods or goddesses and the rules that go along with the new deities.[16] Richard Gere, a popular actor and follower of eastern religious philosophies, sums up the spirit of the age: "Cosmically, there's nothing wrong with being heterosexual, homosexual or omnisexual—with being anything, as long as you don't hurt anybody, yourself included."[17]

Jesus is Dead—Buddha Lives!

Americans are searching for religious and personal truth in unprecedented numbers, similar to the way Saul was seeking knowledge. Eastern religions, or at least eastern religious forms, are the most popular. Once religious pluralism is accepted as valid, all religious expressions, no matter how irrational or illogical, are considered genuine as long as they work for the practitioner. In fact, the more esoteric and non-Western, the better. The following is a description of some of the unique features of eastern religions that have become commonplace in our culture. These beliefs are described as "mysticism" because they have no rational basis. They are "eastern" because of their geographical source.

1. Eastern Mysticism is irrational

In Zen Buddhism, for example, intuition is pitted against reason. The Hindus consider the mind to have all the stability and perception of a "drunken monkey" while the Hare Krishnas refer to the mind as a "garbage pail." All this might seem contradictory to the Western mind, and it is. But remember, the West has given up on rational explanations for the way the world works. Maybe East is best. If man is nothing more than a machine, and machines are often destructive, and rational scientists developed these destructive machines, why should we hold rationality in such high regard anyway? Western rationalism has failed to give answers.

> Perhaps another reason behind the popular abandonment of rationalism in the West is its inability to provide spiritual satisfaction. As Zen master D. T. Suzuki explains, "Zen has come to the definite conclusion that the ordinary logical process of reasoning is powerless to give final satisfaction to our deepest spiritual needs."[18]

We are often confused by the incessant chanting and intellectually void meditation. But these are simply the ways of the East. Much of eastern thought is without intellectual content and meaning. The goal is to transcend the world of things and to reach a spiritual world beyond. The point is not to understand but only to do. This is the appeal of the East. The Western reliance on rationalism has failed. In the West, the law of non-contradiction reigned (A is not non-A). The East knows nothing of such distinctions. In Western rationalist terms, "to know reality is to distinguish one thing from another, label it, catalog it, recognize its subtle relation to other objects in the cosmos. In the East to 'know' reality is to pass beyond distinction, to 'realize' the oneness of all being one with the all."[19] Even a rationalist like Marilyn Vos Savant, who writes for *Parade* magazine, has fallen for the trap when she writes, "It's not hard to hold conflicting beliefs *if* one of them comes from the heart—like religion—and the other one comes from the head—like science."[20]

2. Eastern Mysticism is monistic

The Christian believes in a *personal* God who is separate from His creation. The Bible teaches that there is a distinction between the Creator and the creature. God did not create the world out of Himself (*ex deo*), using the "stuff" of His own being to bring the universe and man into existence. Pagan creation myths abound with this notion. According to one Babylonian account, Marduk, the great stone god, "killed the dragon Tiamat and split her body in half. The upper half was made into the sky, and the lower half the earth."[21] The Bible describes creation in a radically different way: "By faith we understand that the worlds were prepared by the *word of God*, so that what is seen *was not made out of the things which are visible*" (Heb. 11:3; cf. Gen. 1:1-2).

Eastern thought makes no distinction between man and cosmos. The name for this is *monism*. Monism "is the belief that all that is, is one. All is interrelated, interdependent and interpenetrating. Ultimately there is no difference between God, a person, a carrot or a rock."[22] Consider the ethical implications of such a view. The way you treat a person and the way you treat an animal are no different.[23] This is why much of monism is vegetarian. An animal is sacred; therefore, it cannot be killed for food. All is one. God and evil transcend the world of forms and plurality. God does not overcome evil. There is no value judgment in "good" and "evil." Ultimate reality is beyond good and evil. These rational and biblical concepts must be jettisoned in favor of an undifferentiated oneness.

The entertainment business has been quick to pick up on monism. In the *Star Wars* series, monism is quite evident in "the Force," a seemingly benign entity that neither condones the good nor suppresses the evil. Value judgments come from those who use the force. We never learn why something is good or bad. It's obvious that Western, that is, Christian, values have been imported into George Lucas's benign Star Wars universe. But he doesn't tell us how he has been able to do it given his non-Christian emphasis.

The music industry was invaded in the early sixties by The Beatles who held a monistic worldview.

> In 1967, the Beatles made their now-famous link-up with a then-unknown guru, Maharishi Yogi and his occult-sounding product, Transcendental Meditation. In that same year Paul McCartney and John Lennon wrote "I am the Walrus" which opened with the pantheistic declaration: "I am he as you are he as you are me and we are all together." "Instant Karma" followed in 1970 and the next year saw the release of George Harrison's "My Sweet Lord" with its alternating chorus of "Hallelujah" and "Hare Krishna."[24]

Charles Manson adopted the monistic worldview of the Beatles. At the LaBianca murder scene in 1969, his followers scrawled in blood on the refrigerator door "Helter Skelter," a song title from the Beatles' controversial *White Album*. The ambiguity of right and wrong became a reality for Manson and his "family." In Manson's words, "If God is One, what is bad?"[25]

3. In Eastern Mysticsim All is god

It follows from monism that if there is a god, then all is god. Pantheism (*pan* means all; *theos* means god) is the theology of the East. There is no personal God who stands above creation. In fact, there is no creation as such. To speak of a creation would mean to postulate a Creator, someone distinct from the cosmos. Thus, the pantheist agrees with the naturalist that there is just one level of reality, although the naturalist would not consider it to be "spiritual" or "divine." In pantheism, there is no God who is "out there." God and the material world are one and the same. The word "god" refers to the sum total of reality rather than to some being distinct from the rest of reality.

In Christianity, God is distinct from creation (transcendant). God is certainly present *with* His creation (immanent), but He is in no way a *part of* creation. To destroy the created order would in no way affect the existence of God. "The Creator God is not an impersonal force, energy or consciousness, but a living, personal Being of infinite intelligence, power and purity. God is not an amoral entity, but a moral agent who says 'Thou shalt not' and calls people to repentance and faith."[26]

4. In Eastern Mysticsim the individual is a god

The consistency of monism brings us to one of its most bizarre features. If all is god, then man is god in some form. "Swami Muktananda—a great influence on Werner Erhard, founder of est and Forum—pulls no pantheistic punches when he says: 'Kneel to your own self. Honor and worship your own being. God dwells within you as You!'"[27]

Eastern mysticism teaches some form of "chain of being" or "continuity of being," the idea that man and God are of one essence, and that in time, through an evolutionary process or a series of reincarnations, man becomes divine. Ray Sutton writes:

> Life according to this system is a *continuum*. At the top is the purest form of deity. At the very bottom is the least pure. They only differ in *degree*, not in kind. God is a *part of* creation. Man, who is somewhere in the middle of the continuum, is god in another "form." In other words, god is just a "super" man, and man is not a god... yet![28]

Of course, Christianity teaches that there is only one God: "And you are My witnesses. Is there any God besides Me, or is there any other Rock? I know of none" (Isa. 44:8). Man's first sin was the attempt to "be like God," determining good and evil for himself (Gen. 3:5).

5. In Eastern Mysticsim there is no death

Eastern mysticism makes its "leap of being" from mere man to god through raising the state of consciousness, evolutionary development, reincarnation, or some combination of the three. Death is simply the final stage of growth; it is an illusion. Human beings, because they are of a "divine essence," are immortal. Ultimately, death does not exist. For death to exist would mean the extinction of part of the One. A little bit of God would be gone forever.

Reincarnation is a fundamental pillar of New Age thinking. It "solves" the question of death. Reincarnation has been popularized over the years through the writings of Edgar Cayce[29] and most recently, Shirley MacLaine. The Eastern variety of reincarnation would have never been accepted in the Christian West if it had not been stripped of the hideous concept of the "transmigration of the soul."

Reincarnation as it is usually understood in Hinduism states that all life is essentially one (monism): plant, animal, and human life are so interrelated that souls are capable of "transmigrating" from one form of life to another. A person could have been an animal, plant, or mineral in some previous existence. However, this version is unpalatable to American tastes, so in the newer version the movement of human souls is limited to human bodies.[30]

Modern proponents of reincarnation have cleaned up the Eastern variety. You don't hear Shirley MacLaine telling people that she was a rock or a slug in a former life. The typical reincarnationist usually believes that he was once some exotic personality. This is not true reincarnationism. This is "I've always been a star" reincarnationism.

6. Eastern Mysticsim overreacts to modern technology

In 1909 Gandhi denounced medical science as "the concentrated essence of black magic."[31] In the place of medical science, Gandhi resorted to his own form of medicinal "black magic," for example, refusing to allow doctors to give his wife a shot of the "alien medicine" penicillin for her pneumonia.[32] She died. He prescribed dried dung from India's sacred cow for various ailments.[33] The enema was a sacred rite for the Mahatma. And drinking a daily glass of one's own urine holds similar sanctity among devout Hindus.[34] "As late as 1938 Gandhi still sounded adamant on the absolute superiority of a life with no machinery, let alone technology."[35] He wrote:

> I believe that the civilization that India evolved is not to be beaten in the world… India remains immovable and that is her glory… Our ancestors dissuaded us from luxuries and pleasure. We have managed with the same kind of plow as existed thousands of years ago… We have had no system of life-corroding competition . . . It was not that we did not know how to invent machinery, but our forefathers knew that, if we set our hearts after such things, we would become slaves and lose our moral fibre. They, therefore, after due deliberation decided that we should only do what we could with our hands and feet.[36]

As the irrationalists become consistent with the presuppositions of the East, we will begin to see the decline in civilization as it is exemplified in places like India. Gandhi may be a pacifist hero to some, but he is no builder of culture.

> Great cultures, where the scientific enterprise came to a standstill, invariably failed to formulate the notion of physical law, or the law of nature. Theirs was a theology with no belief in a personal, rational, absolutely transcendent Lawgiver, or Creator. Their cosmology reflected a pantheistic and animistic view of

nature caught in the treadmill of perennial, inexorable returns. The scientific quest found fertile soil only when this faith in a personal, rational Creator had truly permeated a whole culture, beginning with the centuries of the High Middle Ages. It was that faith which provided, in sufficient measure, confidence in the rationality of the universe, trust in progress, and appreciation of the quantitative method, all indispensable ingredients of the scientific quest.[37]

The Christian worldview understands technology to be both a gift and a tool. Like anything in this world, technology can be abused. But the potential abuse does not mean its elimination as a tool.

Conclusion

Eastern Mysticism is attractive as a religious system because it is without rules or creeds. You can be your own god. Sin is not the problem, only a lack of enlightenment. Who or what defines "enlightenment"? Is it simply a benign force? What makes the "dark side" of the force evil? Why were Darth Vader and the Emperor wrong while Luke Skywalker and Obi Wan Kenobi were right? Who or what determines the rules?

Notes

1. Allen Cohen quoted in John H. Garabedian and Orde Coombs, *Eastern Religions in the Electric Age* (New York: Tempo Books, 1969), 9–10.

2. Garabedian and Coombs, *Eastern Religions in the Electric Age*, 15.

3. Attributed to G. K. Chesterton. Another version goes like this: "If people stop believing in religion, they don't then believe in nothing, they believe in everything." (Elizabeth Knowles, ed., *The Oxford Dictionary of Quotations*, 5th ed. [Oxford: Oxford University Press, 1999], 211.22).

4. Os Guinness, *The Dust of Death: The Sixties Counterculture and How It Changed America Forever* (Wheaton, IL: Crossway Books, 1994), 279.

5. "U.S. agencies used psychics," *Atlanta Constitution* (Nov. 29, 1995), A14.

6. James Randi, *An Encyclopedia of Claims, Frauds, and Hoaxes of the Occult and Supernatural* (New York: St. Martin's Press, 1995)

7. Allan Bloom, *The Closing of the American Mind: How Higher Education Has Failed Democracy and Impoverished the Souls of Today's Students* (New York: Simon and Schuster, 1987), 26.

8. Douglas Groothuis, "The Smorgasbord Mentality," *Eternity* (May 1985), 32.

9. Dane Rudyhar, *San Francisco Oracle* (August 1967). Quoted in Garabedian and Coombs, *Eastern Religions in the Electric Age*, 13.

10. Groothuis, "The Smorgasbord Mentality," 33.

11. Cardinal Joseph Ratzinger quoted in Peggy Polk, "Vatican: Other faiths 'defective,'" *Atlanta Constitution* (September 8, 2000), B5.

12. Harvey Cox, *Turning East: The Promise and Peril of the New Orientalism* (New York: Simon and Schuster, 1977), 27–28.

13. "Most mystics have come to the depressing conclusion that a rational understanding of the universe is not really possible. Neither can the universe be understood by experimentation as the empiricists claim. There must be some other way of knowing the truth than by human reason or experience." (Robert A. Morey, *Battle of the Gods: The Gathering Storm in Modern Evangelicalism* [Southbridge, MA: Crown Publications, 1989], 132).

14. Norman L. Geisler and David. K. Clark, *Apologetics in the New Age: A Christian Critique of Pantheism* (Grand Rapids, MI: Baker, 1990), 7.

15. Jeff Nutall, *Bomb Culture* (New York: Dell Books, 1968), 104. Quoted in Guinness, *The Dust of Death*, 94

16. David L. Miller, *The New Polytheism: Rebirth of the gods and goddesses* (New York: Harper & Row, 1974). The first chapter is titled "An Exploded Cultural Sphere: The Death of God and the Rebirth of the Gods."

17. "Covering Sexuality and the Geres," *USA Today* (December 7, 1993), 2D.

18. Pat Means, *The Mystical Maze* (San Bernardino, CA: Campus Crusade for Christ, 1976), 39.

19. James W. Sire, *The Universe Next Door: A Basic World View Catalog* (Downers Grove, IL: InterVarsity Press, 1976), 133.

20. Marilyn Vos Savant, "Ask Marilyn," *Parade Magazine* (October 6, 2000), 22.

21. John J. Davis, *Paradise to Prison: Studies in Genesis* (Grand Rapids, MI: Baker Book House, 1975), 69.

22. Douglas R. Groothuis, *Unmasking the New Age: Is There a New Religious Movement Trying to Transform Society?* (Downers Grove, IL: InterVarsity Press, 1986), 18.

23. Richard Willing, "Under law, pets are becoming almost human," *USA Today* (September 13, 2000), 1A.

24. Means, *The Mystical Maze*, 21.

25. Charles Manson, *Rolling Stone Magazine* (June 25, 1970). Quoted in Guinness, *The Dust of Death*, 195.

26. Groothuis, *Unmasking the New Age*, 21.

27. Groothuis, *Unmasking the New Age*, 21.

28. Ray Sutton, *That You May Prosper: Dominion By Covenant* (Tyler, TX: Dominion Press, 1987), 37.

29. For an insightful analysis and critique of Cayce's views see: Gary North, *Unholy Spirits: Occultism and New Age Humanism* (Ft. Worth, TX: Dominion Press, 1986), 193-225. Cayce was an avid Bible student. It is reported that he tried to read through the Bible once each year. He tried to reconcile his occultism with the Bible and failed, ignoring Hebrews 9:26-27. See Phillip J. Swihart, *Reincarnation, Edgar Cayce & the Bible* (Downers Grove, IL: InterVarsity Press, 1975).

30. John Snyder, *Reincarnation vs. Resurrection* (Chicago, IL: Moody Press, 1984), 19.

31. Stanley L. Jaki, *The Savior of Science* (Washington, DC: Regnery Gateway, 1988), 219, note 25.

32. Richard Grenier, *The Gandhi Nobody Knows* (Nashville, TN: Thomas Nelson, 1983), 34.

33. Grenier, *The Gandhi Nobody Knows*, 46.

34. Grenier, *The Gandhi Nobody Knows*, xxv. Despite Gandhi's "constant campaigning for sanitation, it is hard to believe that Gandhi was not permanently marked by what Arthur Koestler terms the Hindu 'morbid infatuation with filth.' (Decades later, Morarji Desai, a Gandhian and one-time Indian Defense Minister, was still fortifying his sanctity by drinking a daily glass of urine.)" (91).

35. Jaki, *The Savior of Science*, 29.

36. M. K. Gandhi, "A Dialogue between an Editor and a Reader," in *Hind Swaraj or Indian Home Rule*, rev. ed. ([1938] 1946), 43–45. Cited in Jaki, *Savior of Science*, 29. Jaki writes: "No wonder that Gandhi had to dispute time and again the claim that he was against scientific education. The thrust of his utterances concerning science almost invariably aimed at the 'satanic civilization' brought about by the misuses of science and technology" (218, note 25).

37. Stanley L. Jaki, *Science and Creation: From Eternal Cycles to an Oscillating Universe* (Edinburgh and London: Scottish Academic Press, 1974), viii.

11

Raging Against the Machine

It is commonplace that the mind of modern man has been secularized. For instance, it has been deprived of any orientation towards
the supernatural. Tragic as this fact is, it would not be so desperately tragic had the Christian mind held out against the secular drift.
But unfortunately the Christian mind has succumbed to the secular
drift with a degree of weakness and nervelessness unmatched in
Christian history. It is difficult to do justice in words to the complete
loss of intellectual morale in the twentieth-century Church.[1]

A dramatic religious shift was taking place at a time when science
seemed to be reaching for the stars. American scientists landed men on
the moon in 1969. A triumph for the materialists, the culmination of a
belief system that claimed reason, science, and technology were still the
ultimate answers to everything. The first scripted words from Neil
Armstrong, as he made the first human impression on the Moon's surface, are indicative of a conscious worldview shift: "That's one step for
man and one giant leap for *mankind.*" Quite a departure from the first
telegraphed words sent over a great distance by Samuel F. B. Morse in
1844: "What hath God wrought?"

But there were signs of cracks in the materialist worldview. In 1971, Edgar D. Mitchell, the sixth astronaut to walk on the moon, conducted a psychic experiment during his voyage where he attempted "to send information telepathically to four receivers on earth."[2] Mitchell describes himself as "pragmatic a test pilot, engineer, and scientist as any of my colleagues,"[3] and yet he "knew" there was something more. This knowledge, Mitchell recounts, was "gained through private subjective awareness.... [that] was not perceptible by the sensory organs, but it was there nevertheless—an unseen dimension behind the visible creation that gives an intelligent design and that gives life purpose."[4] Mitchell was not alone. An entire generation raised on "the validity of scientific principles and the reliability of the technology built upon those principles"[5] was looking for something more, even if it meant returning to "religion," even if that religion was little more than impersonal cosmic forces.

> For many people, it was once part of growing up to reject religion, with all its apparent dogmatism, its comforting worldviews, and its rituals. In those days and for those people, it seemed part of courage to embrace the scientific conception of the universe and of man: that was almost the definition of realism and clear-mindedness. The vast cosmos was a blind cave, in one tiny corner of which a metaphysical freak called man lived, suffered, and died while projecting into the darkness his fantasies of a universal intelligence. It was the mission of science to show man the truth about the cave and its ironclad laws of mindless energy and indifferent matter.[6]

Where the Beat Generation was mostly a subterranean movement made up of a few poets, musicians, artists, writers, drug addicts, homosexuals, and hangers-on, the Counter Culture of the next decade turned their off-beat worldview mainstream. Is it any wonder that columnist

George Will described the 1960s as "the most dangerous decade in America's life as a nation."[7] Sociologist Robert Nisbet tells us why:

> I think it would be difficult to find a single decade in the history of Western culture when so much barbarism—so much calculated onslaught against culture and convention in any form, and so much degradation of culture and the individual—passed into print, into music, into art, and onto the American stage as the decade of the Nineteen Sixties.[8]

Nisbet's assessment could be multiplied a hundred-fold. The decade of the 1960s was a counter cultural religious revolution.

"Turn On, Tune In, Drop out"

Some turned to drugs to escape what they believed was the failed worldview that declared reason, logic, science, and technology to be personal and cultural saviors. Drugs, such as LSD (lysergic acid diethylamide), mescaline, and marijuana, were seen as routes to other dimensions of reality, mystical higher consciousness, a new religion in a bottle that would offer mind-expanding powers and new rituals of "faith" with no need of a personal god. In fact, drugs were sometimes viewed as sacramental, a form of mystical communion.

Timothy Leary, former Harvard psychology professor and high priest and Pied-Piper of the psychedelic worldview, claimed that LSD is "'the sacrament that will put you in touch with the ancient two million year old wisdom inside you'; it frees one 'to go to the next stage, which is the evolutionary timelessness, the ancient reincarnation thing that we always carry inside.'"[9] Leary stated on a 1967 BBC program called "The Mind Alchemists" that "The LSD kick is a spiritual ecstasy. The LSD trip is a religious pilgrimage."[10] The worldview of naturalism was limited in that it rejected any consideration that there was a spiritual connection to man or the cosmos. Psychedelics, Leary pontificated, would change all of that.

In Christ-like fashion, Leary told his dutiful followers, "Turn on to the scene, tune in to what is happening, and drop out—of high school, college, grad school, junior executive—and follow me, the hard way."[11] This was a mocking reference to Jesus' statement to His disciples to take up the cross of self-denial and follow Him (Matt. 16:24). The first chapter of Leary's book *Turn On, Tune In, Drop Out* is titled "Start Your Own Religion." He writes: "Turn On—find a sacrament which returns you to the temple of God, your own body. Go out of your mind. Get high."[12] Remember, there is no neutrality. The rejection of one religion only means the adoption of another. "You must start your own religion," Leary insisted. "You are God—but only you can discover and nurture your divinity. No one can start your religion for you."[13] He not only told you to start your own religion, he told you how to do it.[14] Throughout his works, Leary constantly reminded his followers—"You are God: Remember!" It was always Leary's stated goal to overthrow the "Judeo-Christian" worldview.[15]

Lucy in the Sky with Diamonds

If defrocked Harvard professor Leary was the high priest of the drug culture, The Beatles were its prophets. *Time* magazine writes, "The fact remains that when the Beatles talk—about drugs, the war in Vietnam, religion—millions listen, and this is the new situation in the pop music world."[16] Many believed that some of their songs were laced with drug themes: A reference to drugs in general in "With a Little Help from My Friends"[17] ("I get high with a little help from my friends"); "Hey Jude" and its allusion to shooting heroin ("The minute you let her under your skin"); "Day Tripper" (a reference to recreational drug use without adopting the drug lifestyle); "A Day in the Life" ("I'd love to turn you on"); and, of course, "Lucy in the Sky with Diamonds," a not-so-veiled reference to LSD and its hallucinogenic images of "tangerine trees," "marmalade skies," "newspaper taxis," and "looking-glass ties."[18] Timothy Leary, after listening to the *Sergeant Pepper's Lonely Hearts Club Band* album, "proclaimed the Beatles 'evolutionary agents sent by God, endowed with a mysterious power to create a new human species.'"[19]

Spiritual Poison

The religious elements in the early drug culture turned out to be a spiritual and sometimes a physical dead end.[20] Before too long drugs lost their initial religious and supposed mind-expanding purposes and became strictly recreational, a simple and immediate form of escape from troubled and confusing times. Drugs allow a person, so the theory goes, to transcend the natural world and enter a dimension of enlightenment, creativity, and spiritual knowledge that resides above and beyond the material. For this reason, drug-induced transcendence is explicitly prohibited in the Bible.

The Greek *pharmakeia* and its word group are most often translated as "sorcery" in the Bible (Gal. 5:20; Rev. 9:21; 18:23; 21:8; 22:15). The words "pharmaceutical" and "pharmacy," both drug-related words, are derived from *pharmakeia*. The connection between drugs and sorcery is due to the fact that drugs were often used as potions and poisons by those practicing witchcraft. Since those who dabbled in the occult had no supernatural powers, they had to find ways to amaze and deceive the superstitious and gullible. Some were illusionists, giving the impression that they had powers when in reality they were no different from today's stage "magicians" (2 Thess. 2:9–10).

The more sinister used herbal concoctions—early forms of mind-altering drugs—to affect a person's consciousness. Some, in order to give the impression of great powers, used these drugs as poisons (e.g., hemlock, aconite, and belladonna) to strike fear into a community of superstitious believers. Their main purpose, however, was to alter the mind to break down inhibitions.

> There are innumerable ways in which the mind may be
> disarmed of its critical faculties: fatigue, strong emotion, faulty
> reasoning, wishful-thinking, drugs, hypnosis, hysteria, enthusi-
> asm, ignorance, prejudice—all these are capable of increasing
> the effect of suggestion.[21]

Drugs are an immediate mind-altering substance that can open a person up to all sorts of suggestive beliefs and behaviors. "There is something in their mysterious chemistry that causes them to loosen the grip that man's will exerts on his own faculties—including his mind and his muscular and nervous responses."[22] The hallucinogenic elements in some of these ancient drugs produced physiological effects, giving some the impression that they could fly.[23]

It is no accident, therefore, that drugs are used when religion and sexual mores are being challenged in order to break down resistance to new ideas. This is why the Bible links "sorcery" with "idolatry" (false religions) and "fornication" (sexual immorality) (Isa. 47:8–9; Rev. 21:8; 22:15).

"More Popular than Jesus"

The 1960s also spawned a spiritual revival of eastern religious practices. Alan Watts (1915–1973), a former Anglican priest, promoted a westernized form of Zen Buddhism that became very popular in America. He described Zen as "a new holistic 'view of life' that cannot be understood by normal mental processes."[24] Once again, we see a reaction against rationalism and biblical Christianity. Watts observed:

> Some of our most brilliant and far out scientists... [know]
> that we have thought ourselves through to the bitter end of intel-
> lection, of rational calculation, and that, operationally, physics
> and chemistry imply fall-out, erosion, smog, and ecological
> imbalance. As. H. G. Wells put it, mind is at the end of its tether.[25]

Popular culture led the way, and The Beatles were in the forefront of both denouncing old religious forms, especially Christianity, and promoting new ones. Their first attack was on Christianity, and it came from John Lennon. "Christianity will go," Lennon said in a March 1966 interview that first appeared in the *London Evening Standard*. "It will vanish and shrink. I needn't argue about that. I'm right, and I will be proven right. We're more popular than Jesus right now. I don't know which will go first. Rock 'n' roll or Christianity. Jesus was alright, but his disciples were thick and ordinary. It's them twisting it that ruins it for me."[26] John W. Whitehead writes: "The importance of this statement cannot be underestimated, for it challenged the basic fabric of Western society. The gauntlet was thrown down by the biggest pop icons of the age."[27] Paul McCartney summed up the beliefs of the Beatles when he described them as "four iconoclastic, brass-hard, post-Christian, pragmatic realists."[28]

Soon after this reportedly anti-Christian bombshell, George Harrison began to move the Beatles into eastern religions, especially Hinduism, believing "much more in the religions of India" than Christianity.[29] They began their introduction in things eastern with the works of Maharishi Mahesh Yogi and Transcendental Meditation and Hindu philosophy in general. At first, TM was viewed more as science than religion. The emphasis was on a positive mental attitude brought on by meditation. Its goal, however, was to transcend present physical reality through eastern meditation practices.

George Harrison promoted "Krishna Consciousness," a form of Hinduism, through his popular song "My Sweet Lord" and the chorus "Hare Krishna" and refrains from Hindu sacred writings. Harrison re-recorded the song on its thirtieth anniversary to remind himself that "there's more to life than the material world."[30] Once again, we see that the rejection of one religion is the conscious acceptance of another. With the rise of religious pluralism, where all religions are one, the conception of god is in the eye of the beholder.

As experimentation with drugs, loosened sexual mores, and the rejection of rationality came to a head, it became evident that the movement "lacked intrinsic moral content."[31] The Haight-Ashbury district of San Francisco became a microcosm of the failure of the grand religious experiment:

> The streets of Haight-Ashbury, even in the best days, had been littered with kids who deranged their senses on drugs—only to experience spiritual stupor. A fair number ended their trips in hospital emergency rooms, possessed of one or another demon. Satanic cults were not unknown in the Haight. One of them, the Process, apparently influenced Charles Manson, a hippie who lived in the neighborhood in 1967 and recruited confused young girls and a few men into his "family." Manson was an "acid fascist" who somehow found in the lyrics of the Beatles license to commit ritual murder.[32]

The Tate-LaBianca murders by the Manson "family" (August 9–10, 1969),[33] the Rolling Stones disastrous Altamont raceway concert where a man was stabbed to death by a group of local Hell's Angels who were hired by the Stones as bodyguards (December 6, 1969),[34] and the shooting of four young people on the Campus of Kent State University by the National Guard (May 4, 1970)[35] brought the counterculture to an abrupt end. Where did the radicals go? They became professors in universities all across America. "While the Right was occupying the heights of the political system, the assemblage of groups identified with the Left were marching on the English department. They were seizing power in women's studies, African-American studies, ethnic studies."[36] They became the teachers of our children.

Stranger in a Strange Land

Even science fiction had a hand in launching a countercultural religious and moral revolution. Robert Heinlein's *Stranger in a Strange Land*

(1961)[37] has been described as a counter culture bible that "gave rise to something of a cult among the love-peace-and-revolution flower children of America's 1960s."[38] Valentine Michael Smith is a Mars-born earthling raised by Martians who comes to Earth as a stranger with paranormal powers. At first, finding the ways of Earth difficult to understand, he is taken under the wing of Jubal Harshaw who instructs Smith to experience everything with his new-found powers and to promote a new religious worldview devoid of Earth-world restrictions. The old faith of Christianity is dismissed as exclusive and declared obsolete. With the arrival of Smith, a messianic character if there ever was one (Michael means "Who is like God?"),[39] everyone is declared to be divine: "Thou art God and I am God and all that groks[40] [understands] is God, and I am all that I have ever been or seen or felt or experienced."

Science fiction works rarely become cult classics. *Stranger in a Strange Land* has been described by Kurt Vonnegut as "One of the greatest science fiction novels ever written." This is an exaggeration, to be sure. What made this book so popular? Heinlein's fictional worldview advocated communal living, cannibalism, sexual liberation—including homosexuality and bisexuality—and new religious forms. Man is God in Heinlein's fictional world. God is in everyone (Smith).

Whether Heinlein meant to promote a "free love" moral order and a new religious consciousness or just wanted to tell a story, we'll never know. But many who read *Stranger in a Strange Land* took its worldview approach seriously. Heinlein himself was a "free love" advocate, although his views were never expressed in his earlier science fiction works that had children as the targeted audience, with *Starship Troopers* being his most popular work. Even before World War II, "Heinlein believed in the philosophies of H.G. Wells and Bertrand Russell that stated free love would cure many of the world's ills."[41] Heinlein's not so subtle worldview "was seized upon by the hippie-cults of the mid-1960s and was readily adopted by Charles Manson into his 'Family' organization."[42]

Stranger in a Strange Land even inspired a new religion, the Church of All Worlds (CAW), where its members greet one another with "Thou Art God," a precursor to New Age religions. CAW has elements of ancient nature religions, combining beliefs from many cultures with other mystic, environmental and spiritual disciplines, including "Shamanism, Witchcraft, Vodoun, Buddhism, Hinduism and Sufism, as well as science fiction, transpersonal psychology, bodywork, artistic expression and paths of service." The founders describe CAW as "Neo-Pagan."[43]

A Seismic Shift

The culmination of these worldview shifts changed American belief patterns in dramatic ways. The old categories were shot full of holes by new religious assumptions that could not be rationally criticized since pluralism and relativism are today's reigning worldviews. A common culture with shared religious assumptions has disappeared.

> The "flower generation" staged a neo-romantic revolt against science, technology, and reason in favor of feeling, sexuality, drugs, rock music, fantasy, and Eastern Mysticism. The new heaven of peace, love, and freedom failed to materialize as expected, but the arational experientalism of these years lingers on in a younger generation of Americans.[44]

Those who were disenchanted with the materialist worldview and what it brought into existence—atomic weapons, the military industrial complex, perpetual wars—could no longer live with its foundational assumptions. There was a general revolt against the worldview that taught that there is no real cosmic meaning to life, that the brain is an organic machine without true mind-consciousness, that science and technology are true saviors, that man is "nothing but" a highly evolved animal, and that all values are subjective and illusory.

And where was the church during this period of religious, moral, and social upheaval? Nearly silent. When John Lennon made his statement that the Beatles were more popular than Jesus, the Christian response was meager. The counter culture was flooding society with a new set of paradigms, and all the church could do was call for the banning and burning of Beatles records. "The failed attempt by fundamentalist groups to ban the Beatles, including burn-ins to torch Beatles records, meant that the old-time religion had lost its 200-year grip on American culture."[45]

Conclusion

The craving for "something more" was not fulfilled by the insistence that the cosmos is all there is or was or ever will be. Some substitute had to be found. The rage that young people felt toward the coldness and impersonalism of materialism led to an anything-goes religious experimentation. Religion had found a new home in a world that often dispensed with logic, reason, and common sense. What had started as a "subterranean" movement in the 1950s by a group of ideological misfits, had become mainstream by the 1970s.

Notes

1. Harry Blamires, *The Christian Mind* (London: S.C.P.K., 1963), 3.

2. Edgar D. Mitchell, "Introduction: From Outer Space to Inner Space," *Psychic Exploration: A Challenge for Science*, ed. John White (New York: G.P. Putnam's Sons, 1974), 25.

3. Mitchell, "Introduction: From Outer Space to Inner Space," 28–29.

4. Mitchell, "Introduction: From Outer Space to Inner Space," 29.

5. Mitchell, "Introduction: From Outer Space to Inner Space," 29.

6. Jacob Needleman, "Introduction," *Religion for a New Generation*, eds. Jacob Needleman, A.K. Bierman, and James A. Gould (New York: Macmillan, 1973), 1.

7. George F. Will, "1968: Memories That Dim and Differ," *Washington Post* (January 14, 1988), A27. Quoted in Os Guinness, *The Dust of Death: The Sixties Counterculture and How It Changed America Forever* (Wheaton, IL: Crossway Books, 1994), xii.

8. Robert Nisbet, *The Twilight of Authority* (New York: Oxford University Press, 1975), [67]. Quoted in Guinness, *The Dust of Death*, 12.

9. Theodore Roszak, *The Making of a Counter Culture* (Garden City, NY: Doubleday, 1969), 167.

10. Quoted in Roszak, *The Making of a Counter Culture*, 167.

11. Quoted in Burton H. Wolfe, *The Hippies* (1968), 13. Cited in Allen J. Matusow, *The Unraveling of America: A History of Liberalism in the 1960s* (New York: Harper & Row, 1984), 275–276.

12. Timothy Leary, *Turn On, Tune In, Drop Out* (Berkeley, CA: Ronin Publishing, Inc., [1965] 1999), 3.

13. Leary, *Turn On, Tune In, Drop Out*, 7.

14. Leary, *Turn On, Tune In, Drop Out*, 8–15.

15. Leary states his opposition to the "Judeo-Christian" worldview in a 1976 interview. See "Leary vs. Linkletter" at www.camguys.com/tv.timebombs/top.html.

16. *Time* (September 22, 1967), 62. Quoted in David A. Noebel, *The Legacy of John Lennon: Charming or Harming a Generation?* (Nashville, TN: Thomas Nelson, 1982), 60.

17. "Vice President Spiro Agnew conducted an unsuccessful crusade in 1970 to have 'With a Little Help from My Friends' banned from U.S. radio, charging that the line 'I get high with a little help from my friends' was a drug reference." (Judson Knight, *Abbey Road to Zapple Records: A Beatles Encyclopedia* [Dallas, TX: Taylor Publishing Company, 1999], 239).

18. John Lennon denied an LSD connection. See MacDonald, *Revolution in the Head: The Beatles' Records and the Sixties* (New York: Henry Holt and Company, 1994), 190–191; Hunter Davies, *The Beatles*, rev. ed. (New York: McGraw-Hill, 1978), 281; and *The Beatles Anthology* (San Francisco, CA: Chronicle Books, 2000), 242.

19. Matusow, *The Unraveling of America*, 296.

20. Gary J. Katz, *Death by Rock and Roll: The Untimely Deaths of the Legends of Rock* (New York: Citadel Press, 1995).

21. D. H. Rawcliffe, *Occult and Supernatural Phenomena* (New York: Dover Publications, 1987), 43. This book was originally published under the title *The Psychology of the Occult* (1952) and was reprinted by Dover in 1959 under the title *Illusions and Delusions of the Supernatural and the Occult.*

22. McCandlish Phillips, *The Bible, the Supernatural, and the Jews* (Minneapolis, MN: Bethany Fellowship, 1970), 243–244.

23. Thomas Szasz, *Ceremonial Chemistry: The Ritual Persecution of Drugs, Addicts, and Pushers* (Garden City, NY: Anchor Press/Doubleday, 1974), 64.

24. Richard Kyle, *The Religious Fringe* (Downers Grove, IL: InterVarsity Press, 1993), 229.

25. *The Alan Watts Journal* (March 1970), 4. Quoted in John Charles Cooper, *Religion in the Age of Aquarius* (Philadelphia, PA: The Westminster Press, 1971), 72.

26. The interview was later published in American magazines and newspapers. See *New York Times* (August 5, 1966), 20. The account is retold by the Beatles in *The Beatles Anthology,* 223–226.

27. John W. Whitehead, "Who's Afraid of . . . the Exorcist?," *Gadfly* (October 1998), 10. "Some defended Lennon, including a Wisconsin minister who said that anyone outraged by the remark should 'take a look at their own values and standards. There is much validity in what Lennon said. To many people, the golf course is also more popular than Jesus Christ.'" (*John Whitehead, Grasping for the Wind: The Search for Meaning in the 20th Century* [Grand Rapids, MI: Zondervan, 2001], 216–217)

28. *Time* (September 6, 1968), 60.

29. *New York Times* (December 12, 1966), 57.

30. Quoted in Dean Goodman, "George Harrison says 'The World Is Going Mental,'" Reuters News Service (December 21, 2000).

31. Matusow, *The Unraveling of America,* 303.

32. Matusow, *The Unraveling of America,* 303.

33. Vincent Bugliosi with Curt Gentry, *Helter Skelter: The True Story of the Manson Murders* (New York: W.W. Norton, 1974).

34. Jonathan Eisen *Altamont: Death of Innocence in the Woodstock Nation* (New York: Avon Books, 1970) and David Dalton, "Altamont: An eyewitness Account," *Gadfly* (November-December 1999), 41–43, 62–65.

35. William A. Gordon, *Four Dead in Ohio: Was There a Conspiracy at Kent State?* (Laguna Hills, CA: Northridge Books, 1995). Includes an extensive bibliography. After the killings, more than 450 universities and colleges closed because of student or faculty protest strikes. Riots broke out on some campuses. By the end of May, the National Guard had been called out 24 times at 21 campuses in 16 states.

36. Todd Gitlin, *The Twilight of Common Dreams: Why America is Wracked by Culture Wars* (New York: Metropolitan Books, 1995), 148. "Although the right gained some important political victories in the 1980s and early 1990s, it failed to transform the opportunities opened up by this position of state power into dislodging the Left from its dominance of university humanities and social science departments and the more intellectual side of journalism, film, and broadcasting. In terms of richness and innovative quality of cultural theory and impact on the educated middle class, the story of the Left since the mid-1960s has been one of broad and

persistent success." (Norman F. Cantor, *The American Century: Varieties of Culture in Modern Times* [New York: HarperCollins, 1997], 326).

37. The 1961 edition of *Stranger in a Strange Land* is an edited version of the original manuscript. After Heinlein's death in 1988, his widow resubmitted the original manuscript for publication. She writes in the "Preface" to the 1991 edition "that the editors required some cutting and removal of a few scenes that might then have been offensive to public taste" (1). What was considered radical and offensive in 1961 is now touted as normative.

38. Robert Holdstock, ed., *Encyclopedia of Science Fiction* (London, England: Cathay Books, [1978] 1983), 30.

39. "The given names of the chief characters have great importance to the plot. They were carefully selected: Jubal means 'the father of all,' Michael stands for 'Who is like God?' I leave it for the reader to find out what the other names mean." (Virginia Heinlein, "Preface," in Robert A. Heinlein, *Stranger in a Strange Land* [New York: Ace/Putnam, 1991], 3).

40. "Grok" is Heinlein's Martian word for "to comprehend fully." The dedication to science fiction writer Wilson Tucker's *The Year of the Quiet Sun* (1970) reads: "For the Fifteen and their mates, who are looser because they grok a lot."

41. James Gifford, *Robert A. Heinlein: A Reader's Companion* (Sacramento, CA: Nitrosyncretic Press, 2000), 187.

42. Brian Ash, ed., *The Visual Encyclopedia of Science Fiction* (New York: Harmony Books, 1977), 229. For a discussion of the influence *Stranger in a Strange Land* had on Charles Manson, see Gifford, *Robert A. Heinlein*, 247–248, note 78. Of course, Heinlein cannot be held responsible for the actions of Charles Manson.

43. David V. Barrett, *Sects, 'Cults' and Alternative Religions: A World Survey and Sourcebook* (London, England: Wellington House, [1996] 1998), 215–216.

44. John Jefferson Davis, *Foundations of Evangelical Theology* (Grand Rapids, MI: Baker Book House, 1984), 127.

45. Whitehead, "Who's Afraid of... the Exorcist?," 11.

12

Living Between Two Worlds

[W]e're riding that great divide between reason and unreason,
between naturalism and spiritualism. The pendulum of public
acceptance has been swinging between the two philosophies for
the last two hundred years at least, first one way and then the
other. Right now we seem to be in the midst of a resurgence of the
irrational, the *un*rational; there is a burgeoning of belief in the
supernatural—and not necessarily in any occult sense, although
that usually follows. The present mood might be characterized as
an atmosphere of public willingness to accept the weird, the
strange, the unexplained and chalk it up to supernatural agencies
beyond the ken and control of man.[1]

The extremely popular *X-Files* television series, which first aired in
the Fall of 1993, in some respects is an updated version of *Science Fiction Theatre* (*SFT*) which made its television debut in April 1955. Even
though the innovative Sci-Fi show only ran for two years, 78 episodes
were produced. Brief mention of *SFT* is made in *Back to the Future* by
Marty's science-fiction-loving father. "Each drama was based on scientific fact, dealing with such subjects as UFOs, mental telepathy, psy-
chokinesis, robots, man's first flight into outer space, and the possibility
of thawing out frozen prehistoric animals."[2]

SFT was an inventive concept for the time, a mix of rationalism and irrationalism that today's materialists would reject and consider dangerous in terms of our newly adopted Enlightenment worldview. Investigating paranormal claims was given legitimacy on the show because "real-life scientific experts served as advisors in this series to insure authenticity."[3] The line between real science and the paranormal was being blurred at a time in America's history when academic establishments and government actions were becoming increasingly more secularized.

X-Files is also indebted to *Kolchak: The Night Stalker*. This series "was an odd mixture of reality and fantasy" with an occult touch. Newspaper reporter Carl Kolchak, played by Darren McGavin, "kept running into vampires, werewolves, zombies, and other esoteric phenomena. If he was sent to cover a crooked politician, he would find that the man had sold his soul to the Devil—literally. If he was covering a museum opening, a 500-year-old Aztec mummy would come to life."[4] Sure, it was fiction, but its reality-based script writing put it into the realm of the possible.

The Night Stalker introduced the occult to television viewers in a way that *The Twilight Zone*, which mainly dealt with irony rather than the paranormal, could not.[5] In a reprisal of *The Night Stalker* series in 1974, the Kolchak character relocated from Las Vegas to Chicago, "where he took on werewolves, mummies, zombies, Indian demons, sewer-roaming creatures, and, of course, aliens."[6] Kolchak endures ridicule and opposition at every turn in his attempts to prove that there's something out there. One fan of the show compares the efforts of Kolchak to Galileo.[7] This is odd, since Galileo is most often cited by materialists and secularists as an exemplary scientist who would never consider delving into the paranormal to interpret seemingly unexplainable phenomena. Galileo was a hard science man.

Is the Truth "Out There"?

These shows reintroduced American television viewers to a broader worldview that is once again accepting of phenomena beyond physics. Metaphysical explanations are becoming credible, even in a time when secularism has become the nation's official civil religion. But *X-Files* accomplishes the metaphysical reentry with an interesting twist that keeps one foot in both worlds. The rationalist Dana Scully is pitted against the open-minded genuine seeker Fox Mulder as they explore supposed unsolved FBI cases that have no rational explanation. Scully is assigned to Mulder to keep his paranormal exuberance in check.

X-Files is a metaphor for American belief patterns. Scully represents the materialist who is skeptical of anything paranormal, believing that everything has a logical, scientific explanation. Mulder is open to all things paranormal, from UFOs and ESP to spontaneous human combustion and telekinesis and everything in between. Chris Carter, the show's creator, describes this conflict as his own and probably that of much of America:

> "Mulder and Scully are equal parts of my nature, I guess." Chris Carter muses. "I'm a natural skeptic, so I have much of the Scully character in me, yet I'm willing to take leaps of faith, to go out on a limb. I love writing both those characters, because their voices are very clear in my head." He does admit however, that as the series has progressed, Scully's skepticism has been somewhat eroded. "But she is a scientist first and foremost," he says. "What she sees, what is unexplainable, what seems fantastic to her, she believes, truly, can be ultimately explained scientifically. She is a scientist and will always be one, so she maintains a scientific distance from things, whereas, Mulder leaps in and wants to believe."[8]

But what standard should be used to distinguish between these two opposing positions? How does anyone know whether one of those "leaps of faith" isn't a leap off a cliff? What all of these shows lack is an epistemological standard, a place to stand to assess claims of the paranormal. Just because something cannot be explained scientifically does not mean that there is always a supernatural, preternatural, or paranormal explanation. There may be a rational, scientific solution that we have not discovered.

Will Scooby-Doo Do?

As one might expect, materialists don't like shows that showcase paranormal events, even if the shows are fictional. *X-Files* is criticized by the late Carl Sagan because it "is skewed heavily towards the reality of alien abductions, strange powers and government complicity in covering up just about everything interesting. Almost never does the paranormal claim turn out to be a hoax or a psychological aberration or a misunderstanding of the natural world."[9] Sagan would prefer an adult series similar to the *Scooby Doo* cartoon approach "in which paranormal claims are systematically investigated and every case is found to be" explained in common terms.[10]

Notice Sagan's operating presupposition. He begins by assuming that everything can be explained in terms of present naturalistic assumptions. This would go for any miracle recorded in the Bible, including predictive prophecy. There is no possible way that Jesus could have risen from the dead or performed any of His many miracles given Sagan's presuppositions. A stolen body, yes, but a resurrection? Certainly not. Sagan's presuppositions won't allow it. (See chapter 13.)

Pure materialists like Sagan have no trouble, however, explaining evolution in terms of unseen natural forces. "Natural selection is not random, nor does it operate by chance. Natural selection preserves the gains and eradicates the mistakes."[11] The author of this assertion is describing what a *person* with innate intelligence would do. How does this unseen force do these things? How does "it" know whether what's evolved is a "gain" or a "mistake"? Never mind that no one has actually seen this process take place. Given the criteria of what constitutes the paranormal, evolution would be considered paranormal. There are mysterious unseen forces at work shaping and fashioning life forms into new life forms. Even so, evolution is believed with religious fervor. I wonder what Scooby Doo would think of that?

A Prior Commitment to Materialism

Those who claim that there is always a rational and naturalistic explanation for every seemingly unexplainable phenomenon have a serious problem with elements in their own worldview. Consider the following faith-based irrationalism disguised as "science" from an avowed materialist:

> We take the side of science *in spite* of the patent absurdity of some of its constructs, *in spite* of its failure to fulfill many of its extravagant promises of health and life, *in spite* of the tolerance of the scientific community for unsubstantiated just-so stories, because we have a prior commitment, a commitment to materialism. It is not that the methods and institutions of science somehow compel us to accept a material explanation of the phenomenal world, but, on the contrary, that we are forced by our *a priori* [prior commitment] adherence to material causes to create an apparatus of investigation and a set of concepts that produce material explanations, no matter how counter-intuitive, no matter how mystifying to the uninitiated. Moreover, that materialism is an absolute, for we cannot allow a Divine foot in the door.[12]

In effect, materialists like this author believe in rationalistic scientific explanations even if the explanation is absurd. How does commitment to his worldview differ from those who claim that there are paranormal explanations for some phenomena that seem to the materialist to be absurd? Is it any wonder that there is a mistrust of science and an interest in the paranormal?

"I Do Believe... I Do Believe... I Do Believe!"

Interest in the paranormal—events, abilities, and matters not defined or explained by rational means—has increased as people have lost faith in a purely materialistic worldview. Chris Carter describes it this way:

> I have a pet theory that everyone wants to have that experience where they're driving through the desert at night, and they see something and can't explain what it is. I think it's all about religion. Not necessarily Christian religion, but it's about beliefs—and meaning and truth and why are we here and why are they here and who's lying to us. It's religion with a lowercase "r." Encountering a UFO would be like witnessing a miracle.[13]

David Duchovny, who plays Fox Mulder, agrees with the notion that the appeal of X-Files, and I would add, any show that suggests that there are paranormal explanations that science cannot answer, is a religious quest. (Mulder has been replaced in the new X-Files series by Robert Patrick who played the T-1000 fluid terminator in Terminator 2: Judgment Day [1991].) "Obviously, it's tapping in to something the nation wants. I think it has to do with religious stirrings—a sort of New Age yearning for an alternate reality and the search for some kind of extrasensory god."[14] Sagan and other naturalists, in their attempt to rid the world of demons, sprites, and spirits, have opened Pandora's Paranormal Box. "Western society is currently floundering between a hardball, reason-based, naturalist philosophy which says in effect, 'If it ain't in the atom, it ain't,' and a soft-soap supernaturalism that claims, 'The spirit world is really where it's at.'"[15]

Spiritual Flim-Flam

While there may be unexplained phenomena that some people want to pass off as paranormal, most if not all of them turn out to be bogus, what James Randi has described as "flimflam."[16] Some people are ready to believe almost anything. Such a predisposition opens them up to the spiritual con job. Even in an era in which science is still king, a good many suckers are still born. Some of the most rational people become unbelievably irrational when it comes to psychic "stuff." Even highly intelligent people are sucked into groups and belief systems that promote themselves through flimflam, convincing new adherents that its leaders "have the power." Electrical engineers, CEOs of some of America's largest computer technology companies, and marketing analysts are turning to psychics, tarot card readers, and parapsychology in general to gain some idea of what the future holds for them and their companies during times of uncertainty, especially when "things are falling apart."[17]

Tricks of Religious Charlatans

For many religious seekers, belief in the supernatural is attractive, no matter what the source. "Human beings are spiritual creatures. We hunger for an encounter with the spiritual. We seem to know instinctively that there is more to this life than what we are able to experience with our five physical senses. Implanted in all of us is a desire to understand the ultimate meanings of things." As a result, "millions of people are turning to occult practices for answers to life's questions."[18] John W. Whitehead expresses a similar sentiment: "Ultimately, it seems that people are generally hungry for transcendence. Many want to know God or a God-force. Seeking spirituality, they investigate the occult, astrology charts, angels, UFOs, and extraterrestrial beings. This sometimes leads to tragedy, as in the March 1997 mass suicide of thirty-nine Heaven's Gate cult members who sought union with extraterrestrials supposedly following the Hale-Bopp Comet."[19] This one fact is used by

some very talented but evil people to draw spiritual seekers into dangerous metaphysical movements. The vulnerable and desperate are the most
susceptible. They may be shown what seems to be supernatural phenomena to attract them to a particular cult, pseudo-Christian religious
group, or the paranormal worldview in general. If these genuine seekers
are particularly depressed, confused, or just desperate for answers, they
can find themselves attracted to some of the most bizarre and sinister
religious movements. It happened to 913 reckless souls in Guyana, South
America, on November 18, 1978:

> "Reverend" Jim Jones was as charismatic a leader as any
> who ever swayed reason. Despite his farcical philosophy, he
> managed to convince a considerable number of California's popu-
> lace that he had a direct pipeline to the gods and to salvation.
> With the kind of sleight of hand and sleight of mind that char-
> acterizes such charlatans, he "proved" that he could raise the
> dead—he performed the "miracle" forty-seven times in his
> church—and showed his followers that he was able to cure can-
> cer and other afflictions by removing masses of organic junk
> from their bodies. After his death, cult members came forward
> to testify that, after threats from Jones, they had agreed to fake
> death and then stage instant resurrections. The surgery was even
> simpler than that still being performed by "psychic surgeons" of
> Brazil and the Philippines. Jones merely reached beneath the
> clothes of the intimidated faithful and pulled out chicken giz-
> zards and other material, according to witnesses. Those who did
> not see through the tricks were convinced.[20]

Jones had his followers believing that he had supernatural powers.
They would do anything for such a "gifted" spiritual leader, especially if
he had power over life and death. But Jones had no special powers. He
used deception and the irrational willingness of people to believe in any
claimed supernatural feat to hold them under his spell.

Here's how it worked. On one occasion Jones became angry with a worker, Jean Brown, because of a disruption during a meeting. Jones blamed Brown for the disturbance. "Looking directly at Brown, he said, 'Drop dead.' She fell forward from her chair, rolled over on the platform knocking over chairs.... Then she 'died.'" Jones went on with the meeting, telling those in the congregation "not to look at the body, since the cause of her death was contagious and they too might perish."[21]

As you can imagine, many were upset and frightened. They had just seen a woman drop dead at the command of Jim Jones! Would they be next?

> Several minutes later, Jones, proving that his awesome power was tempered by his bountiful mercy, decided to give Jean another chance. He raised his uplifted arms in her direction and commanded her spirit to return to her body. The spirit apparently responded, because Jean began to stir. She moved stiffly at first, but as life returned, she thanked her savior for his love and promised to do better in the future.[22]

The "death and resurrection" event had been planned and staged for the trusting audience. Jean Brown was in on the deception. Their performance was designed to manipulate the people and to empower Jim Jones. Jones "was a master confidence man."[23] After seeing Jones "raise people from the dead," did his followers believe that he could resurrect them even if they drank from a tub of grape-flavored Fla-Vor-Aid laced with potassium cyanide and tranquilizers? The evidence seems to indicate that most of his followers took the poison willingly possibly expecting to be brought back to life once the fact-finding mission to investigate reports of human rights violations left.[24] They had seen Jones raise the dead before.

A Magician Among the Spirits

Most people are aware of the exploits of Sherlock Holmes, the fictionalized English master detective. Holmes's creator was Sir Arthur Conan Doyle. Holmes the character is quite different from Doyle the author. As a detective, Holmes was scrupulously rational. He could deduce the most fantastic clues from only a few scraps of evidence. The angle of a stab wound would tell him the height of the assailant. A whiff of tobacco smoke left lingering at the scene of a crime would enable him to trace the thief through a local tobacco shop that blended the odd mixture. Everything was logical and reasonable. There had to be a rational explanation for even the most suspicious circumstances, even those in which the clues seemed to point to the paranormal. For Holmes, there was always some logic behind the unexplained evidence.

But when it came to psychic phenomena, Doyle was especially irrational. He was willing to believe any fragment of claimed evidence to support his unbending belief that mediums could communicate with departed spirits through supernatural efforts. Then he met up with Harry Houdini (1874–1926), the "Handcuff King."

Houdini's name is synonymous with magic. He could escape from any and all restraining devices: handcuffs, straight jackets, safes, locked boxes, and jails. He once escaped from Scotland Yard. He even escaped after being placed *inside* a locked safe. Actually, Houdini preferred to be locked inside. It enabled him to line up the exposed tumblers to the correct combination.

Houdini, while fascinated with life beyond the senses, had a running battle with Conan Doyle about the legitimacy of contacting the spirit world. Doyle believed that certain people had the "gift" of being able to break through to the other side. Doyle was an international spokesman for spiritualism, believing it a "'more virile and manly doctrine' than Christianity."[25] He believed that spiritualism as a system of thought "can be reconciled with any religion."[26] Houdini was opened

to believe, but could not. "I'm not denouncing spiritualism. I'm showing up frauds. If there is an honest medium, trot her out."[27] Houdini
believed in God and the afterlife, so he did not deny that supernatural
events could not take place. "Gladly would I embrace Spiritualism," he
wrote in the preface to his *A Magician Among the Spirits*, "if it could
prove its claims, but I am not willing to be deluded by the fraudulent
impositions of so-called psychics, or accept as sacred reality any of the
evidence that has been placed before me thus far."[28]

No one ever passed Houdini's investigative analysis. In his early
years, Houdini practiced the fine art of deception by playing the role of
a medium at seances, "but stopped when he found the locals taking his
off-the-cuff predictions and spirit messages to heart."[29] He was an admitted fraud who became a "medium" to make money. "It takes a flimflammer to catch a flimflammer," Houdini told a reporter in 1924.[30]

Doyle was convinced that Houdini was himself a medium and
capable of supernatural feats using occult powers. He believed that
Houdini could only perform some of his tricks by dematerializing.
Houdini objected.

> I do claim to free myself from the restraint of fetters and
> confinement, but positively state that I accomplish my purpose
> purely by physical, not psychical means. The force necessary to
> "shoot a bolt within a lock," is drawn from Houdini the living
> human being and not a medium. My methods are perfectly natu-
> ral, resting on natural laws of physics. I do not *dematerialize* or
> *materialize* anything; I simply control and manipulate natural
> things in a manner perfectly well known to myself, and thor-
> oughly accountable for and adequately understandable (if not
> duplicable) by any person to whom I may elect to divulge my
> secrets.[31]

As a skeptic of the paranormal, Houdini should be an example to
all of us. Don't be afraid to question claims of preternatural or

supernatural phenomena. If you are ever tempted to believe, investigate, question, and doubt: "The first to plead his case seems just, until another comes and examines him" (Prov. 18:17). Paul tells us, "See to it that no one takes you captive through philosophy and empty deception, according to the tradition of men, according to the elementary principles of the world, rather than according to Christ" (Col. 2:8). Don't be fooled either by the materialist (man-centered "philosophy") or the magician ("empty deception"), both are the "tradition of men."

Conclusion

Dan Korem, a world-famous magician who is a student of magic, deception, and the Bible, writes that it is possible "to convince almost anybody—under the right circumstances and through the use of trickery—that one may have supernatural powers." Korem argues "that unless one is schooled in how the mind can be deceived, one is at a potential disadvantage when trying to objectively report so-called manifestations of occult powers."[32] Unfortunately, many Christians begin with the mistaken assumption that the seemingly unexplainable deserves a paranormal interpretation.

Notes

1. Stephen R. Lawhead, *Turn Back the Night: A Christian Response to Popular Culture* (Westchester, IL: Crossway Books, 1985), 26.

2. Tim Brooks and Earle Marsh, "Science Fiction Theatre," *The Complete Directory to Prime Time Network and Cable TV Shows: 1946-Present*, 7th rev. ed. (New York: Ballantine Books, 1999), 894.

3. Brooks and Marsh, "Science Fiction Theatre," 894.

4. Brooks and Marsh, "Kolchak: The Night Stalker," 548.

5. The devil is featured in a number of *Twilight Zone* episodes, once as a Faustian character ("Escape Clause") and as the author of all things evil ("The Howling Man"). In both cases the devil is real.

6. Ted Edwards, *X-Files Confidential: The Unauthorized X-Philes Compendium* (Boston: Little, Brown and Company, 1997), 3.

7. Edwards, *X-Files Confidential*, 4.

8. Edwards, *X-Files Confidential*, 4.

9. Carl Sagan, *The Demon-Haunted World: Science as a Candle in the Dark* (New York: Random House, 1996), 374.

10. Sagan, *The Demon-Haunted World*, 374.

11. Michael Shermer, *Why People Believe Weird Things: Pseudo-Science, Superstition, and Bogus Notions of Our Time* (New York: MJF Books, 1997), 150.

12. Richard Lewontin, "Billions and Billions of Demons," *The New York Review* (January 9, 1997), 31. Italics in original.

13. Edwards, *X-Files Confidential*, 14–15.

14. Edwards, *X-Files Confidential*, 17.

15. Lawhead, *Turn Back the Night*, 26.

16. The art of flim-flam is portrayed wonderfully in *The Flim-Flam Man* (1967), starring George C. Scott and Michael Sarrazin, and *Paper Moon* (1973), starring Ryan O'Neal and his daughter Tatum.

17. Marci McDonald, "Psst! Want a hot tip? Try a crystal ball," *U.S. News & World Report* (January 8, 2001), 34.

18. Bill Myers and David Wimbish, *The Dark Side of the Supernatural* (Minneapolis, MN: Bethany House, 1999), 16.

19. John W. Whitehead, *Grasping for the Wind: The Search for Meaning in the 20th Century* (Grand Rapids, MI: Zondervan Publishing House, 2001), 268–269.

20. James Randi, *Flim-Flam: Psychics, ESP, Unicorns and other Delusions* (Buffalo, NY: Prometheus Books, [1982] 1987), 248–49. See his chapter on "Medical Humbugs," 173–95. For a Christian critique of the paranormal, see Danny Korem and Paul Meier, *The Fakers: Exploding the Myths of the Supernatural* (Grand Rapids, MI: Baker Book House, [1980] 1981).

21. Mark Lane, *Strongest Poison* (New York: Hawthorn Books, 1980), 47.

22. Lane, *Strongest Poison*, 47.

23. Lane, *Strongest Poison*, 48.

24. For an account of the tragedy, see Phil Kearns with Doug Wead, *People's Temple—People's Tomb* (Plainfield, NJ: Logos International, 1979).

25. Kenneth Silverman, *Houdini: The Career of Erich Weiss* (New York: HarperCollins, 1996), 250.

26. Arthur Conan Doyle, *The History of Spiritualism*, 2 vols. (New York: Arno Press, [1926] 1975), 2:247.

27. Milbourne Christopher, *Houdini: The Untold Story* (New York: Pocket Books, [1969] 1975), 215.

28. Harry Houdini, *A Magician Among the Spirits* (New York: Harper & Brothers, 1924), xi.

29. Silverman, *Houdini*, 254.

30. *Los Angeles Times* (October 28, 1924). Quoted in Silverman, *Houdini*, 247.

31. Quoted in Loraine Boettner, *Immortality* (Philadelphia, PA: Presbyterian and Reformed, 1956), 156.

32. Korem and Meier, *The Fakers*, 17. Korem illustrates his point by convincing a student at Tulane University that he, Korem, is from the Planet Pluto and possesses supernatural powers.

13

Magic, Mechanics, or Miracles?

If Jesus Christ was a magician, then His illusions were totally different from anything any other magicians have done before or since.[1]

The Bible states, without apology, that miracles do happen, from the creation of the universe in Genesis 1 to the new creation in Revelation 21, and everything in between. Even so, the Bible also offers a warning to be discerning, watchful, and even skeptical, especially when people claim to have special powers. This is fundamental straight thinking when God is claimed as the source for their supposed supernatural abilities. Jeremiah writes, "Then the LORD said to me, 'The prophets are prophesying falsehood in My name, I have neither sent them nor commanded them nor spoken to them; they are prophesying to you a false vision, divination, futility and the deception of their own minds'" (Jer. 14:14). We are told, "do not believe every spirit, but test the spirits to see whether they are from God" (1 John 4:1).

Of course, there's a very good reason for these precautions. "Because many false prophets have gone out into the world" (1 John 4:1). Claims of supernatural abilities are legion, so much so that even the best minds are fooled, "so as to mislead, if possible, even the elect" (Matt. 24:24). Christians in Ephesus in the first century were commended because they didn't take a person's word as being the final authority. "I know your deeds, and your toil and perseverance, and that you cannot endure evil men, and *you put to the test* those who call themselves apostles, and they are not, and *you found them to be false*" (Rev. 2:2). An investigation took place to learn the truth. Scripture describes the spiritual counterfeiters as *"false* prophets" (Matt. 24:11, 24; 2 Peter 2:1) and their so-called miracles as *"false* wonders" (2 Thess. 2:9, 11). Bible commentator R.C.H. Lenski characterizes the nature of their supposed "powers" as "lie-signs":

> This explains Matt. 24:24: "pseudo-Christs and pseudo-prophets (none of them real) and they shall give great signs and wonders so as to deceive," etc.; none of these great signs and wonders are real, all of them are deception only, or, as Paul qualifies: "lie-signs and wonders." This is the extent of Satan's power.[2]

There were "magicians, conjurers, and sorcerers" in Babylon who served under Nebuchadnezzar (Dan. 2:1). If they truly had supernatural powers, they would have been able to interpret the king's dream as well as to tell him what he dreamed. This they could not do (2:4–14). In fact, they admitted that it was impossible: "'There is not a man on earth who could declare the matter for the king. . . .'" (2:10). Daniel tells us that only God has the power to reveal "the profound and hidden things; He knows what is in the darkness" (2:22). The devil has no such power. Daniel not only was able to interpret the king's dream, he also told the king what he dreamed in great and exact detail (2:27–49).

If the "magicians, conjurers, and sorcerers" had psychic abilities, then how could Daniel have distinguished himself as a true prophet? Their demonic powers would have been equal to his. There was no contest. Nebuchadnezzar did the right thing by testing the spirits. Christians need to follow his example and do the same.

Science and Miracles

The December 1996 issue of *Popular Mechanics* (*PM*) carried an article that claimed that "science" has solved a number of ancient Bible mysteries. Miracles are out, mechanical explanations are in. According to the people at *PM* there has to be a "scientific" explanation for the "stories' implausible aspects." Implausibility is the operating presupposition of the anti-supernaturalistic worldview of modern science and the editors at *PM*: "Technology and a better understanding of natural processes may explain how these seemingly impossible events occurred."[3]

The folks at *PM* do not come out and say it, but the Bible is assumed to be a compilation of myths and superstitions that are naturally a part of the pre-scientific ancient era. There are staggering theological consequences for those who follow this operating presupposition. If the biblical writers do not give an accurate assessment of historical events, then their judgment in *all* matters must be considered suspect. There is no neutrality on this issue. *PM* concludes that the biblical authors could not tell the difference between a miracle and a phenomenon of nature.[4] This is nothing more than chronological snobbery, the assumption that something is false or unscientific just because it is old. Modern man, looking down the corridors of more than 2000 years of history and with high-tech instruments, is supposedly in a much better position to evaluate these events than those who were actually eyewitnesses. "Now— with the help of high-tech methods including radar imaging, computer simulation and chemical analysis—scientists are becoming convinced that there may be another dimension to these miraculous tales."[5] These are the same people who can't explain how the pyramids were built.

Following anti-supernatural presuppositions, the author of "Bible Mysteries" offers what he believes are rationalistic and scientific explanations for what were once considered miraculous events by well intentioned religionists who wanted people to believe in God.

Noah and the Ark

The first supposed miracle that has a purely scientific explanation is the story of Noah's Ark. *PM* admits that an ark with the same dimensions as Noah's Ark "was found not on Mount Ararat but on a remote site about 20 miles away."[6] Since it was not found on what is today Mount Ararat in Turkey, *PM* concludes that the vessel is not Noah's Ark. A careful reading of the biblical text will show that the ark "rested upon the mountains of Ararat" (Gen. 8:4). In biblical times Ararat was a range of mountains, not unlike our Appalachian or Rocky Mountains. Twenty miles is not a great distance when considering that a mountain range might cover a thousand miles.

But how do scientists explain this huge ship-like structure so high in the mountains? "[It could have been] an astronomical event causing gravitational pull in the ocean waters that forced the boat into the mountains," David Fasold, a shipwreck specialist, hypothesizes. And they say Christians believe in miracles.

Lot's Wife is Turned into a Pillar of Salt

The Dead Sea is the lowest body of water on earth (1,344 feet below the mean level of the world's oceans). The biblical cities of Sodom and Gomorrah were located in the Dead Sea region. Scientists theorize that the twin cities of depravity were "destroyed by an earthquake that toppled buildings and liquified the rocks and soil underneath the cities."[7] Other cities have been lost through liquification: the town of Helice in ancient Greece in 37 B.C., thousands of miles of area in China in 1921, and most recently, a section of Valdez, Alaska, in the 1950s. In a similar way, God destroyed Sodom and Gomorrah, probably through volcanic activity which liquified the surrounding salt and bitumen (asphalt) mines.

But what of Lot's wife? Did she turn into a pillar of salt? Yes and no. The text does not demand that Lot's wife be transformed into salt through and through as those who looked at the snaked-haired Medusa were turned to stone. As Lot's wife "looked back," she got caught in the spray of molten salt and was encased in the mixture, "and she became a pillar of salt" (Gen. 19:26). Henry Morris writes:

> One possibility is that the explosions in the region threw great quantities of its salt deposits into the air, and that some of these fell on her and buried her under a great pile of salt. Another is that she was buried by volcanic ash or other materials and that, gradually, over the following years, her body became petrified, "becoming salt" in fashion similar to that experienced by the inhabitants of Pompeii and Herculaneum when they were buried by the eruption of Mount Vesuvius.[8]

The miracle was that God did it at the time He said He would, for the purpose of ridding the region of the degrading influence of the Sodomites. *PM* dismisses the notion of divine intervention, offering no explanation as to how only Lot and his family knew to escape the impending destruction.

Moses Parts the Red Sea

The *PM* version of Moses parting the Red Sea is inventive but not very original. Liberals have been pushing the strong-wind view for decades. It goes like this: "Because of the peculiar geography of the northern end of the Red Sea, a moderate wind blowing constantly for about 10 hours could have caused the sea to recede about a mile and the water level to drop 10 ft., leaving dry land for a period of time before crashing back when the winds died down."[9] A few questions immediately come to mind. First, has anyone observed such a phenomenon happening again since the time of Moses? Second, is it possible that the sea bottom would be dry enough for the Israelites to pass through? The mud would have been at least a foot thick, and ten hours of wind would not be enough time to dry the ground. Ten days would not have been enough time to fulfill the biblical requirement that "the sons of Israel went through the midst of the sea on dry land" (Ex. 14:22). Third, how did Moses know that this unique phenomenon, never witnessed before and never to be repeated again, would take place at this precise time?

Lazarus is Raised from the Dead

Was Lazarus really dead or was he in a coma? Dr. Gerald A. Larue, former professor of biblical history and archeology at the University of Southern California and president of the Committee for the Scientific Examination of Religion, a secular humanist organization, says it is possible Lazarus was either in a coma or a catatonic state. Again, citing a pre-scientific bias toward medical ignorance, Dr. Larue surmises that those who placed Lazarus in the tomb probably buried him alive. Since, according to the good doctor, "hearing is often the last sense lost," Lazarus heard Jesus' loud voice telling him to "come forth" (John 11:43). Hearing Jesus' voice supposedly shocked him right out of the coma.

Hogwash. A sick man, four days without food and water, and bound from head to toe would have had little chance of survival in a rock tomb. Jesus states emphatically that Lazarus was dead (v. 14). How coincidental that Jesus arrives in the nick of time to shout his friend out of his coma. Another miracle of extraordinary timing. In addition, Lazarus's body would have been handled to make it ready for burial. They would have noted that the body was still warn, a sure sign of life.

A Plague of Locusts

How do we explain plagues of locusts? Some insect plagues could be explained in terms of environmental changes: "The locusts followed unseasonable rains that fell in the form of hail in the seventh plague" on

Egypt.[10] But how would Moses know that the locusts would fly just when he gave the command? *PM* finally acknowledges that timing is the key element in all their mechanistic scenarios. "There remains, however, this mystery. Most of the plagues were produced at Moses's command, in one case at a time set by the Pharaoh himself, and ceased at his prayer."[11] There was no *Farmer's Almanac* in Moses' day that predicted a locust plague at a particular time.

Moses and the Burning Bush

Did Moses mistake "the angel of the Lord" for "a natural gas seep that was ignited by lightning"?[12] Once again we are forced to believe that Moses was an ignorant and superstitious bedouin who did not have the sense to check out what *PM* maintains was a common occurrence in the desert. Do such phenomena happen today? The Bible tells us that Moses, taking on the role of a scientist, walked around the bush: "I must turn aside now, and see this marvelous sight, why the bush is not burned up" (Ex. 3:3). Moses was looking for a rational, scientific explanation. He did not immediately assume that the event was miraculous. Moses spent forty years in the wilderness. Are we to assume that he was not familiar with desert phenomena?

PM has added nothing new to skeptical analysis. Others have attempted to explain away the miraculous. Consider the following:

> [A]mong the commentators who think that a natural explanation can be found, some think that the phenomenon of the bush that "burned with fire" and yet "was not consumed" can be explained as a variety of the gas plant or *Fraxinella*, the *Dictamnus Albus L.* This is the plant with a strong growth about three feet in height with clusters of purple blossoms. The whole bush is covered with tiny oil glands. This oil is so volatile that it is constantly escaping and if approached with a naked light bursts suddenly into flames.[13]

Another writer attempts to explain the flames as "the crimson blossoms of mistletoe twigs… which grow on various prickly Acacia bushes… When this mistletoe is in full bloom, the bush becomes a mass of brilliant flaming color and looks as if it is on fire."[14] Here's one that would suit the people at *PM*: "Electrical energy of an extremely high voltage would readily produce the phenomenon which Moses witnessed as fire burning without consuming it."[15] In all of these explanations, Moses is a dupe who had not learned anything about his desert environment in the forty years he spent there.

Miracles Or Magic?

Were the miracles in the Bible tricks? Was Jesus an extraordinary stage magician? Did He pretend to raise people from the dead, walk on water, and feed thousands? Was Jesus like Jim Jones, using some of His followers to concoct an elaborate deception on the people to build a following of nationalist zealots to overthrow the Romans? Some people believe this, even though Jesus rejected any notion of armed revolt or refusal to pay taxes.

Walking on Water

The miracles that Jesus performed have never been duplicated. Today's magicians require numerous assistants, tens of thousands of dollars worth of special equipment, and days of preparation time to perform their elaborate tricks, and walking on water would have been an elaborate piece of prestidigitation. Imagine the type of gear Jesus would have needed to convince His disciples that He was actually walking on water during a violent storm in the middle of a large lake where their boat was "battered by the waves" (Matt. 14:24). Here's how Christian magician André Kole describes the impossibility of a walk-on-water trick:

On several occasions I have been asked to perform before magicians' conventions. One time a convention host asked me to perform on the beach before 700 magicians from around the world. He wanted me to create an illusion in which I would get out of a boat and walk on the water a short distance to land.

After spending many weeks trying to formulate all the methods we could use for such an illusion, it was finally scrapped. It was impossible to create any type of effect that would convince anyone I was really walking on water.

This experience showed me that, even with all our modern technology, we can't come close to duplicating many of the things Jesus did nearly 20 centuries ago.[16]

Keep in mind that Jesus walked on water during a storm "many stadia away from the land" (Matt. 14:24). A stadium is approximately 600 feet. The conditions in first-century Israel were far from optimal for such an elaborate trick, especially during a time when engineering knowledge was minimal.

Giving Sight to the Blind

Jesus' healing miracles were different from the modern variety of so-called faith healers because He healed people with obvious maladies that could be investigated and validated. He restored the sight of a man who was known by the people of his town as someone who had been "blind from birth" (John 9:1). John adds that "since the beginning of time it has never been heard that any one opened the eyes of a person born blind" (9:32). The man was known by his "neighbors" (9:8). It was not a case of mistaken identity (9:9). The miracle was thoroughly investigated because the religious skeptics did not believe the man's testimony, "that he had been blind, and had received sight" (9:18). So they questioned "the parents of the very one who had received his sight" (9:18). The parents gave the following answer, "We know that this is

our son, and that he was born blind; but how he now sees, we do not
know. Ask him; he is of age, he shall speak for himself" (9:20–21).
John's gospel anticipates the objections to the miraculous and meets
them head-on by recounting the investigative process for its readers.

Feeding, Healing, and Raising the Dead

Jesus performed many miracles in front of numerous eyewitnesses.
He fed more than five thousand people, multiplying the food from five
loaves of bread and two fish (Matt. 14:17). Where did he hide all the
food if this was a trick? He healed ten lepers and sent them to have their
healing verified (Luke 17:11–19). Leprosy was the most dreaded disease in Jesus' day. The priests had a record of those who had the disease
(Lev. 13:2–3). They would have examined the ten men thoroughly before declaring them "clean."

Of course, the resurrection of Jesus is the most significant New
Testament miracle. If Jesus has not been raised from the dead, then the
Christian's faith is "in vain" (1 Cor. 15:14). None of the popular de-
bunking theories by atheists, rationalists, and materialists can withstand
investigative scrutiny. The swoon theory and the stolen body theory,
two of the most popular explanations for the resurrection, do not hold
up when the New Testament record is studied. How does a beaten and
battered Jesus roll a huge stone from the mouth of a cave where He was
buried after an excruciating beating and crucifixion, walk a few miles
on feet that had large spikes driven through them, and then convince
His disciples that He had risen from the dead? If the disciples had stolen
the body, then it's amazing that they suffered martyrdom for a lie. If
Roman officials had stolen the body, then all they had to do to prove
that Jesus had not risen from the dead was to display his crucified corpse.

The Bible goes a step further by including the testimony of eyewitnesses. Thomas was a "hands-on" eyewitness (John 20:24–29). Luke, the
disciple who wrote that he had "investigated everything carefully from

the beginning," even interviewing "eyewitnesses" (Luke 1:2–3), reports that Jesus "presented Himself alive after His suffering, by many convincing proofs, appearing to them over a period of forty days" (Acts 1:3). Paul tells us that Jesus "appeared to more than five hundred brethren at one time, most of whom remain until now" (1 Cor. 15:6). As Paul tells King Agrippa, "For the king knows about these matters, and I speak to him also with confidence, since I am persuaded that none of these things escape his notice; for this has not been done in a corner" (Acts 26:26).

Conclusion

The Bible anticipates modern-day skeptics. All the criteria for determining if a miracle has taken place are evident in the biblical text. The miracles have not been duplicated under identical circumstances by any modern magician. None of these miracles could have been accomplished either by mechanical or magical means, either then or now. The miracles of the Bible are unique because Jesus is unique.

Notes

1. André Kole and Al Janssen, *Miracles or Magic?* (Eugene, OR: Harvest House, [1984] 1987), 113.

2. R.C.H. Lenski, *The Interpretation of St. Paul's Epistles to the Colossians, to the Thessalonians, to Timothy, to Titus and to Philemon* (Minneapolis, MN: Augsburg Publishing House, [1937] 1961), 427

3. Mike Fillon, "Science Solves Ancient Mysteries of the Bible," *Popular Mechanics* (December 1996), 39.

4. Fillon, "Science Solves Ancient Mysteries of the Bible," 40.

5. Fillon, "Science Solves Ancient Mysteries of the Bible," 39.

6. Fillon, "Science Solves Ancient Mysteries of the Bible," 40.

7. Fillon, "Science Solves Ancient Mysteries of the Bible," 41.

8. Henry M. Morris, *The Genesis Record: A Scientific and Devotional Commentary on the Book of Beginnings* (Grand Rapids, MI: Baker Book House, 1976), 356.

9. Fillon, "Science Solves Ancient Mysteries of the Bible," 41–42.

10. Fillon, "Science Solves Ancient Mysteries of the Bible," 42.

11. Fillon, "Science Solves Ancient Mysteries of the Bible," 42.

12. Fillon, "Science Solves Ancient Mysteries of the Bible," 43.

13. Werner Keller, quoting Harold N. Moldenke, in *The Bible as History* (New York: William Morrow, 1956), 131.

14. Smith quoted by Werner Keller in *The Bible as History*, 131.

15. Howard B. Rand, *Primogenesis* (Haverhill, MA: Destiny Publishers, 1953), 142.

16. Kole and Janssen, *Miracles or Magic?*, 110.

14

Lost in Space

Flying saucers are just one more manifestation of the ever-present religion of humanism: evolutionary, self-salvational, and gnostic. Flying saucerism's theology is not that unique. Its pseudo-technology is impressive to those who see it, but not many do see it up close, and in any case, major religious movements are not based on technology—influenced by it, yes, but not based on it. They are based on specific *presuppositional* views of God, man, law, and time. They are also based on a view, pro or con, of final judgment.[1]

People who are looking for a way to fill the spiritual vacuum left by atheistic materialism want to do it on their own terms, even if what they advocate is more science fiction than true science. "The chariots of the gods from outer space replace the chariots of fire in the Bible. Men believe that they can preserve their metaphysical autonomy of the ancient spacemen"[2] and escape final judgment on God's terms. There are a number of theories to explain what many people believe are extraterrestrials. Are they visitors from other solar systems who travel among the galaxies via highly sophisticated spacecraft, beings from a parallel universe, spiritual creatures from a different dimension who live among us unseen by our three-dimensional eyes, or are they demons posing as benevolent space aliens?

The materialists are still trying to prove that God does not exist. If they could only find another highly evolved civilization among the multitude of unexplored galaxies, then such a discovery would prove that no god is needed to explain how life came to Earth. Actually, Francis Crick, co-discoverer of the structure of the DNA molecule, for which he received a Nobel Prize, proposes a theory called "directed panspermia."[3] Crick thinks "that life on earth may have begun when aliens from another planet sent a rocket ship containing spores to seed the earth."[4] The most natural question is, Where did the aliens come from? Was there an alien race that seeded the planet of aliens that seeded Earth? Crick's hypothesis only pushes the argument back several steps with no final resolution. "This scenario still leaves open the question of who designed the designer [aliens]—how did life originally originate?"[5] Crick and other advocates of "directed panspermia" have no way to account for the *original* seed bearers. Crick's extraterrestrial quest, even though it has the trappings of science, is religious nonetheless. He is searching for ultimate meaning in terms of what the stars *might* reveal about how life originated on Earth.

Looking Heavenward for a "Savior"

On July 4, 1947, Roswell, New Mexico, was visited by extra-terrestrials. So says a group of enthusiastic ufologists. For years the Air Force insisted that the entire affair was a case of mistaken identity. Hoping to put the controversy to rest, Air Force representatives issued an official 25-page report of its investigation involving official CIA photo analysis, interviews, and archival searches claiming that the crash-landing was nothing more than a weather balloon that bit the dust. Or was it? Die-hard believers smell a cover up. UFO buffs believe that the United

States government has been hiding the truth about what happened in Roswell and other sightings, hoping to avert panic among the citizenry. The latest explanation offered by governmental officials is that the people saw crash dummies. Some remain skeptical. Walter Haut, president of the Roswell UFO Museum, is not convinced by the Air Force explanation: "It's a bunch of pap…. Basically I don't think anything has changed. Excuse my cynicism, but let's quit playing games."[6]

Americans are experiencing a crisis in faith where many no longer believe that science can explain everything. A sizeable number consider traditional religions to be narrow minded, quick to dismiss anything that does not fit into their rigidly constructed worldview. They want more, and they are willing to reach toward the heavens to get it. "Many flying saucer buffs are believers precisely because aliens may offer hope, much like a deity…. Americans are desperately searching for hope in an increasingly cynical age."[7] Carl Sagan makes a similar point:

> The interest in UFOs and ancient astronauts seems at least partly the result of unfulfilled religious needs. The extraterrestrials are often described as wise, powerful, benign, human in appearance, and sometimes they are attired in long white robes. They are very much like gods and angels, coming from other planets rather than from heaven, using spaceships rather than wings. There is a little pseudoscientific overlay, but the theological antecedents are clear.[8]

When surveys were taken in the 1940s, most people did not believe that UFOs were extraterrestrial in nature. "A 1947 Gallup poll found that 'virtually no one considered the objects to be from outer space.' Most people considered the sightings to be either hoaxes, secret weapons, illusions of some kind, or some phenomenon that could be scientifically explained."[9] Even through the 1950s, UFOs were mostly explained as Soviet test planes. The Cold war was running full throttle. With the arrival of Sputnik in 1957, the suspicions of many people were confirmed. By 1973, more than ten percent of Americans claimed to have seen a UFO. The increase in sightings followed the increase in religious skepticism and paranoia regarding Russian space superiority.

As a candidate for president, Jimmy Carter promised the American people that he would open up the files on UFOs. Carter filed a "sighting report" to the International UFO Bureau in Oklahoma City on September 18, 1973. The incident occurred, according to Carter, in October 1969 in Albany, Georgia. "It seemed to move toward us from a distance, stop, move partially away, return, then depart," Carter wrote. He described it as "bluish at first, then reddish, luminous, not solid."[10] Carter was the first presidential candidate to make the topic of UFO study a plank in his presidential platform:

> If I become President, I'll make every piece of information
> this country has about UFO sightings available to the public,
> and the scientists.
> I am convinced that UFOs exist because I have seen one.[11]

Carter's belief in UFOs did not seem to hurt his run for the presidency. No extraordinary information came out of the Carter presidency (1976–80) to throw any additional light on the topic. Did he know too much? Was there a conspiracy of silence among government officials to keep the truth of UFOs from getting out to the general public? Many conspiracy theorists know a whole lot more than they are telling us. The conspiracy theme has become part of UFO lore and the storylines in alien movies like *Men in Black* (1997), released fifty years after Roswell, and *Independence Day* (1996).

Of course, lots of people see UFOs. What they see is at first *unidentified*. An unidentified object—whether flying or earthbound—is not necessarily an extraterrestrial, that is, a visitor from another planet. Most UFO sightings are easily explained. "There are hundreds of varieties" and an equal number of plausible explanations.[12] What was part of the fringe in the 1940s had become mainstream in the 1970s. Certainly the modern space age made belief in planetary travel a more realistic possibility. Inhabitants of an insignificant planet in an obscure solar system had landed on the moon in 1969, and probes had gone to Venus and Mars in the 1970s. If earthlings were reaching for their moon and neighboring planets, then why couldn't a more advanced planetary civilization reach for a distant solar system like ours? What we've learned since putting men on the moon in 1969, is that space travel is complicated, expensive, and time-intensive.

Modern Fiction

While 1947 seems to be the turning point for the serious study of UFOs, sightings had been reported much earlier. In 1896 and 1897, a number of unexplained phenomena were observed. People reported seeing cigar-shaped airships in California. Thousands of people across the United States affirmed that they had also seen such ships. These sightings, which were dutifully reported in hundreds of newspaper accounts, might explain the April 1897 publication of a series of stories written by British science-fiction writer H. G. Wells, *The War of the Worlds*. *Pearson's Magazine* began publishing *War of the Worlds* as a serial which concluded in December of 1897. The movie version of *War of the Worlds* was released in 1953. *Independence Day* is a high-tech remake of the H.G. Wells' classic space-invader movie. For nearly a century, science fiction writers have been supplying popular culture with dreams of interplanetary travel and "men from Mars," the origin of Wells' sinister invaders.

"Klaatu Barada Nikto"

After the Roswell incident, Hollywood jumped on the UFO bandwagon with *The Day the Earth Stood Still* (1951), one of the most respected science fiction films of all time that seems to evade the ravages of time, even though its special effects are minuscule compared to today's big-budget sci-fi thrillers. The visiting alien in *The Day the Earth Stood Still,* Klaatu, was quite different from Wells' menacing destroyers. He was an interplanetary benefactor who "came in peace" to warn Earth of its headlong rush toward nuclear oblivion. If earthlings did not get their collective act together, he warned that a planetary council might unleash a giant robot like Gort, an intergalactic RoboCop, who had the power and autonomy to wipe out all aggressors.

In the same year, another alien hit the big screen—*The Thing (From Another World).* The frozen invader was anything but benevolent. He was a destroyer, similar to the alien antagonists of Wells' earlier work. Another film, *This Island Earth* (1954), combined alien encounters with space travel. Exeter, the top alien, kidnaps two earth scientists to help him save his planet, Metaluna. *This Island Earth* added a new dimension to UFO interest, a Close Encounter of the Fourth Kind (CEIV), an abduction aboard a spacecraft. (The movie never explains how a superior race of aliens needs help from a technological backward planet like Earth.)

A series of nasty-alien encounters were depicted in *Invasion of the Body Snatchers* (1956), *The Blob* (1958), *I Married a Monster from Outer Space* (1958), and the eerie *Village of the Damned* (1960). Many of these movies were not-too-subtle parables about the growing menace of Communism in America.

A friendly alien encounter that turned sinister was the story-line behind the television series *V.* Alien reptiles disguised themselves as humans to gain the trust of earthlings. The Visitors' planet is running out of water and food. The seemingly benevolent space travelers, who come bearing gifts of new technology and ways to fight diseases, plan to suck Earth dry and breed humans for food.

Messianic Hopes

From *The Day the Earth Stood Still* to Carl Sagan's *Contact* (1997), alien encounter movies are projections of evolutionary optimism and messianic hope. The rationalistic worldview of secularism was not meeting the needs of the spiritually deprived. Science needed to be resuscitated and infused with special meaning. More than this, science needed a resurrection of monumental proportions. Hollywood gave science a way out of its materialistic and anti-supernatural dilemma by turning to the heavens. The comic book super hero Superman was the first inter-galactic messianic figure: He was sent to Earth by his father, kept his identify secret, exhibited extraordinary powers, emerged to the public when he was about thirty years old, and went about doing good works. In the movie version of *Superman*, "upon his arrival, [the infant] gives us one more less-than-subtle hint as he opens his arms wide [to his adoptive parents] to suggest a miniature Christ."[13]

Messiahism hit the silver screen in a more indirect way when Klaatu landed with Gort in Washington, D.C. in broad daylight.

> Scriptwriter Edmund H. North transformed the alien emissary Klaatu into a Christ-figure, implying that extra-terrestrials would be the true saviors of mankind. He did this in a subtle manner, having Klaatu adopt the earth name Carpenter[14] and through the alien's death and resurrection.[15]

The resurrection takes place after a fearful military establishment kills Klaatu for being a "threat" to the nation. Does any of this sound familiar? (Luke 23:2)

Close Encounters of the Third Kind (1977) also depicts aliens as saviors, as beneficent gods who draw their "chosen ones" to themselves. "It is the alien landing as Epiphany, the coming of the gods rather than extra-terrestrials" as menacing destroyers.[16] The aliens choose only the "elect."

Similar to Klaatu in *The Day the Earth Stood Still*, *E.T., The Extra-Terrestrial* (1983) personified the alien as savior. An infant alien is left on earth where he is taken in by a family in turmoil. "He hides in a shed (a manger) and is discovered and cared for by children (the disciples), persecuted by adult authorities, killed, and then raised from the dead. His ascension is witnessed by a newly formed community of believers."[17] All the elements of religion are present.

> Here was the scientific savior who was sent to earth from above (fulfilling the promise of its "shining spaceship"), performed healing-type miracles in exchange for faith, produced conversion experiences in the innocent and pure ("the little children who come unto it") and died and was resurrected before its ascension to its "home."[18]

The parallels with Christianity are unmistakable. Al Millar, in his "E.T."—You're More Than a Movie Star, lists thirty-three parallels between E.T. and Jesus Christ.[19] The underlying premise is that there are aliens in our universe who can perform "miracles" in the same way that Jesus did. The purpose of this idea is to minimize the uniqueness of Jesus. Atheists like Arthur C. Clarke, author of 2001: A Space Odyssey, downplay the religious overtones in works of science fiction, but they can't escape them. "If certain parallels exist between E.T. and the Christ story, they are not unlike similar religious parallels contained in the many science fiction works (film or literature) that have been created before."[20] There is no need for God, even though these aliens display god-like attributes. If we can just contact our distant alien brothers, we will learn the age-old mysteries of the universe and attain eternal life. "Alien supermedicine" will save us all.[21]

For many secularists, "God" is nothing more than a highly evolved super-scientist who can perform what we call "miracles." Just like the light bulb, airplane, and computer would amaze ancient cultures, these highly advanced super-aliens amaze us. Among some UFO enthusiasts, Jesus was an alien who was able to manipulate nature with His superior alien technology. In the movie Forbidden Planet (1956), Dr. Morbius, played by Walter Pidgeon, was able to build a robot with the help of

Krell super-science that enabled him to manufacture everything from precious stones and lead to food and alcohol. Similarly, Jesus was able to produce enough food to feed the masses by means of superior alien science unknown in the first century and today. In the *Star Trek* episode "Who Mourns for Adonis?,"[22] it is suggested that the gods of Greek and Roman mythology, and by implication the God of the Bible, were really aliens with super powers. Gene Roddenberry, an avowed atheist, transferred his religious allegiance from the true God of the Bible to the alien gods of his own imagination.

> Many contemporary films, especially sci-fi films, reflect this longing for a sense of meaning outside of ourselves. Since our God-framework (we have a personal Creator and are created for God's pleasure) has been taken away, we are forced to dream up our own meaning. The *Star Trek* series is a perfect example. The crew of the *Enterprise* travel through space to other worlds only to be reminded that humanity is its own meaning. There is no higher reality than the finer instincts within us. No one questions too much where these instincts come from. The *Enterprise* may go in search of God (*Star Trek 5*) but it always comes back to Captain James T. Kirk.[23]

Those who are looking outside Earth for spiritual help are also looking beyond God. At its core, belief in extraterrestrials is little more than science-fiction humanism—the creation of another man-made religion based on what some people *think* is out there. Syracuse University professor Robert Thompson explains, "In an era where the old traditional social systems have really begun to break at the seams, these unexplained phenomenon programs give an appearance that maybe there are some other forces out there. And even in the scary cases, this is quite comforting."[24]

Chariots of the UFOnauts

Hoping to hold on to the Bible as a special book, some have gone so far as to turn it into a UFO manual. Elijah, for example, is said to have ascended into the atmosphere in a "chariot of fire" (spaceship) caught in a whirlwind (exhaust gases). Jacob's vision of angels ascending and descending on a ladder has been interpreted as a UFO event described in ancient pictography. The pillar of fire that preceded the Israelites as they passed through the Red Sea and led them in the wilderness is thought to be an alien encounter. Here is how Presbyterian minister Robert H. Downing describes the Red Sea crossing:

> The heart of the Old Testament religion is the Exodus, which reported that something resembling a space vehicle—a "pillar of cloud by day, and pillar of fire by night"—led the Hebrew people out of Egypt up to the "Red Sea," hovered over the sea while it departed, and then led them into the wilderness, where an "angel" proceeded to give them religious instructions. The fact that some sort of Unidentified Flying Object—UFO—was reported to have been present at the Red Sea at the time of the parting should cause us to desire a closer look. The parting of the sea was, of course, in itself unique—so much so, in fact, that we should think seriously about the outside force reported to have been present at the time of the parting. I personally find the suggestion that the parting of the Red Sea was deliberately caused by intelligent beings in some sort of space vehicle to be the most persuasive explanation available at the present time.[25]

Ezekiel's vision of "wheels within wheels" gets special attention by the UFO enthusiasts. All the necessary spaceship "nuts and bolts" are present: "fire flashing forth," "glowing metal," a description of a spaceship that had passed through the earth's atmosphere (1:4); "living beings" with alien characteristics (1:5–6, 10–11); "burnished bronze" for spaceship landing legs (1:7); the ability to hover (1:12); and a propulsion mechanism "that looked like burning coals of fire, like torches darting back and forth among living beings" (1:13).

While Ezekiel interpreted this sight as "the appearance of the likeness of the glory of the LORD" (1:28), "some UFO enthusiasts have seized on the vision describing the arrival of an extraterrestrial spaceship."[26] Josef F. Blumrich, an engineer with NASA, designed a spacecraft based on Ezekiel's vision. Blumrich "found that the description could be adapted into a practical design for a landing module launched from a mother spaceship (in the prophet's vision, the glowing metal godhead). Blumrich worked out the design in detail and published an account of it in a 1973 book titled *The Spaceships of Ezekiel*."[27]

The New Testament is also ufologized by proponents of alien encounters. As you might suspect, Jesus ascending to heaven in a cloud is said to be a primitive description of an ancient astronaut (Jesus) returning to the mother spaceship via teleportation: "He was lifted up while they were looking on, and a cloud received Him out of sight" (Acts 1:9).

Even the tabloids have jumped on the bandwagon. The front page of the May 17, 1994 issue of *Sun* reads: "God Sent Aliens to Create the World." The article also explains that Adam and Eve arrived by UFO and that the tree of knowledge was a computer. We're told why man stopped living to age 900 and how a laser engraved the Ten Commandments on stone tablets. In all of these cases twentieth-century technology, space-travel theories, science fiction writing, and wild speculation about extraterrestrials are read back into ancient texts. My guess is that the Bible can be made to say anything if this method is practiced consistently. Don't forget that Hal Lindsey was able to turn the locusts of Revelation 9 into Vietnam-era "Cobra helicopters."[28]

From a Galaxy Far, Far Away

In terms of what we know about physics, long-distance space travel is near impossible. For example, Voyager 2 was launched on August 20,

1977, traveling at 33,000 miles per hour, and yet it took seventeen years to travel a mere 4.3 billion miles. The closest star, Alpha Centauri, is 4.3 light years away. That's roughly thirty-six trillion miles from earth. "Scientists calculate that to cross such vast distances in a human lifetime, the first starship would have to cruise at one-third the speed of light: 150 million miles per hour or so."[29] Even at that speed, a spacecraft would need thirteen years to make the trip, and another thirteen to make the return, with no guarantee of finding anything once it got there. H.G. Wells at least had the good sense to base his planetary invaders on Mars.

Science fiction writers work within the framework of accepted scientific theory. Realizing the physical obstacles to space travel, they turned to "warp drives" and light-speed travel ala *Star Wars*. Warp drive, a mainstay for travel in the *Star Trek* storyline, is being used less and less. David Brin, author of *The Postman* and other sci-fi novels, understands the technological problems associated with space travel. "We're starting to face the fact that space is very, very big and we're probably not going to be able to cheat.[30]

One way out of the problem is to maintain that our interstellar neighbors have taken a different evolutionary path. The bodies of alien beings are not carbon-based, and so they can travel at speeds faster than light without disintegration. But this theory begs the question. While evolution might be accepted among the majority of scientists, it has little evidential support. It's more a religious theory than science. Since evolution cannot account for life on earth, how can we assume that it can account for life anywhere else, non-carbon-based aliens included?

Welcome to the Flatland Universe

In 1884 Edwin Abbott published the story about an imaginary two-dimensional world called "Flatland."[31] The people are circles, triangles, and squares. They live in pentagons. A three-dimensional object passing through Flatland would only be visible in segments to a resident of the two-dimensional world. A sphere would appear as a series of slices in the form of a circle. There is no "up" or "down," only left and right, forward and backward.

Abbott's fictional world has been adapted by advocates of alien civilizations: alien encounters could be visits from a different dimensional world right next door. Time and distance are not factors in a multi-dimensional universe since the worlds are parallel. They are next to one another, and in some cases may overlap, and yet are virtually invisible because of dimensional differences. Sometimes a fourth dimensional traveler, so the theory goes, passes through our three-dimensional world. Such a passage would explain the odd shapes and ultra-super sonic speeds that are often described as UFO sightings. The oddities are explained in terms of fourth-dimensional reality that do not comport with known physical laws of the third dimension. In a fourth or fifth dimensional world, such phenomena would make perfect sense. Such a theory is based on faith. No one has documented such a case.

The Spirit World

Of course, such a theory does not substantiate the reality of alien beings crossing dimensional lines; it only makes such encounters plausible given what we know about physics. The Bible describes reality in a multi-dimensional format. God is near. In fact, Jesus is called "Immanuel, which translated means, 'God with us'" (Matt. 1:23). We are told that where "two or three have gathered together" in Jesus' name, He is "in their midst" (Matt. 18:20). Angels appear and disappear at will (Luke 1:11, 26). After His resurrection, Jesus seemed to appear out of thin air: "When therefore it was evening, on that day, the first day of the week, and when the doors were shut where the disciples were, for fear of the Jews, Jesus came and stood in their midst (John 20:19). Paul was taken up into the "third heaven," whether "in the body" or "out of the body" he did not know (2 Cor. 12:2). The Bible is forthright about the realities of a spiritual world beyond our physical world. That world does not seem to be separated by distance. Notice that in every case, God is in control of this world.

The Devil Rides a Spaceship

A popular Christian explanation for alien encounters is that they are demonic. John Keel, a private reporter who began to collect information on UFOs in the mid-1960s, concluded that "The UFOs do not seem to exist as tangible, manufactured objects. They do not conform to the accepted natural laws of our environment.... The UFO manifestations seem to be, by and large, merely minor variations of the age-old demonological phenomenon."[32] If God's angels, who are spirits, can travel interdimensionally, then why can't Satan's angels?

While this proposed solution solves some problems and fits well with the biblical framework of what spiritual beings can do, it is still fraught with difficulties. Does the devil have the authority and freedom to act in this way? Does the Bible give any indication that this is the way Satan operated in biblical times? Has the status of the devil changed since the death, resurrection, and ascension of Jesus so that he has more freedom and power? How can this be when the Bible says Satan has been "disarmed" and "thrown down" (Col. 2:15; Rev. 12:9)?

Popular prophecy writer Hal Lindsey speculates that increased interest in UFOs fulfills Jesus' prediction that there will be "terrors and great signs from heaven" just before His return (Luke 21:11).[33] Such terrors and great signs from heaven, Lindsey believes, are unidentified flying objects of the demonic kind disguised as benevolent aliens! Following the studies of unnamed "authorities, Lindsey concludes:

> Authorities now admit that there have been confirmed
> sightings of unidentified flying objects. There are even some

baffling cases where people under hypnosis say they were taken aboard UFOs by beings from space.

Reports held in U.S. Air Force files reveal that whatever these flying objects are, they move and turn at speeds unmatched by human technology.

It's my opinion that UFOs are real and that there will be a proven "close encounter of the third kind" soon. And I believe that the source of this phenomenon is some type of alien being of great intelligence and power.

According to the Bible, a demon is a spiritual personality in a state of war with God. Prophecy tells us that demons will be allowed to use their powers of deception in a grand way during the last days of history (2 Thessalonians 2:8–12). I believe these demons will stage a spacecraft landing on Earth. They will claim to be from an advanced culture in another galaxy.

They may even claim to have "planted" human life on this planet and tell us they have returned to check on our progress.[34]

All of this is pure speculation. Lindsey is operating under the assumption that extraterrestrial UFOs are a reality. He assumes, without a thorough study of the Bible, that the reality of UFOs are somewhere hidden in Scripture. How can the average Christian pick up a Bible and come to these fantastic conclusions? The great signs from heaven that Matthew, Mark, and Luke describe in their accounts of Jesus' Olivet discourse were reported by first-century historians. For example, the respected Jewish historian Josephus recounts that "there was a star resembling a sword, which stood over the city [of Jerusalem], and a comet, that continued a whole year."[35] In A.D. 66, just four years before the destruction of Jerusalem, Halley's comet passed over Jerusalem. There is no need to concoct a speculative theory about space aliens to make the Bible fit with a dubious hypothesis about demonic aliens.

Hal Lindsey is not alone in finding UFOs in Scripture. Charles Ryrie, a popular prophecy writer and author of the notes in the best selling *Ryrie Study Bible*, asks this question about the figurative language found in Revelation: "How do we make sense out of all those beasts and thrones and horsemen and huge numbers like 200 million? Answer: Take it at face value. If God intended to disclose something to us in a book, then we can be confident He wrote it in such a way as to communicate to us, rather than confuse us."[36]

Ryrie gives an example on how we should interpret the Bible at "face value" by looking at Revelation 9:1–12 (the locusts from the abyss): "John's description sounds very much like some kind of war machine or UFO. Demons have the ability to take different shapes, so it is quite possible that John is picturing a coming invasion of warlike UFOs. Until someone comes up with a satisfactory answer to the UFO question, this possibility should not be ruled out."[37] Revelation needs to be interpreted in its first-century context and against the backdrop of Old Testament events and symbols. The events communicated to John are said to take place "shortly" (1:1). The first-century readers were told to "heed the things which are written in it; for the time is near" (1:3). The time was "short" for *them*; it was "near" for *them*.[38] John is not describing prophetic events in the distant future but events that were in the near future of the first readers.[39]

Is finding UFOs in the Bible interpreting Scripture at "face value"? Belief in UFOs is a rather recent curiosity based on evolutionary presuppositions. Christians from time immemorial knew nothing of such happenings.[40] If UFOs are the interpretative key to this section of Scripture, then God's Word would have remained a mystery for millions of Christians for centuries who were bound by scientific limitations. Until someone like Klaatu lands in Washington, D.C., in front of thousands of people and goes to a famous scientist to show him how to do his math, I contend that UFO sightings should be filed under "wishful thinking."

The Return of the Nephilim?

One last alien theory needs to be put to rest. Some Christian writers believe that demons co-habited with women and had children by them called the Nephilim (Gen. 6:1–5). Supposedly, the offspring of these semi-demonic beings caused God to destroy the ancient world by a flood (6:5–7). Accordingly, these Nephilim will appear in the future as seemingly benevolent aliens similar to the reptilian aliens in the television mini-series *V.* This hypothesis is based more on pagan mythology and medieval superstition than on sound Bible interpretation.[41]

The Nephilim theory is based on the premise that the "sons of God" in Genesis 6 are demonic beings. In reality, the "sons of God" are related to Seth, the son of Adam (Gen. 4:23; 5:3). Seth was the father of Enosh. Notice the genealogy listed in Luke's gospel: "The son of Enosh, the son of Seth, the son of Adam, *the son of God*" (Luke 3:38). Those faithful to God are described in Scripture—whether men or angels—as sons or children of God. "The daughters of men" are related to Cain's progeny (Gen. 6:2). The Sethites compromised their faith and yoked themselves with the ungodly Cainite line.

> What is revealed, then, is that these two lines did not maintain their distinctiveness. The "seed of the woman" and the "seed of the serpent" [Gen. 3:15] became mixed by way of intermarriage. The first step in this direction was taken by the god-fearing line. They were attracted by the beautiful daughters of their godless neighbors who undoubtedly were consciously seducing them. Thus they were lured into mixed marriages with all the devastating consequences of such unions.[42]

The Israelites are constantly warned not to marry the "daughters of" the ungodly. Isaac was not to take for himself a wife "from the *daughters of the Canaanites*" (Gen. 24:3). The same charge was given to Jacob (28:1). Esau, the rejected son, "took his wives from the *daughters of Canaan*" (36:2). One of the signs of apostasy is when the godly intermarry with non-believers: "While Israel remained at Shittim, the people began to play the harlot with the *daughters of Moab*" (Num. 25:1). Paul takes up this theme in the New Testament:

> Do not be bound together with unbelievers; for what partnership have righteousness and lawlessness, or what fellowship has light with darkness? Or what harmony has Christ with Belial, or what has a believer in common with an unbeliever? (2 Cor. 6:14–15)

God tells His people to "come out from their midst and be separate" (2 Cor. 6:17). To those who remain faithful to the things of Christ, God says, "I will be a father to you, and you shall be sons and daughters to Me" (2 Cor. 6:18; also see Matt. 5:9; Luke 20:36; Rom. 8:14, 19; Gal. 3:26). Faithful Israelites are said to be "sons of the living God" (Hosea 1:10). Gleason Archer offers a helpful summary of the Sethite position:

> Instead of remaining true to God and loyal to their spiritual heritage, they allowed themselves to be enticed by the beauty of ungodly women who were daughters of men—that is, of the tradition and example of Cain.[43]

There is some debate over whether the Nephilim are the offspring of the union between the "sons of God" and the "daughters of men" or that the Nephilim just lived at the same time this happened. "The Nephilim were on the earth in those days, and also afterward, when the sons of God came in to the daughters of men, and they bore children to them" (Gen. 6:4). We read about the Nephilim after the flood. "There also we saw the Nephilim (the sons of Anak are part of the Nephilim)… (Num. 13:33). The sons of Anak are said to be "great and tall" (Deut. 9:2). Being tall may have been unusual in Israel, but it's hardly an indication of a union between a demon and human. Saul is described as "taller than any of the people" (1 Sam. 9:2), and he is neither part of the Nephilim or a son of Anak. The sons of Anak couldn't have been that superior, because the Bible says that Caleb "drove out from there the three sons of Anak" (Joshua 15:14).[44]

Conclusion

The Bible is its own best interpreter. There is no justification for turning to the latest headlines of today's tabloid newspapers to give meaning to the Bible. The idea that Genesis 6:1–4 is describing fallen angels marrying humans and creating a race of semi-demonic supermen cannot be proved by an appeal to Scripture.

Notes

1. Gary North, *Unholy Spirits: Occultism and New Age Humanism* (Tyler, TX: Institute for Christian Economics, 1986), 327.

2. North, *Unholy Spirits*, 328.

3. Francis Crick, *Life Itself: Its Origin and Nature* (New York: Simon and Schuster, 1981).

4. Michael J. Behe, *Darwin's Black Box: The Biochemical Challenge to Evolution* (New York: The Free Press, 1996), 248.

5. Behe, *Darwin's Black Box*, 249.

6. Bruce Handy, "Roswell or Bust," *Time* (June 23, 1997), 60–71.

7. Quoted in Bill Hendrick, "UFOs and the Otherworldly: Do You Believe?," *Atlanta Journal/Constitution* (June 25, 1997), B1.

8. Carl Sagan, *Broca's Brain: Reflections on the Romance of Science* (New York: Random House, 1979), 56.

9. Ron Rhodes, *The Culting of America: The Shocking Implications for Every Concerned Christian* (Eugene, OR: Harvest House, 1994), 184.

10. This description of Carter's sighting is found in Colin Bessonette, "Q&A on the News," *Atlanta Constitution* (November 5, 1997), A2.

11. Quoted in North, *Unholy Spirits*, 288.

12. Donald H. Menzel, "UFOs–The Modern Myth," *UFOs: A Scientific Debate*, eds. Carl Sagan and Thornton Page (New York: Barnes & Noble Books, [1972] 1996), 141–143.

13. Robert Short, *The Gospel from Outer Space: The Religious Implications of E.T., Star Wars, Superman, Close Encounters of the Third Kind and 2001: A Space Odyssey* (San Francisco, CA: Harper & Row, 1983), 42.

14. Jesus was a carpenter. Get it?

15. Bobby Maddex, "The Gospel According to E.T.," *Rutherford Magazine* (October 1996), 22.

16. Baird Searles, *Films of Science Fiction and Fantasy* (New York: AFI Press, 1988), 128.

17. Peter Fraser and Vernon Edwin Neal, *ReViewing the Movies: A Christian Response to Contemporary Film* (Wheaton, IL: Crossway Books, 2000), 31.

18. Maddex, "The Gospel According to E.T.," 23.

19. Al Millar, *"E.T." You're More Than a Movie Star* (New Port News, VA: privately published, 1982), 4–5. See Donald R. Mott and Cheryl McAllister Saunders, *Steven Spielberg* (Boston, MA: Ywayne Publishers, 1986), 126, 167, note 41.

20. Matt and Saunders, *Stephen Spielberg*, 126–127.

21. Searles, *Films of Science Fiction and Fantasy*, 116.

22. "Who Mourns for Adonis?" is episode 33 and aired on September 22, 1967.

23. Alan MacDonald, *Movies in Close-Up: Getting the Most from Film and Video* (Downers Grove, IL: InterVarsity Press, 1992), 118.

24. Quoted in Alan Bush, "More paranormal programming sighted in prime time," USA Today (October 4, 1994), 3D.

25. Barry H. Downing, *The Bible and Flying Saucers* (Philadelphia, PA: J.B. Lippincott, 1968), 9.

26. George Constable, ed., *The UFO Phenomenon* (Alexandria, VA: Time-Life Books, 1987), 14.

27. Constable, ed., *The UFO Phenomenon*, 14.

28. Hal Lindsey, *There's a New World Coming* (New York: Bantam Books, [1973] 1984), 124.

29. Mike Toner, "So much space, so little time: Dreams of star travel fading," *Atlanta Journal/Constitution* (September 11, 1994), A16.

30. Toner, "So much space, so little time," A26.

31. A brief description of the Flatland universe is given in Carl F. Ellis, Jr., *Beyond Liberation: The Gospel in the Black American Experience* (Downers Grove, IL: InterVarsity Press, 1983), 17–20.

32. John Keel, *UFOs: Operation Trojan Horse* (New York: Putnam's, 1970), 299. Quoted in North, *Unholy Spirits*, 291.

33. For a discussion of this theme in Lindsey's work, see Timothy Weber, *Living in the Shadow of the Second Coming: American Premillennialism, 1875–1982* (Grand Rapids, MI: Zondervan/Academie, 1983), 218.

34. Hal Lindsey, *The 1980s: Countdown to Armageddon* (King of Prussia, PA: Westgate Press, 1980), 34–35.

35. Josephus, *The Wars of the Jews*, 6:5:3, 742.

36. Charles C. Ryrie, *The Living End: Enlightening and Astonishing Disclosures about the Coming Last Days of Earth* (Old Tappan, NJ: Fleming H. Revell, 1976), 37.

37. Ryrie, *The Living End*, 45.

38. See Kenneth L. Gentry, Jr., *Before Jerusalem Fell: The Dating of the Book of Revelation*, 3rd ed. (Atlanta, GA: American Vision, 1999).

39. Gary DeMar, *Last Days Madness: Obsession of the Modern Church*, 4th ed. (Powder Springs, GA: American Vision, 1999).

40. Of course, if Erich Von Däniken is to be believed, the Earth was visited by extraterrestrials centuries ago. See Erich Von Däniken, *Chariots of the Gods?: Memories of the Future: Unsolved Mysteries of the Past*, trans. Michael Heron (New York: G. Putnam's Sons, 1970) and *Gods from Outer Space: Return to the Stars or Evidence for the Impossible*, trans. Michael Heron (New York: G. Putnam's Sons, 1970). For an evaluation of Von Däniken's theories, see William M. Alnor, *UFOs in the New Age: Extraterrestrial Messages and the Truth of Scripture* (Grand Rapids, MI: Baker Book House, 1992) and John Allan, *The Gospel According to Science Fiction* (Milford, MI: Quill Publications, 1975), 19–58.

41. Chuck Missler and Mark Eastman, *Alien Encounters: The Secret Behind the UFO Phenomenon* (Coeur d'Alene, ID: Koinonia House, 1997), 203–213, 240–242.

42. G. Ch. Aalders, *Bible Student's Commentary: Genesis*, trans. William Heynen, 2 vols. (Grand Rapids, MI: Zondervan, 1981), 1:154.

43. Gleason Archer, *The Encyclopedia of Bible Difficulties* (Grand Rapids, MI: Zondervan, 1982), 80.

44. For an alternate theory, see John H. Walton, Victor H. Matthews, and Mark W. Chavalas, *The IVP Bible Background Commentary: Old Testament* (Downers Grove, IL: InterVarsity Press, 2000), 36.

15

The Devil's Playground

There are two equal and opposite errors into which our race can
fall about the devils. One is to disbelieve in their existence. The
other is to believe, and to feel an excessive and unhealthy interest
in them. They themselves are equally pleased by both errors and
hail a materialist or a magician with the same delight.[1]

Popular culture is one way to track shifting opinions about paranormal and occult experiences. Before television's debut soon after the second world war, music, literature, and film were expressions of popular culture for the masses. Film gave life to literary works that many people talked about but rarely read. Abraham "Bram" Stoker's *Dracula* (1897) was the first novel of its type to make it to the big screen, although there were earlier stage productions of the work.

Silent film star Lon Chaney, Sr., "the man of a thousand faces," captivated and frightened audiences with his performances of strange and sympathetic characters. He was born to deaf parents and traveled in a theatrical troupe where he "befriended outcasts, misfits and the deformed, seeing the humanity in each."[2] Chaney was the first choice to play Dracula, but his untimely death in 1930 meant the part would go to Hungarian-born stage actor Bela Lugosi. With the production of *Dracula* in 1931, a dramatic shift in worldviews was noticed. While Chaney's "most terrifying disguises were in the final analysis, *human* stories. This *Dracula* was about a bloodsucking demon from hell!"[3] But this living-dead demon could be destroyed. A crucifix could keep him at bay.[4] The light of day would turn Dracula to dust. A wooden stake driven into his undead heart would send him to eternal damnation. Of course, these remedies against the demonic are nothing more than superstitions.

Elements of the Christian worldview are still evident in this early horror film with its obvious occult themes. "Both Christ and Dracula deal with blood and eternal life. Vampirism is, as Renfield [Dracula's insect-eating slave] makes clear, the antithesis of Christianity. Whereas Christ shed his blood so that his followers could have eternal life; Dracula shed his followers' blood so that he could have eternal life."[5]

At the end of the movie, as sun light streams through the windows of the dank and dark English castle, church bells are heard in the distance. The film reminds us that while God is still alive, demons roam the earth in the form of squares of celluloid whose images are projected by light onto a silver screen. Script writers and novelists form the modern conception of God, Satan, and evil. Dracula was a kindly old uncle compared to today's devil-inspired monsters.

God's Competitor

Christian writers unwittingly impute powers to Satan that are God's alone. Neil Anderson, author of *Bondage Breaker* writes, "I have no question that [the occult] works."[6] Merrill F. Unger, author of several books on demonology, believes that "though Scripture condemns magic, it clearly recognizes the reality of its power."[7] C. Fred Dickason writes in *Demon Possession and the Christian*, "Occult magic includes demonic forces that actually produce detectable phenomena."⁸ If the occult "works," and Satan can impute real powers to those who ask for it, then Satan is God's true spiritual competitor. This cannot be, since Satan is a mere creature, just one of many angels. "When Peter preached at Pentecost, he attested that Jesus was 'accredited by God to you by miracles, wonders and signs, *which God did* among you through him [Acts 2:22].' Hebrews 2:3, 4 indicates that the message of Christ's followers was also authenticated by miracles of God. The power of Satan, on the other hand, is *deception*, not miracle. If he could really work a miracle, it would suggest that he is divine. That's why 2 Thessalonians 2:9 reads, 'The coming of the lawless one will be in accordance with the work of Satan displayed in all kinds of *counterfeit* miracles, signs and wonders.'"⁹ Why couldn't Peter's critics claim, since Satan can also "produce detectable phenomena," that these miracles were demonic? Why should they follow this Jesus when Satan might have equal power? Maybe Satan has something better to offer, and God is hiding powerful secrets from us (Gen. 3:1–7).

Jesus makes it clear that His miracles should not and cannot be attributed to Satan. Satan might try to fool people into believing that he can duplicate the miracle-working power of Jesus, but Jesus assures us that Satan has no such power (Matt. 12:29). While Satan can possess a man, this does not mean that he can give him occult powers to compete with those of Jesus and His disciples. Having the ability to break chains does not mean that occult powers are present (Mark 5:4). There are people today who can do similar feats of strength with much stronger metals than were available in the first century. If this demon-possessed man had occult powers, then he should have been able to disappear, make the chains disappear, float through the air, or do some other incredible feat.

As we study this fascinating and controversial topic, the following questions should be paramount in our mind:

- Does man have the power to create life by occult means?
- Does the devil have power to resurrect the dead?
- Can the devil empower humans to perform miracles comparable to the miracles of Christ?
- Is the devil in charge of this world?
- Just because some people do evil acts "in the name of Satan," does this mean that the devil gave them power to perform these acts?
- Is the modern portrayal of the devil and his works accurate?
- Has Hollywood misrepresented the power of the devil be cause its scripts follow Christian misrepresentations of the devil's power?

"To a New World of Gods and Monsters"

The horror genre matured rapidly with the release of *Frankenstein* (1931), *The Mummy* (1932), *The Bride of Frankenstein* (1935), and *The Wolf Man* (1941). The monsters in *Frankenstein* and *The Bride of Frankenstein* were brought to life with elements from nature—electricity— the symbol of the new Enlightenment scientist. In the eighteenth and nineteenth centuries, electricity was more than just a symbol of scientific discovery. Some were touting it as the substance of life. Electricity was seen as a "life force" independent of the need for a divine Creator similar to the way that mathematics was being used to unravel the orderliness of the universe independent of any divine intervention.

The theme of reanimation in Mary Wollstonecroft Shelley's *Frankenstein, or the Modern Prometheus* (1818), the novel on which the first movie is loosely based, was written against the backdrop of an emerging humanistic science. The study of electricity was all the rage in Shelley's day, from Benjamin Franklin's experiments with kites and keys to European scientists who had applied electrical currents using batteries "to dead animals and human cadavers, creating muscular contractions."[10] (Some have suggested that the "Frank" in *Frankenstein* may have been

inspired by the electrical experiments done by Benjamin *Frank*lin.[11])
Mary Shelley's husband experimented very early with electricity and
dead animals. Like any good science fiction writer, Shelley wove contemporary science and character traits of people she knew into a powerful literary metaphor infused with moral lessons.

Incantations, witches, and magic spells play no role in the creation
of Frankenstein's monsters. These are purely man-made beasts, even
though the devil lurks just below the surface of their work. Keep in
mind, however, that there is no way to avoid God as creator in these
movies since Dr. Frankenstein reanimates only what God first animated.
Frankenstein's monster was put together from other humans of God's
making. There is no *ex nihilo* creation, a creation from nothing, or even
a creation from the "dust of the ground" (Gen. 2:7). Even so, it still
would have been God's dust.

In the *Bride of Frankenstein*, Dr. Septimus Pretorious, played creep-
ily by Ernest Thesiger, beguiles Dr. Frankenstein into playing God. He
convinces his former pupil of the unlimited possibilities of science with
no religious restraints. The spooky doctor, dressed in black clothes, including a medieval alchemist's skull cap, shows Frankenstein some of
his latest creations, seven miniature, toy-like beings in jars. If there is a
hint of the demonic, it's here. When Henry Frankenstein gazes upon
the little people, he comments appropriately, "But this isn't science. It's
more like Black Magic." Pretorious dismisses the notion, informing
Frankenstein that he grew them "as Nature does—from seed." True
Satanism is not in occult powers but in the high-handed notion that
man can be god (Gen. 3:5), a much more subtle and prevalent practice.

In Johann Goethe's nineteenth-century drama *Faust* (1773), the
title character creates a living homunculus, or "little human being," in
a vessel over a fire. Faust, you will recall, sells his soul to the devil in
exchange for esoteric powers and hidden (occult) knowledge. Shelley
has Dr. Frankenstein studying the medieval works of Cornelius Agrippa,

Paracelsus, and Albertus Magnus who were noted for their work as astrologers, mystics, and alchemists.

One of Dr. Pretorious's creations-in-a-jar is the devil. Pretorious asks Frankenstein if he notices the resemblance.[12] "The next one is the very Devil—very bizarre, this little chap. There's a certain resemblance to me, don't you think? Or do I flatter myself? I took a great deal of pains with him. Sometimes I have wondered whether life wouldn't be much more *amusing* if we were *all* devils, and no nonsense about *angels* and being *good*."[13] Spoken like a true humanist.

But it's the laboratory with its machines and electrical current that will bring life to the pieced-together remains of the dead. Even so, the story line of *The Bride of Frankenstein* leaves the dulling impression that there is something behind it all. Prior to meeting Pretorious, Frankenstein reveals his misgivings to his wife: "I've been cursed for delving into the mysteries of life. Perhaps death is sacred, and I profaned it.... I dreamed of being the first to give to the world the secret that God is so jealous of—the formula for life." Elizabeth warns Henry: "Don't say those things. Don't *think* them! It's blasphemous and wicked. We are not *meant* to know those things." Henry won't give up the wonder and exhilaration of it all. Deep down he believes that he is "*intended* to know the secret of life. It may be part of the Divine Plan." Elizabeth knows better. "No, no! It's the *Devil* that prompts you. It's death, not life, that is in it all and at the end of it all."

The creation of Frankenstein's monster was Shelly's indictment of scientific pursuits that had gone astray. Henry Frankenstein (Victor in the novel), played by Colin Clive, was tampering with God's realm by creating autonomous man's version of Adam and Eve. In fact, the Motion Picture Association of America (MPAA) demanded that Clive's line, "I know what it feels like to be God," be cut from the *Frankenstein* film.[14]

[Joe] Breen, a Catholic journalist prior to his appointment [to the Production Code Administration], immediately noted the story's irreverent tone. "Throughout the Script," he wrote, "there are a number of references to Frankenstein which compare him to God and which compare his creation of the monster to God's creation of Man. All such references should be eliminated."[15]

Breen missed the depiction of the Monster, played by Boris Karloff, arms outstretched as he is tied to a pole, as a man-made Christ figure in the *Frankenstein* sequel and his encounter with a blind hermit in the forest. "Trussing the Monster up in a Christ-like pose by a mob of jeering villagers is a heavyhanded conceit. The religious overtones are in full force in the hermit sequence. The Monster feasts on bread and wine, the Holy Sacrament, and the scene fades to black with the camera lingering on the luminous after-image of the crucifix."[16]

The point of the novel and first two movies is an indictment of rationalism and scientism gone mad. Man without moral restraints can only create monsters. Shelley's work was a "rebellion against scientific rationalism."[17] The French Revolution of the late eighteenth century had such high hopes for the materialists who made reason a god, until blood literally ran in the streets. The concluding line uttered by the monster in *The Bride of Frankenstein*, as he brings the castle tower down upon himself, his "bride," and Dr. Pretorious, is an appropriate conclusion to what life is like without God: "We belong dead."

These classic horror movies were not about occult powers but of man assuming the role of God, the very temptation that led to Satan's fall. Satan still tempts us with it today.

It was not long before the devil found a new role in Hollywood. The temptation to be as God gave way to Satan becoming a god, or at least sharing many of God's divine attributes. "If God is nothing," according to Russian novelist Feodor Dostoyevsky (1821–1881), "everything is permitted; if God is nothing, everything is a matter of indifference."[18] Unbelievably, this "everything" includes giving Satan a lofty position, not only in film, literature, and song but also in modern-day religious choices. There are those who will try anything to find fulfillment. Unfortunately, the occult is no longer off-limits to a nation looking for spiritual satisfaction. "People do not live well by illusions. Rather, they will fill the vacuum of their hearts with something... anything... if need be."[19] Blaise Pascal (1623–1662), mathematician, scientist, and philosopher, declared, "In the heart of every man there is a God-shaped vacuum which only God can fill through His Son, Jesus Christ."[20] Anything else is a poor and damning substitute.

"Hail, Satan!"

While Hollywood tampered with the edges of the demonic, the 1968 production of *Rosemary's Baby* brought an end to the ambivalence. Prior to this time, the devil always knew his place. He was a defeated and doomed creature whose power was limited by God and the forces of morality and the Christian religion. *Angel on My Shoulder* (1946) and *The Devil and Daniel Webster* (1941) are two of the best examples of the devil under God's thumb. The devil is real but under control. The modern devil of religious pluralism is new and improved, no longer so accommodating.

Rosemary's Baby[21] is based on the novel by Ira Levin (1967). The setting for Levin's story takes place, not in the dark shadows of a haunted mansion, but among seemingly ordinary people who live in a gothic-style New York apartment building resembling a medieval cathedral called the Bramford.[22] Levin uses real events in telling his story: the 1965 visit of the Pope to New York, the November 1965 New York City blackout, and the 1966 *Time* magazine cover that asks, "Is God Dead?" *Rosemary's Baby* unequivocally says yes to the question.

Everything seems so normal when Rosemary (Mia Farrow) and her actor husband Guy Woodhouse (John Cassevetes) move into what they soon learn is an apartment building with a history. During dinner with a friend, the young couple learn about the building's dark past:

> Are you aware that the Bramford had a rather unpleasant reputation around the turn of the century? It's where the Trench sisters conducted their little dietary experiments. And Keith Kennedy held his parties. Adrian Marcato lived there too. . . . The Trench sisters were two proper Victorian ladies—they cooked and ate several young children including a niece.... Adrian Marcato practiced witchcraft. He made quite a splash in the 1890s by announcing that he'd conjured up the living devil. Apparently, people believed him, so they attacked and nearly killed him in the lobby of the Bramford.... Later, the Keith Kennedy business began and by the 1920s, the house was half empty.... World War II filled the house up again.... They called it Black Bramford.... This house has a high incidence of un-pleasant happenings. In 1959, a dead infant was found wrapped in newspaper in the basement.

Even though they know the building's macabre history, Rosemary and Guy move into the malevolent-looking Gothic structure, next door to an elderly couple, Minnie and Roman Castevet, who happen to be part of a coven of devil worshippers. Roman is the son of a witch, Adrian Marcato, who once lived in the Bramford. Roman Castevet is an ana-gram[23] for his given name, Steven Marcato.

Rosemary's Baby is an overtly mocking reversal of everything Chris-tian. Guy, an unemployed and struggling actor, sacrifices his wife by making a pact with a coven of devil worshippers, who want to force her to bear Satan's son in return for fame and fortune as a broadway actor. A drugged and hallucinating Rosemary, having partaken of the "cup of demons" (1 Cor. 10:21), is raped by the devil in what appears to be a dream sequence that replicates a Black Mass. A beast-like figure resembling the devil, with yellowish eyes and clawed, scaly hands, rapes Rosemary. Anton LaVey, the founder of the Church of Satan and author of the *Satanic Bible*, plays the role of the devil during the rape scene. Rosemary conceives and gives birth to the son of Satan. The year is 1966. More precisely, it's the sixth month of 1966—666!

At first, Rosemary is told the baby has died. In fact, the baby was kidnapped by her devil-worshipping neighbors. Rosemary, hearing the cries of a baby in her neighbors' apartment, sneaks through the closet passageway between their two apartments intent on killing her "demon seed." She finds the coven (including her husband), encircling a black-draped bassinet paying homage to the son of Satan. Devil worshippers from around the world comprise a group of adoring Satanic Magi.

Rosemary finally learns the horrible truth that she was impregnated by the devil and the baby is the offspring of Satan. Like Mary who was chosen by God to give birth to His Son, the devil has chosen Rose-*Mary* to give birth to his son.

> **Roman:** Satan is his father, not Guy. He came up from hell and begat a son of mortal woman. (The coven members cheer "Hail, Satan!") Satan is his father and his name is Adrian. He shall overthrow the mighty and lay waste their temples. He shall redeem the despised and wreak vengeance in the name of the burned and the tortured. "Hail, Adrian! Hail, Satan!" (Others in the room repeat the incantation.) "Hail, Satan!"
> **Minnie:** He chose you out of all the world—out of all the women in the whole world, he chose you. He arranged things, because he wanted you to be the mother of his only living son.
> **Roman:** His power is stronger than stronger! His might shall last longer than longer.

Roman Castevet declares, "God is dead! God is dead and Satan lives! The year is One, the first year of our Lord! The year is One, God is done!" A chorus of voices declare in unison, "Hail, Satan!" "In Levin's novel, though not in the film, the assembled guests are shouting their ave marias, 'Hail Rosemary.'"[24] The birth of Rosemary's baby, the antichrist, takes place in the "Year One." This is another self-conscious, parallel reference to the year of Jesus Christ's birth, also in Year One, A.D.—*Anno Domini*, the year of Our Lord. Now there is a new lord, Satan's son.

> So part of the point of the film is to suggest the connection between the death of God and the emergence of the occult underground. Witchcraft, necromancy, astrology, the occult—all these have indeed risen rapidly to the surface in the past several years. The astrology columns are no longer the refuge of the lonely, poor, and troubled. They are of the first part of the daily paper our college students turn to today.[25]

The occult is no longer underground. Religious pluralism has enshrined it as just one of many spiritual options open to today's spiritual seekers. By the end of *Rosemary's Baby*, "Rosemary's home is destroyed and evil has triumphed."[26]

Of course, *Rosemary's Baby* has no basis in biblical fact. Satan has no such power, although there are many Christians who believe he can perform innumerable miraculous feats. When Christians impute such powers to Satan, they in effect defame God's character and call into question His omnipotence and sovereignty.

A Floodgate of Films

Following *Rosemary's Baby* in popularity, there was *The Exorcist* (1973). While the crucifix repels Dracula in 1931, it is abused and rendered powerless in 1973. The movie ends with the devil leaving the possessed girl, only to enter and destroy the well meaning but powerless exorcist. Father Karras "defeats" the demon by hurling himself out the window in an act of desperation. The audience is left with the impression that the devil will return. The devil is a spirit. He can always enter another body. One possession is just as good as any other.

> More than any popular film in recent history, *The Exorcist* leads us patiently to a confrontation with the Devil. It takes the quest seriously and asserts the primacy of religious and mystical accounts of evil over that of Enlightenment science. All this makes the film as serious and potentially edifying exploration of evil. But, even as it strives to vindicate the ultimate power of goodness, it unleashes the complex and powerful forces associated with the aesthetics of evil.[27]

From this point in film history, a flood of occult- and evil-inspired films rolled through theaters. Stephen King's first book, *Carrie*, was published in 1974, with the movie adaptation following in 1976. Carrie is a "gifted" but misunderstood high school girl who can move things by force of will. Carrie's mother is depicted as a Bible-selling, Bible-thumping, psycho-religious fanatic who cannot control her daughter's powers.

In *The Omen*, the devil is incarnated in the form of a five-year old-boy sired by the devil himself, and adopted by an unsuspecting wealthy American couple. A script similar to that of *Rosemary's Baby* is designed to give the devil's efforts a global dimension. While the devil may have been confined to a bassinet and a bedroom in the two earlier occult blockbusters, the *Omen* trilogy unleashes his power on the world. Damien is a "Jekyll/Hyde, with Hyde triumphant."[28] Once again, as in *The Exorcist*, the Church is powerless to stop the inevitability of demonic evil.

> In the *Omen* trilogy, the Catholic Church and its agents play Don Quixote to some very gigantic windmills. Audience sympathies may be with the "impossible dream," but the foe

definitely looks unbeatable. A measure of the demon's modern powers can be gleaned from the fact that "the desolate one" wins Round One, *The Omen* (1976), quite convincingly; annihilates his opponents in Round Two, *Damien—Omen II* (1978); and declares Round Three, which includes incidentally a melodramatic "Second Coming of Christ, *The Final Conflict—Omen III* (1981), a pyrrhic victory for his opponent, remind the Nazarene he has "won nothing."[29]

Lessons Learned

Did these movies teach any good lessons? The devil is portrayed as a real entity, not a phantasm concocted from the imagination of deeply disturbed individuals who have psychological problems. The producers did not attempt to explain away evil on naturalistic or psychological grounds. "*The Exorcist* set out to present the mysteries of faith in a rational world."[30] These films alert "us to the fact that spiritual evil is a reality within history, that it is a part of the human predicament, not a remote metaphysical speculation."[31]

But we are left without a solution. "Despite psychology and philosophy, modern man does not know how to handle what bubbles up from the subconscious. Denying the existence of true moral guilt and at the same time plagued by guilt feelings, he is unable to deal with either on naturalistic or humanistic grounds."[32] Once the devil was let out of his box, few in Hollywood knew how to get him back in, or cared to, since horror movies with an occult theme mean big business and big bucks. There are five sequels of Freddy Kruger in *Nightmare on Elm Street* if you count *Freddy's Dead: The Final Nightmare* in 1991. Don't forget the continued resurrection of Michael in the *Halloween* saga, now numbering four. Or is it five? No, it's seven, if you count *Halloween H2O* (1998). And Jason is always back, eight times to be exact, in *Friday the 13th*. There were eight *Amityville Horror* movies made from 1979 to 1996. The two *Ghostbusters* (1984, 1987) movies

bring the horror genre full circle. While electricity was used to ani-
mate Frankenstein's monsters, atomic energy is the only power that
can defeat the forces of darkness in the modern era. Ministers, priests,
and rabbis remain powerless on the streets below as the Ghostbusters
take on the occult powers with their nuclear backpacks.

Conclusion

None of these movies accurately depicts the biblical view of the
devil and his limited powers. Similarly, many Christians impute much
more power to the devil than the Bible ever does. In one sense, it's
Christian misconceptions about the devil that help script writers with
their story lines. Even the screen adaptation of Frank Baum's *Wizard of
Oz* continued the process of distorting the effect of evil by giving us
both good and bad witches. A child can choose one form of magic over
another. Autonomous power is what matters. Disney's Mickey Mouse
made believing in occult powers cute. Mickey became the "Sorcerer's
Apprentice" in a clip from Disney's *Fantasia*. Unfortunately, it seems
that "Our image of witches comes to us from the three hags in *Macbeth*,
stirring their filthy cauldrons and muttering weird chants; from Grimm's
Fairy Tales, where the long crooked fingers point their warts at you
while the witch cackles; and from the late Walt Disney who filled our
eyes with such monstrous females in his cartoon films,"[33] rather than
from the Bible.

Notes

1. C. S. Lewis, *The Screwtape Letters* (New York: Macmillan, [1942] 1946), 9.

2. Bob Longino, "More to actor Lon Chaney than even his '1,000 faces,'" *Atlanta Constitution* (October 24, 2000), D3. James Cagney starred in the film biography of Chaney, *The Man with a Thousand Faces*. His son, Lon Chaney, Jr., carried on his father's talents by starring in a number of horror movies, most notably *The Wolf Man*.

3. David J. Skal, *The Monster Show: A Cultural History of Horror* (New York: W.W. Norton, 1993), 115.

4. When Renfield cuts his finger on a paper clip, Dracula reacts eagerly to the sight of blood and moves closer with a ravenous, blood-maddened look. Before the Count can get closer, a crucifix falls from Renfield's neck and dangles over his hand, sending Dracula reeling backwards. As to shield himself, Dracula throws his arm over his eyes.

5. E. Michael Jones, *Monsters from the ID: The Rise of Horror in Fiction and Film* (Dallas, TX: Spence Publishing Co., 2000), 124.

6. Neil T. Anderson, *The Bondage Breaker* (Eugene, OR: Harvest House, 1990), 115.

7. Merrill Unger, *Demons in the World Today* (Wheaton, IL: Tyndale, 1971), 79.

8. C. Fred Dickason, *Demon Possession and the Christian* (Chicago, IL: Moody Press, 1987), 218.

9. André Kole and Jerry MacGregor, *Mind Games: Exposing Today's Psychics, Frauds, and False Spiritual Phenomena* (Eugene, OR: Harvest House, 1998), 79.

10. David J. Skal, *Screams of Reason: Mad Science and Modern Culture* (New York: W. W. Norton & Co., 1998), 37.

11. Skal, *Screams of Reason*, 43.

12. Jeremy Dyson, *Bright Darkness: The Lost Art of the Supernatural Horror Film* (London, England: Cassell, 1997), 55.

13. James Whale, the director of *Frankenstein* and *The Bride of Frankenstein*, was a prominent and public homosexual in Hollywood. Dr. Pretorious is Whale's alter ego. Frankenstein and Pretorious "work together to 'give birth' to a woman, two homosexuals replacing the heterosexual model of male and female parenting and replacing God—annihilating those noxious enemies of homosexuality, society and religion in one blow." (Gary Morris, "Sexual Subversion," *Bright Lights Film Journal*, Issue 11 [1993]). The article can be found at www.brightlightsfilm.com/19/19_bride1.html.

14. Skal, *The Monster Show*, 137.

15. Skal, *The Monster Show*, 187.

16. Michael Brunas, John Brunas, and Tom Weaver, *Universal Horrors: The Studio's Classic Films, 1931–1946* (Jefferson, NC: McFarland & Company, 1990), 120.

17. Skal, *Screams of Reason*, 33.

18. Feodor Dostoyevsky, *The Devils (The Possessed)*, trans. David Magarshark (Harmondsworth, Middlesex: Penguin Books, 1953), 126. Quoted in Vincent P. Miceli, *The Gods of Atheism* (New Rochelle, New York: Arlington House, 1971), 141.

19. Theodore Roszak, *Where the Wasteland Ends: Politics and Transcendence in Postindustrial Society* (Garden City, NJ: Doubleday, 1972), xxix.

20. Cited in Gary A. Wilburn, *The Fortune Sellers: The Occult Phenomenon of the 20th Century* (Glendale, CA: Gospel Light, 1972), 27.

21. It's ironic that Roman Polanski directed *Rosemary's Baby*, and his wife, Sharon Tate, was the victim in one of the worst crimes of the twentieth century. Tate was murdered by the disciples of Charles Manson. She was pregnant at the time. Her movie debut was *Eye of the Devil* (1965), in which she "played a country girl with bewitching powers." In the film, "[David] Niven became the victim of a hooded cult which practiced ritual sacrifice." (Vincent Bugliosi, *Helter Skelter: The True Story of the Manson Murders* [New York: W. W. Norton, 1974], 27). In 1967 Sharon Tate appeared in another Polanski Production, *The Fearless Vampire* Killers. "A victim of the vampire early in the picture, in the last scene she bites her lover, Polanski, creating still another monster" (28).

22. The movie was filmed at the Dakota where John Lennon of the Beatles lived and was murdered by Mark David Chapman in 1980.

23. An anagram is a word or phrase scrambled into another word or phrase using the same letters.

24. John C. Cooper and Carl Skrade, *Celluloid and Symbols* (Philadelphia, PA: Fortress Press, 1970), 73. The Roman Catholic version of the "Hail Mary" goes like this: "Hail Mary, full of grace. The Lord is with you. Blessed art thou among women and blessed is the fruit of thy womb, Jesus. Pray for us sinners, now and at the hour of our death. Amen."

25. Cooper and Skrade, *Celluloid and Symbols*, 72–73.

26. Stuart M. Kaminsky, *American Film Genres*, 2nd ed. (Chicago, IL: Nelson-Hall, 1985), 127.

27. Thomas S. Hibbs, *Shows About Nothing: Nihilism in Popular Culture from The Exorcist to Seinfeld* (Dallas, TX: Spence Publishing, 1999), 50–51.

28. Kaminsky, *American Film Genres,* 129.

29. Les and Barbara Keyser, *Hollywood and the Catholic Church: The Image of Roman Catholicism in American Movies* (Chicago, IL: Loyola University Press, 1984), 229.

30. Bob McCabe, *The Exorcist—Out of the Shadows: The Full Story of the Film* (London, England: Omnibus Press, 1999), 26.

31. Donald J. Drew, *Images of Man: A Critique of the Contemporary Cinema* (Downers Grove, IL: InterVarsity Press, 1974), 78.

32. Drew, *Images of Man*, 79.

33. John Kerr, *The Mystery and Magic of the Occult* (Philadelphia, PA: Fortress Press, 1971), 79. Cited in Wilburn, *The Fortune Sellers*, 135, note 3.

16

The Bible, the Devil, and God

And though this world, with devils filled, should threaten to
undo us, we will not fear, for God hath willed His truth
to triumph through us.
The prince of darkness grim we tremble not for him;
his rage we can endure, for lo! his doom is sure,
one little word shall fell him.[1]

The Bible describes the devil as tempter, adversary, and accuser but always under God's control (Job 1:6-22; Matt. 4; Luke 4). Satan is a creature who does not share God's attributes of omniscience, omnipresence, or omnipotence, that is, Satan does not know everything, cannot be everywhere, and cannot do everything. Satan is nowhere near God's co-equal. Demons, "under certain circumstances, can control (1 John 3:10; John 8:44), invade (Luke 22:3), blind spiritually (2 Cor. 4:4), deceive (Rev. 20:7–8), and trap (1 Tim. 3:7)"[2] unbelievers. Demonic possession is a reality in rare cases (Acts 19:16). Concerning Christians, demons "can tempt (1 Chron. 21:1), harass or afflict (Job 2:7), oppose (Zech. 3:1), and deceive (2 Cor. 11:3).... They can also disguise demonic works as godly (2 Cor. 11:4–15)."[3] There is no biblical example, however, of a believer being possessed by the devil.

If Satan is tempting a person in one locale, he cannot be tempting someone else somewhere else. This limitation is true of demons in general. They are *creatures*, not gods. The devils have no more power than angels, since demons are fallen angels. In the spiritual realm, angels (fallen or otherwise) have powers that humans do not possess. Satan was able to show Jesus "all the kingdoms of the inhabited earth in a moment of time" (Luke 4:5). In a similar action, an angel showed the events of the Book of Revelation so that John could see them (Rev. 22:8–9). But nowhere in Scripture do we find Satan being able to transfer this ability to humans.

At the same time, the Bible says that Satan is defeated, disarmed, and spoiled (Col. 2:15; Rev. 12:7; Mark 3:27), "fallen" (Luke 10:18), and "thrown down" (Rev. 12:9). He was "crushed" under the feet of the early Christians (Rom. 16:20). He has lost "authority" over Christians (Col. 1:13) and has been "judged" (John 16:11). He cannot "touch" a Christian (1 John 5:18). His works have been "destroyed" (1 John 3:8). He has "nothing" (John 14:30). He "flees" when "resisted" (James 4:7) and is "bound" (Mark 3:27; Luke 11:20; Rev. 20:2).

But can the devil perform miracles? Can he consign people to hell? Can he grant powers to humans? If we view pop-culture as the standard for outlining an authoritative demonology, then the devil has almost as much power as God. In some examples, as we've seen with *Rosemary's Baby*, he has more power than God. Even some Christians have imputed god-like powers to the devil. Satan is considered to be "alive and well on planet earth," while God seems "to be holed up in his corner of the universe sulking."[4] Even a cursory study of the Bible will show that Satan has no miraculous powers, at least none he can transfer to humans. He can deceive people into believing he has such powers, but when called on to demonstrate the reality of those powers, he comes up empty. We saw with the magicians and conjurers in Babylon that they had no preternatural powers. They told king Nebuchadnezzar that reading a person's mind was impossible. "There is not a man on earth who could declare the matter for the king..." (Dan. 2:10, cf. v. 27).

The "mediums and spiritists" are ridiculed by God because all they can do is "whisper and mutter" (Isa. 8:19). Those who call on the "ghosts of the dead" through "mediums and spiritists" receive no answer (19:3). Those who claim to have powers bestowed upon them from demonic forces can only hope that there are enough people out there who are actually gullible enough to believe them. But God calls on His people to put such claims to the test.

> Stand fast now in your spells and in your many sorceries with which you have labored from your youth; perhaps you will be able to profit, perhaps you may cause trembling. You are wearied with your many counsels, let now the astrologers, those who prophesy by the stars, those who predict by the new moons, stand up and save you from what will come upon you. . . . There is none to save you (47:12–15).

To put it simply, God says, "Put up or shut up." If the agents of the devil really have powers, they would be able to demonstrate them.

Satan had a perfect opportunity to display his power when Elijah challenged the prophets of Baal by devising a simple test. Elijah called on the true God, and the prophets of Baal called on their god to act on command. The prophets of Baal "cried with a loud voice and cut themselves according to their custom with swords and lances until the blood gushed out on them" (1 Kings 18:28). They did this for hours, "but there was no voice, no one answered, and no one paid attention" (1 Kings 18:29). When Elijah called on God, He acted without hesitation: "Then the fire of the LORD fell, and consumed the burnt offering and the wood and the stones and the dust, and licked up the water that was in the trench. And when all the people saw it, they fell on their faces; and they said, 'The LORD, He is God; the LORD, He is God'" (18:38–39). If Satan truly had power to duplicate God's miracles, then this would have been the perfect time to imbue the prophets of Baal with supernatural powers.

The "Magicians" of Egypt

Christian commentators often turn to the story of Moses and Aaron and their encounters with the magicians of Egypt as evidence that demonic miracles are real and can rival God's miraculous works. If miracles are a way to demonstrate God's power and authority over the created order, then "if something or someone other than God can perform miracles, then the value of miracles for attesting to Christ's divinity is negated."[5]

When Aaron threw down his rod before Pharaoh (Ex. 7:8–12), it became a serpent by the power of God. We shouldn't be surprised that God can perform such a miracle since He created man from the dust of the ground (Gen. 2:7). For God, turning a dead stick into a serpent is child's play. Could Pharaoh's sorcerers and magicians also perform creation miracles? The Bible describes their "powers" as "secret arts," or more accurately, "deceptive arts" (Ex. 7:11). These were developed skills—conjurors' tricks—that were concealed from Pharaoh and the general public. The livelihood of the magicians depended on their ability to convince Pharaoh that they had miraculous abilities. Pharaoh's tricksters had no more power than the "magicians" who served in Nebuchadnezzar's court and could not tell the king the contents of his dream.

Turning a staff into a serpent was a simple magician's trick. Jannes and Jambres, the names that Paul gives to Pharaoh's court magicians (2 Tim. 3:8), probably performed this spectacle quite often. It was their signature trick. But how did they create the illusion? Dan Korem, a trained magician, reminds us of similar illusions performed today. "The most practical method to duplicate the magicians' feat is similar to a trick performed today where a magician changes a cane to a silk handkerchief, rope or a handful of flowers."[6] Modern magicians regularly work with animals, so we shouldn't be surprised if ancient magicians did the same. Here's how it could have been done. Susan Schaffer, a reptile curator at the San Diego Zoo,

> explained that to measure the length of a snake, she takes a tightfitting tube and coaxes the snake into it, as snakes like dark, tight-fitting environs. To replicate the illusion of changing a rod into a snake, a telescopic shell must be constructed to house the snake. Given the materials available during that time period, such as a piece of pliable papyrus, this could easily be made. With the snake concealed inside the "staff," the magician would simply have to pass his hand over the shell, collapsing it at the same time, leaving the snake in its place. This action could be covered by the motion of throwing the staff to the ground, creating the illusion that the staff visibly changes to a snake.[7]

Lighting would have been poor indoors, so the sleight of hand would have been easily concealed. A good magician could come up with several ways to perform this trick in a way that would convince the casual observer who probably saw what happened around Pharaoh's court from a distance.

But didn't Pharaoh's magicians turn water into blood and produce frogs on command, replicating the miracles brought about through Moses? The miracle performed by Moses turned the Nile into blood as well as the "rivers... streams... pools... reservoirs" as well as the water in "vessels of wood and in vessels of stone" (Ex. 7:19). Pharaoh's magicians did the same "with their secret arts" (7:22). Their trick was to turn a small amount of water into blood. They must have gone to Pharaoh with a small pot of water and showed him how they too could turn it into blood. Magicians turn milk into confetti, a common trick performed by many stage illusionists.[8] Turning clear water into "blood" would be simple. Holding a pouch of blood in the palm of the hand—there was enough of it around—it would have been a simple thing to open it into the water. "Presto-changeo"—water into blood! The real miracle would have been for the magicians to turn the bloodied water throughout Egypt back into fresh water! This they could not do.

The plague of frogs, like the bloodied waters, occurred throughout Egypt. Once again, the court magicians went to Pharaoh and showed him that they could also produce frogs. "Magicians today produce live doves in the middle of a stage from handkerchiefs; and doves are far more difficult to handle than a docile frog."[9] Like with the bloody water, the real miracle would have been to rid the land of frogs. Reginald Scot, author of *The Discoverie of Witchcraft* (1584), takes an equally skeptical view of miraculous demonic powers being attributed to Pharaoh's magicians. "If Pharaoh's magicians had suddenly made frogs, why could they not drive them away again? If they could not hurt the frogs, why should we think that they could make them? …Such things as we are being bewitched to imagine, have no truth at all either in action or essence, beside the bare imagination."[10] If someone begins with the assumption that the devil can impart the ability to perform miracles, then he will see miracles in what is really the ancient art of stage magic. The replication of frogs was the last trick performed by Pharaoh's magicians. They ran out of tricks. By the third miracle, "the magicians said to Pharaoh, 'This is the finger of God'" (8:19). They knew a miracle when they saw it.

Raising Dead Spirits

A popular practice among self-appointed mediums is the claim that they can contact the dead on behalf of the living. The movies *Ghost*

(1990) and *The Sixth Sense* (1999), which emphasized this theme through emotional story lines, were hugely popular with audiences. But is it possible for the dead to communicate with the living through a medium? Unquestionably, the Bible teaches that there is life after death. In some rare cases, the dead manifest themselves to the living: Moses, Elijah, and Jesus (Matt. 17:3; Acts 1:3). But do humans have power, through demonic avenues, to reach departed souls?

Saul and the "medium" in 1 Samuel 28 is offered as evidence that the dead can be contacted by the living. Did the witch or medium of En-dor actually "conjure up" Samuel at the request of King Saul (1 Sam. 28)? Not all commentators think so. There is no indication in Scripture that Satan or any human in league with the devil has such power. Only God has authority over life and death: "But I will warn you whom to fear; fear the One who after He has killed has authority to cast into hell; yes, I tell you, fear Him!" (Luke 12:5). Many assume that the events surrounding Jesus' death were orchestrated by Satan. Jesus' words contradict this assumption: "I lay down My life that I may take it again" (John 10:17; cf. 13:37). Satan's power is expressly limited by God (Job 1:6–12).

If the medium of En-dor did not have the power to "conjure up" Samuel, then how should the biblical text be interpreted? One view maintains that God "brought up" Samuel since God controls life and death. This explains why the medium of En-dor expressed surprise that Samuel appeared (1 Sam. 28:12). "When the woman saw Samuel, she cried out with a loud voice; and the woman spoke to Saul, saying, 'Why have you deceived me? For you are Saul.' And the king said to her, 'Do not be afraid; but what do you see?' And the woman said to Saul, 'I see a divine being coming up out of the earth'" (1 Sam. 28:12–13). She was surprised because she knew that she had not really contacted Samuel's spirit on her own. Like a rigged seance meeting, the medium thought she was in control of the situation until the real Samuel actually appeared and spoke.[11] There is not a single place in the Bible where Satan conjures up the dead. There is, however, evidence that God, has brought back departed saints on rare occasions. On the mount where Jesus was transfigured before His disciples, "Moses and Elijah appeared to them, talking with Him" (Matt. 17:3).

More Frauds Exposed

"In the book of Acts," Clinton E. Arnold writes that "Luke records four separate instances involving the use of magic. In three of these instances Luke directly connects the magic with the work of Satan or his demons."[12] This author assumes that in three of the four cases demonic *power* was used to enable these magicians, fortunetellers, and exorcists to perform supernaturally. A careful study of Scripture and what we know about the limited power of Satan from Scripture will show that in none of these instances was demonic power being used.

Simon the Magician (Acts 8)

Philip encounters Simon, "who formerly was practicing magic in the city, and astonished the people of Samaria, claiming to be someone great" (Acts 8:9). Those who saw him perform believed that he was "the Great Power of God" (8:10), because "he had for a long time astonished them with his magic arts" (8:11). But it was Simon who was amazed "as he observed signs and great miracles taking place" (8:13). Simon knew that these were not the usual tricks. Wanting a piece of the action, Simon offered money so he could perform the same tricks (8:19). Even today, magicians pay for tricks developed by other magicians.

The Jewish Magician and False Prophet (Acts 13)

Paul encounters "a certain magician, a Jewish false prophet whose name was Bar-Jesus" (13:6). The Bible tells us that Bar-Jesus, who claimed to be a magician, was a "false prophet." Paul, after fixing his gaze upon him, said, "You who are full of all deceit and fraud, you son of the devil, you enemy of all righteousness, will you not cease to make crooked the straight ways of the Lord?" (13:10). Bar-Jesus was a false prophet, full of deceit, and a fraud who did not have demonic or any other powers. While Bar-Jesus aligned himself with the devil, this does not mean that the devil was able to give him occult powers.

The Slave-Girl with the "Python Spirit" (Acts 16)

Paul encounters a demon-possessed slavegirl who was being used by her masters to make money for them by "fortune-telling" (16:16). Could she truly foresee the future? If magicians and sorcerers are unable to read the mind of a king (Dan. 2:27), how is it possible for a demon to read the mind of God? God is in control of time, not the devil. The slave-girl is said to have "a spirit of divination" (16:16). Actually, the Greek states that she had a "python spirit." What does this mean?

> That phrase means she was used by the priests of the Delphic Oracle to predict the future. The word literally means "pregnant with a god," or in more modern terms, a "ventriloquist." Here's how the scam worked: The person with the python spirit would mutter unintelligible phrases that were alleged prophecies, then the priests would translate. The fact that the slave girl earned a lot of money for her masters doesn't mean her predictions were correct any more than the psychics answering the "900" telephone lines are correct. As far as we know, the only thing this girl got correct was that Paul and Silas were servants of the most high God.[13]

Why would a demon-inspired girl point out to people the "way of salvation"? (16:17). "Since salvation was a popular topic of conversation in those days, even if it meant different things to different people,

it is not in the least strange that the girl should have hailed the mission-
aries as teachers of 'the way of salvation'."[14] But why would a demon
want to promote the work of Christ? "Perhaps the ulterior motive was
to discredit the gospel by associating it in people's minds with the occult."[15] In effect, her "endorsement" of their miracles was an attempt to
give credibility to her fraudulent predictions by rightly identifying the
work of Paul and Silas.

The Jewish Exorcists (Acts 19)

When "God was performing extraordinary miracles by the hands
of Paul," some of the Jewish exorcists attempted to duplicate them.
They could not (19:13–16). Those who claimed to have "practiced
magic" (19:19) confessed that their performances were tricks to fool
the people. "Many also of those who had believed kept coming, *confess-
ing and disclosing their practices*" (19:18). In demonstration of the rejection of their fraudulent practices, "many of those who practiced magic
brought their books together and began burning them in the sight of
all; and they counted up the price of them and found it fifty thousand
pieces of silver" (19:19).

A Speaking Statue (Revelation 13:15)

New Testament scholar George Eldon Ladd comments that the
"power to make statues speak was well known in the ancient world.
There grew up a cycle of legend around the person Simon Magus (Acts
8:9ff.), and early Christian literature relates stories of how he [seem-
ingly] brought statues to life."[16] In fact, the literature of that era is
abundant with stories of "speaking statues" and other "miracles":

> The ancient pagan priests had for centuries practiced de-
> ceiving superstitious worshipers into believing images made of
> stone, metal and wood could talk. Many of them used drugs or

self-hypnosis to induce a trance in which they claimed to be speaking oracles from the gods or images. One such was the "oracle at Delphi," a Greek temple inhabited by priestesses and from which Alexander the Great demanded a revelation. Ventriloquism was a highly skilled and widely practiced art in heathen idolatry. Eurycles of Athens was the most celebrated of Greek ventriloquists. They were called *engastrimanteis*, or "belly prophets" because the ancients believed the voices came from the bellies of the oracles. Priests of ancient pagan religions were masters of this art and to ventriloquism may be ascribed the alleged miracles of the "speaking statues" of the Egyptians, Greeks and Romans.... Modern archaeologists have found devices used for secretly piping the human voice beneath altars bearing the statues of pagan gods.[17]

A study of the history of the first century abounds with accounts of events similar to those described in Revelation 13. "The command to perform idolatry alludes partly to the pressure placed on the populace and the churches in Asia Minor to give homage to the image of Caesar as a divine being. By the end of the first century A.D. all the cities addressed in the Apocalypse's letters had temples dedicated to the deity of Caesar, the first established in 29 B.C."[18]

The Bible clearly teaches that man-made images cannot come to life, even by the power of Satan: "Idols of gold and of silver and of brass and of stone and of wood . . . can neither see nor hear nor walk" (Rev. 9:20). The Psalmist writes that idols "have mouths, but they cannot speak.... They cannot make a sound with their throat" (Ps. 115:5a, 7c; cf. Isa. 46:7; Jer. 10:5).

Is It Safe?

If the devil's powers are overrated, does this mean that it's safe to dabble in the occult? Not at all. The purpose of the occult practitioners is to get around God's way of doing things. In all occult techniques, the practitioner either wants something that God forbids or pursues a good thing contrary to God's expressed will. As the perpetual rebel, man believes that he can subvert God's moral order by going to a lesser self-appointed god, Satan, to get what he wants. But even Satan-worship exacts a price, not from Satan, but from God: Adam and Eve lost Paradise (Gen. 2:15–17; 3:5, 14–24), Saul lost his kingdom (1 Sam. 28:3–19), and Judas most certainly lost his soul (Luke 22:21–23). The following is a list of the Bible's prohibitions against dabbling in the black arts:

> Witchcraft (sorcery)—Exodus 22:18
> Necromancy-Spiritualism—Leviticus 19:31; 20:6;
>   Deuteronomy 18:11
> Astrology—Isaiah 47:13
> False prophecy
>   inaccurate—Deuteronomy 18:2022; cf. I John 4:1
>   idolatrous—Deuteronomy 13:1-3
> Divination—Deuteronomy 18:10
>   arrows—Ezekiel 21:21
>   livers—Ezekiel 21:21
>   images—Ezekiel 21:21
> Fire walking—Deuteronomy 18:10
> Omens—Jeremiah 10:2
> Wizardry (secret knowledge)—Deuteronomy 18:11
> Charms (snakes)—Jeremiah 8:17
> Enchantment (spells)—Isaiah 47:9-12
> Times (lucky days)—Leviticus 19:26[19]

The Bible gives us the answers we need to live a full and abundant life. Messing with the promises of forbidden things is messing with trouble. "The secret things belong to the LORD our God, but the things revealed belong to us and to our sons forever, that we may observe all the words of this law" (Deut. 29:29).

To put yourself under the authority, and thus, the power, of another being is an act of rebellion against God. It will lead to disastrous results. But worst of all, submission to occult practices is a way of despising God; it is disobedience of the highest order. "For rebellion is as the sin of divination, and insubordination is as iniquity and idolatry" (1 Sam. 15:23). It is no accident that divination and immorality are so often mentioned in the same context (Acts 15:29; 1 Cor. 10:6–9; Gal. 5:20; Rev. 2:14; 9:21). Those who choose the occult over Christ want power and authority apart from Him. This is the worldview of the Satanist as expressed by Anton Szandor La Vey, founder of the San Francisco-based Church of Satan: "I wouldn't presume to improve on Milton's quote, 'Better to reign in hell than serve in heaven.'"[20]

Why the Interest?

Interest in the occult emerges when the prevailing Christian worldview fails to impact people's lives in concrete, life-transforming ways. When the Christian message becomes defeatist, retreatist, and exclusively otherworldly, the door is opened wide to the occult. When the Church embraces a watered-down Christian message and raises the white flag of cultural surrender, you can expect the devil to march in where he once feared to tread and give the impression that he has the power.[21] Os Guinness describes it this way:

> Early hunters on safari in Africa used to build their fires high at night in order to keep away the animals in the bush. But when the fires burned low in the early hours of the morning, they would see all around them the approaching outlined shapes of animals and a ring of encircling eyes in the darkness. When the fire was high they were far off, but when the fire was low they approached again.[22]

We see the encircling eyes of the occult because the Church has allowed the fires of a vibrant Christian faith to burn low. The Christian message has been diluted: The Bible has answers in death but little to say about life in the here and now. Those looking for answers to problems that confront them daily will try any option, including the occult, if they believe they might get some answers.

Paganism, which supposedly has received a "bum rap" from Christianity and the scientific community (for different reasons), is now seen as a viable worldview option. Witchcraft thrives in a relativistic world where Christianity is only one religious alternative among many, as the following makes crystal clear:

> One need not be a witch—I am not—to understand witchcraft as a valid expression of the religious experience. The religion of witchcraft offers to restore a lost option, paganism, to our religious worldview. Both Christianity and scientism have taught us falsely that paganism is nonsense. We are taught that pagans worshipped idols, that they believed undignified things about a useless variety of silly gods, and that they invented interesting but irrelevant myths…. The religions of Egypt and Canaan, of the Celts and the Teutons, when properly understood, are rich, sophisticated, beautiful, and psychologically full of insight. The neopagan witches are attempting to recreate the positive values of pagan religion.[23]

Once the Bible is dismissed as authoritative or is dismissed because of its inability to deal with "modern" issues, we are left with a free-for-all when it comes to a choice of worldviews. The worldview of relativism makes all other worldviews possible and permissible, even the fraudulent worldview of occult practices.

Conclusion

The man-centered worldview of rationalism and the diminished worldview of Christianity produced a new worldview which is now being identified as the New Age movement, higher consciousness, holistic healing, psychic healing, astrology, eastern mysticism, life readings, and outright Satanism. Actually, there is nothing new about anything we are seeing today. Such fraudulent practices have been with us since the beginning of time. Truth is, God has no competitors.

Notes

1. Martin Luther, "A Mighty Fortress is Our God," third verse.

2. Bob and Gretchen Passantino, *Satanism* (Grand Rapids, MI: Zondervan, 1995), 15.

3. Bob and Gretchen Passantino, *Satanism*, 15.

4. Robert S. Wheeler, *The Children of Darkness: Some Heretical Reflections on the Kid Cult* (New Rochelle, NY: Arlington House, 1973), 31.

5. André Kole and Jerry MacGregor, *Mind Games: Exposing Today's Psychics, Frauds, and False Spiritual Phenomena* (Eugene, OR: Harvest House, 1998), 79.

6. Dan Korem, *Powers: Testing the Psychic and Supernatural* (Downers Grove, IL: InterVarsity Press, 1988), 174.

7. Korem, *Powers*, 174.

8. Korem, *Powers*, 175.

9. Korem, *Powers*, 175.

10. Reginald Scot, *The Discoverie of Witchcraft* (New York: Dover Publications, 1972), 180. Scot's work was originally published in 1584, and only 250 copies were reprinted in 1886. It was reprinted once again in Great Britain in 1930. The 1972 Dover edition is the latest reprint, retaining the spelling of the original edition.

11. Dan Korem takes the position that the entire encounter was staged, that the medium of En-dor was doing nothing more than a modern-day medium who claims to have contacted the dead and speaks for the departed spirit. See Danny Korem and Paul Meier, *The Fakers: Exploding the Myths of the Supernatural* (Grand Rapids, MI: Baker Book House, 1981), 91–101. Reginald Scot makes a similar case in *The Discoverie of Witchcraft*, 83–84.

12. Clinton E. Arnold, *Powers of Darkness: Principalities and Powers in Paul's Letters* (Downers Grove, IL: InterVarsity Press, 1992), 31.

13. Kole and MacGregor, *Mind Games*, 82–83.

14. John Stott, *The Spirit, the Church, and the World: The Message of Acts* (Downers Grove, IL: InterVarsity Press, 1990), 264.

15. Stott, *The Spirit, the Church, and the World*, 264.

16. George Eldon Ladd, *A Commentary on the Revelation of John* (Grand Rapids, MI: Eerdmans, 1972), 184. "Simon was deemed a god at Rome and honored as a god with a statue in the River Tiber between two bridges." For an account of Simon Magus, see Paul L. Maier, ed., *Eusebius: The Church History: A New Translation with Commentary* (Grand Rapids, MI: Kregel, 1999), 71–72. *The Church History* of Eusebius was written in the fourth century and relies on the works of earlier writers.

17. Paul T. Butler, *Thirteen Lessons on Revelation*, 2 vols. (Joplin, MO: College Press Publishing Co., 1982), 2:21.

18. G. K. Beale, *The Book of Revelation: A Commentary on the Greek Text* (Grand Rapids, MI: Eerdmans, 1999), 710.

19. Gary North, *Unholy Spirits*, 65. This is an expanded version of the original title *None Dare Call It Witchcraft* (New Rochelle, NY: Arlington House, 1976).

20. Quoted in John M. Leighty, "Biblical Satan is Lukewarm Topic in Today's Modern World," *The Marietta Daily Journal* (January 29, 1988), 5B.

21. Gary DeMar and Peter J. Leithart, *The Reduction of Christianity: A Biblical Response to Dave Hunt* (Ft. Worth, TX: Dominion Press, 1988).

22. Os Guinness, *The Dust of Death: A Critique of the Establishment and the Counter Culture—and a Proposal for a Third Way* (Downers Grove, IL: InterVarsity Press, 1973), 277.

23. Jeffrey B. Russell, *A History of Witchcraft: Sorcerers, Heretics and Pagans* (London: Thames and Hudson, 1980), 174–175.

17

Testing the Prophets

Ever since human beings first walked the earth, they have
attempted—whether by extension of logic or through the use of
magic—to divine what the unknown future holds in store for them.
For a variety of reasons—to comfort themselves, to prepare
themselves—human beings have been eager to know what
tomorrow, the day after tomorrow, the next month, the next year,
the years to come, will do to them and in what ways the future will
affect their lives and their fate.[1]

The Bible establishes the standard for discerning the claims of a prophet. It's quite simple. He or she must be 100% accurate (Deut. 18:20–22). No mistakes. No adjustments. No *ex post facto* explanations as to why a prophecy did not come to pass as specified. In fact, the Bible bases its authority on its own claim of unquestioned prophetic integrity. With nearly two thousand predictions[2] on everything from the birth of a promised redeemer to the destruction of particular nations, it only takes one failed prediction to call the others into question. God has set the highest standard possible. You will *never* hear modern-day "prophets" make the claim that all their prophecies came to pass as written. They and their reading public are satisfied with a better than average percentage of accuracy.

In biblical terms, it is not enough for a self-proclaimed "prophet" like the late Jeane Dixon (1918–1997) to boast that her "record of accuracy is unequaled."[3] As compared to what? As compared to other self-proclaimed "prophets" who have a lower percentage of accuracy. Today's popular prophets are like baseball players who only like to talk about how many career-hits they got. They don't want to be reminded about how many times they struck out. For example, Babe Ruth is best remembered for hitting a record 60 home runs in 1927[4] and 714[5] in his career. But few Ruth fans want to remember that he struck out 1330 times. Compare Ruth's strike-out numbers to those of Joe DiMaggio who only struck out 369 times in his thirteen-year career. It takes an impartial statistician to keep it all in perspective. While the modern Major League record for the highest season batting average of .426 by Rogers Hornsby in 1924 is impressive by any baseball standard, it is less than remarkable by any biblical standard concerning fulfilled prophecy.

Setting the Standard

Carl Sagan, a skeptic of all supernatural claims, demands the same level of accuracy for prophecy as he does for science. He believes that accuracy is a sign of legitimacy for both science and religion.

> Think of how many religions attempt to validate themselves with prophecy. Think of how many people rely on these prophecies, however vague, however unfulfilled, to support or prop up their beliefs. Yet has there ever been a religion with the prophetic accuracy and reliability of science? There isn't a religion on the planet that doesn't long for a comparable ability—precise, and repeatedly demonstrated before committed skeptics—to foretell future events. No other human institution comes close.[6]

As history attests and Sagan admits, science has not been 100% reliable. "The history of science," Sagan concedes, "is full of cases where previously accepted theories and hypotheses have been overthrown to be replaced by new ideas which more adequately explain the data."[7] To cite just three of hundreds of examples, Louis Pasteur's fellow scientists opposed him on the germ-theory origin of disease. In the 1860s, spontaneous generation was still being debated in the prestigious French Academy of Sciences. Science books more than ten years old are nearly obsolete today. Sagan's claim that the reason science works so well is that it has a "built-in error-correcting machinery"[8] doesn't fly. False prophets are constantly correcting themselves *after the fact* as well. Bible prophecy has a far better record than the history of science. In fact, there is no comparison.

Prophecy and Projection

Not all predictions claim a supernatural source. For example, Andrew M. Greeley, a Catholic priest and professor of Sociology, accurately predicted in the late 1970s that the Communist government of the former Soviet Union would be overthrown "either by a violent revolution or more likely by a 'social democratic' faction within the party."[9] The insightful and correct forecast was based on Greeley's study of history and his understanding of the inherent economic and political flaws of Communism. There was no claim of clairvoyance or precognition on Greeley's part. Social scientists project future trends based on past conditions and present performance in nearly every field of study. For example, "If [as of 1996] current trends in the miniaturization of computer memory continues at the rate of the past twenty years, a factor of 100 every decade, today's eight megabyte memory chips will be able to store ten terabytes in thirty years' time."[10] While this type of futurology is not an exact science, it is necessary for planning. People who project future trends do not use crystal balls, tarot cards, or astrology. "The most reliable way to anticipate the future is by understanding the present."[11] We expect and accept mistakes from this type of futurology.

Jeane Dixon and the "Gift" of Prophecy

Throughout her career, the late Jeane Dixon continually reminded people that she had predicted the assassination of President John F. Kennedy as far back as 1952. Dixon maintained that she had a supernatural gift, unlike someone who forecasts what the future will be like based on the study of past and present trends. To give religious authenticity to her "gift," Dixon claimed the vision of the 1960 presidential death came to her when she was in St. Matthew's Cathedral, Washington, D.C.[12] The prophecy was repeated to investigative reporter Jack Anderson, who published it in the Sunday supplement *Parade* magazine in 1956.[13] Did Dixon really predict Kennedy's assassination? Well, not quite. Here's how Anderson reported the prediction as Dixon related it to him: "As to the 1960 election, Mrs. Dixon thinks it will be dominated by labor and won by a Democrat. But he will be assassinated or die in office, though not necessarily in his first term."[14] In reality, "she merely employed the well-known 20-year cycle that every president elected in an even decade year since 1840 died in office."[15] Dixon did not predict in 1952 that JFK would be the new president in 1960. She never named the winner of the 1960 election. Her prediction that he would be assassinated was based on probability. Ronald Reagan (1980) broke the twenty-year cycle. She had a 50-50 chance on what party would win in 1960. Labor unions usually endorse Democrats.

Overall, how good of a prophet was Dixon? "Among her failed predictions: a world war started by Red China in 1958; Russia to be the first to put a man on the moon[16] and a stunning wave of suicides in the U.S. She also stated repeatedly that President Nixon had 'excellent vibes'[17] and would be remembered as one of the great modern presidents."[18] In 1969, Dixon wrote that Cuba's dictator, Fidel Castro, "is rapidly losing both influence and power in his island government."[19] She predicted that a comet would "strike the earth around the middle of the 1980's" causing "one of the worst disasters of the twentieth century."[20] Dixon was sure that we would have a woman president in the 1980s.[21] She predicted a period of peace that "will lull the majority of our people and many of our political leaders to sleep.... [F]or while peace seems to be on everyone's mind, sudden destruction and war will occur in 1999."[22] Then there is this contradictory prediction:

> A child, born somewhere in the Middle East shortly after 7 A.M. (EST) on February 5, 1962, will revolutionize the world. Before the end of 1999 he will bring together all mankind in one all-embracing faith. This will be the foundation of a new Christianity, with every sect and creed united through this man who will walk among the people to spread the wisdom of the Almighty Power.[23]

At one point in her autobiography, Dixon predicted that the South Vietnamese will "win their war against the Communists," and in the next sentence she leaves open the possibility that the Communists will win.[24] Either way, Dixon could claim that she "predicted" the outcome. She followed a similar win-win pattern when she predicted Walter Mondale would become the Democratic candidate for the presidency in 1980 "unless the people change their thoughts." And when asked about who would win the presidency in 1980, she "predicted" it would be Ronald Reagan, "unless [the people] change an awful lot and switch at the last moment."[25]

On the back cover of *My Life and Prophecies*, Dixon is shown wearing a large crucifix around her neck. She continually quotes the Bible to support her claims. "The Bible is filled with specific tests and requirements a prophet has to be able to meet before he or she can be called 'a prophet of the Most High.'"[26] The book then lists twenty Bible verses to support this assertion. But one verse is conspicuously absent: "When a prophet speaks in the name of the LORD, if the thing does not come about or come true, that is the thing which the LORD has not spoken. The prophet has spoken it presumptuously; you shall not be afraid of him" (Deut 18:22).

With the Bible as the standard, Dixon was a failure, a false prophet. But she was a clever false prophet. She appealed to the Bible for support for her claim that she was endowed with a divine gift. Prophesying in Jesus' name does not make a true prophet.

> Not everyone who says to Me, "Lord, Lord," will enter the kingdom of heaven; but he who does the will of My Father who is in heaven. Many will say to Me on that day, "Lord, Lord, *did we not prophesy in Your name*, and in your name cast out demons, and in Your name perform many miracles?" And then I will declare to them, "I never knew you; DEPART FROM ME YOU WHO PRACTICE LAWLESSNESS" (Matt. 7:21–23; also see 24:5; Mark 13:6; Luke 21:8).

Dixon claimed the name of Christ to lend credibility to her prophetic business. In reality, her predictions were based on historical analysis, probability, good guesses, and the short-term memory of her followers who forgot how many times she got it wrong. Any good student of history could have done as well or better.

Reading the Stars

Many Americans were shocked when they learned that astrology played a role in the presidential life of Ronald Reagan. Through Donald Regan, former secretary of the Treasury and Reagan's White House chief of staff, we learned that Nancy Reagan had been "consulting an astrologer and actually influencing the chief executive's decisions on the basis of astral predictions. The first lady had been dabbling with the occult as early as 1967, when her husband was governor of California, by relying upon the advice of prophetess Jeanne [*sic*] Dixon."[27] Regan writes, "Virtually every major move or decision the Reagans made during my time as White House chief of staff was cleared in advance with a woman in San Francisco who drew up horoscopes to make certain that the planets were in a favorable alignment for the enterprise."[28] The woman from San Francisco was Joan Quigley who is described as "the world's foremost political astrologer." Quigley claims she had guided the fortunes of Ronald Reagan by giving "astrological advice that shaped administration policy with the U.S.S.R and with regard to other crucial matters."[29] She takes credit for every good thing that happened to the Reagans and blames the negatives on astrological inevitability: "From February through May 1987 the indications were terrifying. When I saw them coming, I was fearful that even astrology would not be able to protect him."[30]

Past administrations had similar paranormal interests. "And Nancy Reagan is far from the first First Lady to seek guidance from extrascientific sources. Mary Todd Lincoln attended séances trying to contact her dead son Willie, and Edith Wilson and Florence Harding consulted the same clairvoyant."[31] While we were told that astrology did not affect specific policy issues, "astrological influence dramatically reduced the presidency's effectiveness, at least partly, by keeping Ronald Reagan under wraps much of the time."[32]

Astrology is unbiblical and irrational. The heavenly bodies—sun, moon, and stars—are created objects. They have no personality, godlike qualities, or spiritual forces. The only forces they exhibit are gravity, and in the case of stars, heat. Astrologers point to the Bible's claim that heavenly bodies are "signs," that is, astrological signs that govern personality and destiny (Gen. 1:14). The biblical context tells a different story. They are "signs"—light bearers—to distinguish between "the day from the night... for seasons, and for days and years ... to give light on the earth" (1:14–18). Prior to the compass and other guidance tools, navigators used the stars as fixed markers when sight observations could no longer spot the coastline. Celestial bodies, therefore, were placed in the heavens by God mostly for utilitarian purposes and to display God's glory (Psalm 19:1). Even the star of Bethlehem was little more than a navigational light that shows that God, not the stars, controls the heavens (Matt. 2:2, 9). No special powers are ever attributed to the Star of Bethlehem by the biblical writers.

Because suns, moons, and stars are created things, they can have no religious import other than to point back to their Creator. Paul writes, "for since the creation of the world His invisible attributes, His eternal power and divine nature, have been clearly seen, being understood *through what has been made*, so that they are without excuse" (Rom 1:20). The Psalmist writes, "The heavens are telling of the glory of God; and their expanse is declaring the work of His hands" (Psalm 19:1; 8:3). All things created speak of the Creator (Job 12:7–12). Created things, even stars, have no permanence since the Bible says there will be a "new heaven and a new earth" (Rev. 21:1). Looking to the stars and planets for spiritual guidance is no different from chopping down a tree, calling on a craftsman to shape it into a representation of some false god, and bowing down to worship before it (Isa. 40:18–20).

The Bible condemns astrology but not astronomy, the scientific study of heavenly bodies. In a similar way, the Bible condemns the worship of "birds and four-footed animals and crawling creatures" (Rom. 1:23) but not their study. The sluggard is told, "Go to the ant,... observe her ways and be wise" (Prov. 6:6). The Psalmist tells us, "Do not be as the horse or as the mule which have no understanding" (Psalm 32:9a). We are to "look to the birds of the air" and study their habits (Matt. 6:26), not to worship them (Rom. 1:23). The same is true of the cosmos in general and everything else God has made.

Worshipping the Stars

One of the first reforms that King Josiah implemented during his reign as king was "to bring out of the temple of the LORD all the vessels that were made for Baal, for Ashera, and for all the host of heaven" to be burned (2 Kings 23:4). "All the host of heaven" is defined in the next verse as "the sun... moon... and constellations" (v. 5). The Hebrew is very clear, the phrase "constellations" refers to "the twelve divisions of the zodiac marked by the figures and names of animals: the twelve constellations of the zodiac."[33]

The Bible is clear: "And beware, lest you lift up your eyes to heaven and see the sun and the moon and the stars, all the host of heaven, and be drawn away and worship them and serve them. . ." (Deut. 4:19). Of course, astrologers will claim that they are not worshipping the stars, only consulting their mysterious forces and peculiar influences on our lives. In essence, astrologers and their victims are attributing to the stars the attributes of God. This is the definition of idolatry. God calls on us to put the star readers to the test:

> Let now the astrologers, those who prophesy by the stars, those who predict by the new moons, stand up and save you from what will come upon you. Behold, they have become like stubble, fire burns them; they cannot deliver themselves from the power of the flame; there will be no coal to warm by, not a fire to sit before! So have those become to you with whom you have labored, who have trafficked with you from your youth; each has wandered in his own way. There is none to save you (Isa. 47:13–15).

In addition to being unbiblical, astrology is irrational. A person can't be born under a particular "sign." All the supposed "signs" are made out of non-patterned star points that were formed thousands of years ago before the invention of the telescope. It's like "connect the dots," and you get to pick the dots. Any grouping of stars can be turned into a variety of configurations. Find a book on constellations, choose the constellations Leo and Cancer, redraw the stars as points on a blank sheet of paper, and then hand the paper to a friend and have him connect the dots in the form of a lion (Leo) and crab (Cancer). Then ask someone else to connect the dots to look like two other animals. What's the point? The dots can be made to look like anything.

Astrology is an ancient practice based on ancient science. As we know, much of what people thought they knew about the construction of the cosmos has proved to be wrong. "In essence, astrology is astronomically local; its predictions are based entirely on the behavior of our own solar system. Ancient doctrine held, of course, that it is the earth itself that sits at the center of the solar system; and this pleasant observational error astrologers yet accept."[34] Then there is the problem of alignment. At the moment of birth, the sun, planets, and stars are thought to be in a particular alignment. But are they really? Light from the sun takes 8.3 light-*minutes* to reach earth. Jupiter is nearly 51 light-minutes away from Earth, and Pluto 5.6 light-*hours*, assuming the speed of light today is identical to the speed of light when the universe was created.[35] This means that when you look at the sun, you are actually seeing what happened eight minutes before you actually see it. The closest stars are measured in light-*years*. None of the heavenly bodies are aligned in the way they are actually seen at the moment of birth.

Studies done on thousands of people who were born under the same sign differed radically in terms of personality profiles. When tested under controlled conditions, astrologers are dismal failures.[36] This is why astrologers stick with predictions that can be applied to almost anybody. After a group of people had been given an astrological reading, they were asked if the reading was accurate. They all said it was. They soon learned that they all had received the same reading.

Nostradamus

Michel de Notredame (1503–1566), more popularly known as Nostradamus, was born in the Provincial city of St. Rémy, France, into a Jewish family that had converted to Catholicism when he was nine. He was well educated, "studying the humanities, which in that day were grammar, rhetoric, logic, arithmetic, geometry, music and astronomy. The last consisted of a mixture of what we now know as the science of astronomy and the art of astrology. All of these subjects were taught in Latin."[37] Prior to his university training, Michel learned Greek, Latin, and Hebrew from his grandfather. He continued his education by pursuing medical training at the prestigious University of Montpelier in 1522. His medical skills "distinguished him as a plague doctor."[38]

Following his medical studies, Nostradamus cultivated his early interest in astrology which he had picked up during his university training, a required subject at Montpelier. His attempts at publishing annual almanacs that contained considerable amount of astrological prophetic speculation were an immediate success. An English translation appeared under the title the *Almanacke For 1559*.

Like modern-day "prophets," Nostradamus's enigmatic quatrains (four-line prophecies) were taken as accurate predictions of future events. The accidental death of King Henry II of France in 1559 in a jousting tournament solidified Nostradamus's reputation as a true prophet among the nobility. The following quatrain supposedly predicts the death of the king:

> The young lion will overcome the older one,
> in a field of combat in a single fight:
> He will pierce his eyes in their golden cage;
> Two wounds in one, then he dies a cruel death.

It's a curious thing that if the "prophecy" was designed to predict the king's death, why didn't Nostradamus use the king's name? In addition, if the quatrain was so clear, then why didn't the king refrain from participating in a dangerous jousting contest? And why didn't Nostradamus warn the king? He had corresponded with Henry on March 14, 1557, in which he had predicted great things for the young king. Like so many of Nostradamus's quatrains, the verses must be manipulated to fit actual events. Henry's helmet was not made of gold; there was only a two-year age difference between the king and his jousting opponent which hardly counts as a "young lion" overcoming the "old one"; their jousting did not take place "in a field of combat"; neither man used the lion in his heraldic crest; and in later editions of the work, words were added to the quatrain to make it more prophetically accurate.[39]

Some speculate that the quatrain best fits a *past* event, for example, the imprisonment in the Tower of London and beheading of Sir Thomas More ("older one") by Henry VIII of England ("the young lion") on July 6, 1535. But even if Nostradamus had meant the quatrain to describe some future event, there is little in it that is spectacular since he mentions no names. Kings often engaged in combat and found themselves opposed by "young lions" trying to make a name for themselves on the battlefield. Since the quatrain is enigmatic and potentially symbolic, it could be made to apply to almost any political figure who died during combat. Of course, there is always another explanation: The prophecy did not come pass. It seems that Nostradamus's "prophecies" can only be understood after the fact.

Because Nostradamians believe the French seer envisioned the Great Fire of London (1666), the rise of Napoleon Bonaparte, the cunning brutality of Adolf Hitler, the life of Princess Diana, the coming "third antichrist," and events related to the year 2000 and beyond, Nostradamus is considered be in a prophetic league of his own. Consider a prophecy that supposedly had the late Princess Diana in view:

[I]n 1991, a rift between Princess Diana and Prince Charles became public knowledge. Several newspapers carried reports of an alleged telephone conversation between the Princess and a close friend, James Gilbey. A book detailing the Princess's miserable marriage and rejection by Prince Charles stoked the fires of speculation still further. These events may well be reflected in quatrain VI:74 [of Nostradamus' writings]: "She who was cast out will return to reign; her enemies found among conspirators; more than ever will her reign be triumphant. At three and seventy death is very rare."[40]

The author offers the following interpretation of the supposed uncanny prophetic ability of Nostradamus. "This suggests that in the end the popularity of the Princess will guarantee her a welcome return to the centre of monarchy, with her perhaps living until the age of 73."[41] Now that Diana is dead at a young age, followers of Nostradamus will claim that only the interpretation is wrong. The prophecy must refer to someone else.

When Croesus, the Lydian king famous for his wealth, asked the Oracle at Delphi whether he should go to war against Cyrus of Persia, in 550 B.C., the oracle told him, "After crossing the Halys River, Croesus will destroy a great empire." True to the Oracle's word, Croesus did destroy a great empire. His own.

Like the Oracle at Delphi, the prophecies of Nostradamus are purposefully vague. We are told that "Nostradamus confused the dating of his predictions and wrote in a bewildering mixture of anagrams, symbols, Old French, Latin, and other languages"[42] to hide his special powers so he would not be accused of witchcraft by the Inquisition. This is doubtful since his quatrains were viewed as prophetic, and he was considered a prophet and was received at court.

Like most psychics and fortunetellers, his prophecies, in hindsight, can be made to say anything. Translation has a lot to do with the identification of the historical personages in the Nostradamus quatrains. With the way he used anagrams, symbols, Old French, and a mixture of other languages, a translator would have his pick of what he wanted the "prophecies" to say. In addition, because of the highly symbolic style of his writing, his prophecies were open to wildly speculative interpretations. Here is an example:

> A great swarm of bees will arise but no one will know from whence they come: They ambush by night, the sentinel under the vines, the city handed over to five bribed babblers.

Are the bees literal bees? What about the vines? One believer in the Nostradamus' prophecies interprets the above quatrain this way:

> Nostradamus foresaw that soon the empty Hall of Mars like countless other halls throughout France would be decorated with the bees of Napoleon's coat of arms as a symbol of his coming Empire. The coup d'etat was planned the night before. The "*five babblers*" are the Directory's executive counselors. Two of them conspired with Napoleon, the other three were bribed to look the other way.[43]

It's obvious that the people did know "from whence" Napoleon came; he was from France. Bees must be interpreted figuratively. "Babblers" must mean "conspirators." What is the "sentinel under the vine"? Taking a literal reading, my guess is that Nostradamus foresaw the arrival of African Killer Bees.

Like every self-styled "prophet," Nostradamus presents two future scenarios that cannot co-exist. "The first is total nuclear war by 1999 and the second is a golden age of enlightened peace by the end of this millennium. . . . Nostradamus states clearly that if we survive our next generation we may look forward to thousands of years of Earth-related history."[44] Of course, 1999 has passed and nothing remotely like what Nostradamus predicted came about.

Is it any wonder that the prophecies of Nostradamus have elicited excitement among the "spiritually sensitive"? You can take your pick and always be right. "Again, his prophecies were neither specific nor understandable. Surely if somebody had the power of precognition, he or she could be specific about what the future held. It makes you wonder why people still diligently study his work."[45]

What About Bible Prophecy?

Those who put their faith in the dismal track record of celebrity prophets, who trust the supposed predictive powers of dispassionate heavenly bodies, or who turn to the enigmatic anagrams of Nostradamus for direction and comfort have put their trust in "myths" (1 Tim. 1:4), "worldly fables" (1 Tim. 4:7), "cleverly devised tales" (2 Peter 1:16), and "false words" (2 Peter 2:3). Why do people turn their lives over to those who have a below average predictive success rate when they can turn to the reliability of God's Word where true knowledge about the future is found? Of course, it's possible that many people are not aware of the predictive history of the Bible and how it compares to today's very poor imitations. But people like Nostradamus, Jeane Dixon, and Joan Quigley are safe prophets. They don't make moral demands on people. There is no call to bow down before the sovereign God of the universe. So even though the prophets of the day may not always be accurate, they require nothing from their adherents.

The Bible is not like a horoscope that claims to chart life's opportunities and pitfalls. The Bible's prophecies, like its miracles, are designed to point us to our God and Savior, Jesus Christ (Luke 24:25, 27, 44; John 21:24–25). Biblical prophecy is not a religious curiosity; it's an integral part of God's character which stands as a faithful witness to the outworking of His redemptive plan in time and history.

Carl Sagan asks, "Yet has there ever been a religion with the prophetic accuracy and reliability of science?" Most certainly. Here is a great way to "test the spirits," as the Bible tells us to do. The Old Testament includes numerous prophecies concerning the first coming of Christ. No single person, no matter how clever, could have manipulated the circumstances around his life to fit the prophetic specifics of so many prophecies. There are too many prophecies over which he would have no control. Consider just eight Messianic prophecies (any eight could be used):

1. Place of birth: Bethlehem (Micah 5:2; Matt. 2:5–6; Luke 2:4)
2. Time of birth: based on the seventy weeks of years given to Daniel (Dan. 9:25; Luke 2:25–32)
3. Manner of birth: born of a virgin (Is. 7:14; Luke 1:34)
4. Price of betrayal: thirty pieces of silver (Zech. 11:12; Matt. 26:15; 27:9–10)
5. Manner of death: crucifixion (Ps. 22:16, 18; Matt. 27:35; Luke 23:34; John 19:24; 20:25)
6. Condition of the body: no broken bones (Ps. 34:20; John 19:31–33) but a pierced side (Zech. 12:10; John 19:34, 37)
7. Loyalty of his disciples: deserted by His followers (Zech. 13:7; Matt. 26:31)
8. Burial place: buried in a rich man's tomb (Is. 53:9; Matt. 27:57–30)

The only reason Mary and Joseph were in the insignificant city of Bethlehem in Judea was due to a Roman decree to tabulate a census for tax purposes (Luke 2:1). How could Jesus have been sure that He would be crucified instead of stoned to death, since stoning was the Jewish form of punishment? (John 8:59; Acts 7:58). There was no way that Jesus could have known that the Roman soldiers would not break His legs. Of course, as a dead man, Jesus had no say in where He would be buried.

He could not be sure that the Romans would give up His body to His family for burial. These and many more prophecies were fulfilled in the life of Christ. "It has been calculated that twenty-nine Messianic prophecies were fulfilled in the final twenty-four hours of [Jesus'] life alone."[46]

Peter Stoner, professor of mathematics and astronomy, writes, "we find that the chance that any man might have lived down to the present time and fulfilled all eight prophecies is 1 in 10^{17}."[47] That would be 1 followed by seventeen zeros: 1 chance in 100,000,000,000,000,000 or 1 in 100 quadrillion. Of course, there are more than just eight prophecies. Stoner also considers forty-eight prophecies. "We find the chance that any one man fulfilled all 48 prophecies to be 1 in 10^{157}."[48] That's 1 followed by 157 zeros. This number is so large as to be unimaginable. But there are more than 48 prophecies. Floyd Hamilton calculates that there "are in the Old Testament 332 distinct predictions which are literally fulfilled in Christ."[49]

None of this considers the fulfillment of New Testament prophecy regarding the destruction of Jerusalem in A.D. 70. Dozens of prophecies were given by Jesus and the New Testament writers describing what was to happen within a generation. The prophecies were fulfilled to the letter. Jesus predicted that there would be earthquakes and famines before that first-century generation passed away (Matt. 24:34). There were earthquakes (27:54; 28:2; Acts 16:26) and famines (Acts 11:28; cf. Rom. 8:35), just like Jesus predicted (Matt. 24:7). Paul tells us that the "gospel" had been preached "to all the nations" in his day (Rom. 16:25–26), just like Jesus predicted would happen (Matt. 24:14). Jesus said that the temple would so thoroughly be destroyed that "not one stone... shall be left upon another, which will not be torn down" 24:2). The temple was destroyed in A.D. 70 by Roman armies lead by Titus.[50]

How do critics of biblical predictive prophecy deal with these claims? Tim Callahan, in his *Bible Prophecy: Failure or Fulfillment?*, ignores Stoner's arguments even though he is familiar with his book *Science*

Speaks.[51] Callahan's operating presuppositions won't allow him to assess the prophecies outside the parameters of his anti-supernatural world-view, and because he rejects the Bible as a reliable historical document. His argument is circular: The prophecies aren't truly predictive because the Bible's not a prophetic book, and the Bible's not a prophetic book because the prophecies can't be predictive, because no one can predict the future. Furthermore, Callahan will not believe the Bible's testimony because he claims there are no historical sources to validate the New Testament.

> [T]he historicity of the details of the life of Jesus is not verified outside the New Testament, with the exception of the statement by Tacitus in the Annals of Imperial Rome that Jesus was crucified by Pilate for sedition and a reference in the writings of Flavius Josephus to James, the brother of Jesus. Thus, the validity of the gospels cannot be verified by external sources and must be taken somewhat on faith. As such, using them as fulfillment of Old Testament prophecy is likewise a matter of faith.[52]

We can turn this argument around and claim that since many of the events that Tacitus and Josephus record in their writings are not mentioned in the Bible, their histories are not verifiable. Callahan assumes that only histories outside the Gospels are reliable documents for study.

How many works of the first century can be verified by other contemporary sources? Not many, because most historical records have not survived the ravages of time, wars, and weather. How do we know that these "external sources" are reliable? Where can we turn to validate the testimony of Josephus and Tacitus? Why are their records of history trustworthy while the testimony of the Bible is not?[53] And if we could find contemporary histories that validated the accuracy of Tacitus and

Josephus, where would we go to validate the accuracy of those validating Tacitus and Josephus? The assumption made by non-Christian scholars is that "an assertion made by a pagan writer with his biases is somehow intrinsically more believable than an assertion made by a biblical writer, despite the obvious high moral standards of biblical teaching."[54]

The limited number of references to Jesus Christ in these Roman histories could be the result of Roman prejudices and biases against the New Testament record. Pontius Pilate, a representative of Rome, had Jesus put to death based on false testimony from His enemies (Matt. 26:59–61), even after Pilate declared that he found no guilt in Jesus (Matt. 27:19, 24; Mark 15:14; Luke 23:14; John 19:4, 6). In addition, Callahan fails to point out that Josephus mentions Jesus, His crucifixion under Pilate, and His reported resurrection.[55] He also fails to mention a fragment of Thallos (A.D. 55), Pliny the Younger's books of letters (Book 10) written around A.D. 112 to Emperor Trajan that includes background information on Jesus related to the treatment of Christians, and other historical material.[56]

Callahan's claim that the "fulfillment of Old Testament prophecy is . . . a matter of faith" is true, but so is the denial of the fulfillment of Old Testament prophecy. Josephus and Tacitus do not deny the biblical prophetic record as it relates to Jesus or attempt to refute its claims. In fact, both Josephus and Tacitus acknowledge that Jesus lived and died the way the New Testament said He did. Callahan does not believe the Bible's testimony because of his anti-supernatural presuppositions.

Conclusion

There are *four* gospel accounts that offer testimony to the life and work of Christ and an additional twenty three, the rest of the New Testament. A study of their content will show that they were not copied from a single source. Luke maintains that he "investigated everything carefully from the beginning" (Luke 1:3; see Acts 1:1–3). He examined the claims of "eyewitnesses" (1:2). The author of the fourth gospel writes: "This is the disciple who bears witness of these things, and wrote these things; and we know that his witness is true" (John 21:24). He was an eyewitness. The requirement for replacing Judas was someone who was "a witness... of His resurrection" (Acts 1:22). Such testimony would stand up in a modern court of law. The gospel accounts of the life and work of Christ circulated while these eyewitnesses were still alive.[57] There are no contemporaneous accounts refuting their claims. The fulfillment of these Messianic prophecies meet both the Bible's requirement of 100% accuracy and Sagan's insistence on "accuracy and reliability."

Notes

1. David Wallechinsky, Amy Wallace, and Irving Wallace, *The People's Almanac Presents the Book of Predictions* (New York: William Morrow, 1980), xv.

2. J. Barton Payne, *Encyclopedia of Biblical Prophecy: The Complete Guide to Scriptural Predictions and Their Fulfillment* (New York: Harper & Row, 1873), 631–682.

3. Rene Noorbergen, "Prologue," in Jeane Dixon, *My Life and Prophecies: Her Own Story as told to Rene Noorbergen* (New York: William Morrow, 1969), 17.

4. The record was broken in 1998 by Sammy Sosa, who hit 66, and Mark McGwire, who hit 70.

5. Hank Aaron holds the new record of 755 career home runs.

6. Carl Sagan, *The Demon-Haunted World: Science as a Candle in the Dark* (New York: Random House, 1996), 30.

7. Carl Sagan, "Velikovsky's Challenge to Science," cassette 186–74, produced by the American Association for the Advancement of Science. Quoted in John Blanchard, *Does God Believe in Atheists?* (Auburn, MA: Evangelical Press, 2000), 431.

8. Sagan, *The Demon-Haunted World*, 31.

9. Wallechinsky, Wallace, and Wallace, *The People's Almanac Presents the Book of Predictions*, 42.

10. *Evangelical Times* (September 1996). Quoted in Blanchard, *Does God Believe in Atheists?*, 315.

11. John Naisbitt, *Megatrends: Ten New Directions Transforming Our Lives* (New York: Warner Books, 1982), 2.

12. Justine Glass, *They Foresaw the Future: The Story of Fulfilled Prophecy* (New York: G.P. Putnam's Sons, 1969), 223.

13. Wallechinsky, Wallace, and Wallace, *The People's Almanac Presents the Book of Predictions*, 392.

14. Jack Anderson, *Parade* (May 13, 1956), 5. Quoted in André Kole and Jerry MacGregor, *Mind Games: Exposing Today's Psychics, Frauds, and False Spiritual Phenomena* (Eugene, OR: Harvest House, 1998), 111. Ruth Montgomery has March 11, 1956, as the date for the *Parade* article. See Ruth Montgomery, *A Gift of Prophecy: The Phenomenal Jeane Dixon* (New York: William Morrow, 1965), 6. I've read in several places, that Dixon later predicted that Kennedy would *not* win the presidency. I have not been able to find a reference for this failed prediction.

15. Bill Hendrick, "Believe it … or not," *The Atlanta Constitution* (January 5, 1998), D1.

16. In 1965, Dixon predicted, "Russia will be the first nation to put a man on the moon, probably in about three years' time." Montgomery, *A Gift of Prophecy*, 176.

17. "Sargent Shriver and Richard M. Nixon have 'excellent vibrations' for the good of America and will serve their country well." Montgomery, *A Gift of Prophecy*, 177. Also see *Time* (August 13, 1965), 59. Nixon left office in disgrace in 1974.

18. Wallechinsky, Wallace, and Wallace, *The Book of Predictions*, 394.

19. Dixon, *My Life and Prophecies*, 141.

20. Dixon, *My Life and Prophecies*, 142.

21. Dixon, *My Life and Prophecies*, 153–54.

22. Dixon, *My Life and Prophecies*, 140.

23. Montgomery, *A Gift of Prophecy*, 171.

24. Dixon, *My Life and Prophecies*, 145.

25. Richard Williams, ed., *Quest for the Unknown: Charting the Future* (Pleasantville, NY: Readers Digest, 1992), 59.

26. Dixon, *My Life and Prophecies*, 14–16.

27. Ted Peters, *The Cosmic Self: A Penetrating Look at Today's New Age Movements* (San Francisco, CA: HarperCollins, 1991), 38–39.

28. Donald T. Regan, *For the Record: From Wall Street to Washington* (New York: Harcourt Brace Jovanovich, 1988), 3. See pages 73–74.

29. Joan Quigley, *"What Does Joan Say?": My Seven Years as White House Astrologer to Nancy and Ronald Reagan* (Birch Lane Press, 1990), 11.

30. Quigley, *"What Does Joan Say?,"* 156.

31. Barrett Seaman, "Good Heavens!," *Time* (May 16, 1988), 25.

32. Seaman, "Good Heavens!," 25.

33. "2 Kings" in *Lange's Commentary* (Grand Rapids, MI: Zondervan [1960], 3:169, 186. Quoted in Robert A. Morey, *Horoscopes and the Christian* (Minneapolis, MN: Bethany House, 1981), 10.

34. David Berlinski, *Black Mischief: The Mechanics of Modern Science* (New York: William Morrow and Company, 1986), 83.

35. "Scientists have discovered that light may once have travelled many thousands of times faster than now, posing new questions about Einstein's theory of relativity, which forms the basis for much of our understanding of the universe. Einstein built his theory around the idea that the speed of light in a vacuum is a constant 670,615,000 mph (186,282 miles per second) and that nothing could go faster. New studies suggest, however, that this did not apply in the infancy of the universe, during and soon after the big bang. . ." (Jonathan Leake, "High-speed light casts doubt on Einstein's laws," *The Sunday Times* [December 24, 2000]).

36. André Kole and Jerry MacGregor, *Mind Games: Exposing Today's Psychics, Frauds, and False Spiritual Phenomena* (Eugene, OR: Harvest House, 1998), 194–197.

37. James Randi, *The Mask of Nostradamus* (New York: Charles Scribner's Sons, 1990), 12.

38. Randi, *Mask of Nostradamus*, 12.

39. For a critical analysis of the supposed predictive death of Henry II, see Randi, *The Mask of Nostradamus*, 170–176.

40. Stephen Skinner, *Millennium Prophecies: Predictions for the Year 2000 and Beyond from the World's Greatest Seers and Mystics* (New York: Barnes and Noble, [1994] 1997), 86–87.

41. Skinner, *Millennium Prophecies*, 87.

42. "Europe's Greatest Prophet: The Uncanny Words of Nostradamus," in *Strange Stories, Amazing Facts* (Pleasantville, NY: The Reader's Digest Association, 1976), 511.

43. John Hogue, *Nostradamus and the Millennium: Predictions of the Future* (New York: A Dolphin Books, 1987), 69.

44. Hogue, *Nostradamus and the Millennium*, 188.

45. Kole and MacGregor, *Mind Games*, 113.

46. Blanchard, *Does God Believe in Atheists?*, 561–562.

47. Peter W. Stoner, *Science Speaks: Scientific Proof of the Accuracy of Prophecy and the Bible*, 3rd rev. ed. (Chicago, IL: Moody Press, 1969), 106.

48. Stoner, *Science Speaks*, 109.

49. Floyd E. Hamilton, *The Basis of Christian Faith: A Modern Defense of the Christian Religion*, rev. ed. (New York: Harper & Row, 1964), 160.

50. For a complete discussion of the Olivet Discourse and its relation to the destruction of the temple in A.D. 70, see Gary DeMar, *Last Days Madness: Obsession of the Modern Church*, 4th ed. (Atlanta, GA: American Vision, 1999).

51. Tim Callahan, *Bible Prophecy: Failure or Fulfillment?* (Altadena, CA: Millennium Press, 1997), 98.

52. Callahan, *Bible Prophecy*, 111.

53. For a discussion of this subject, see the interview with Edwin Yamauchi of Miami University (Oxford, Ohio) in Lee Strobel, *The Case for Christ: A Journalist's Personal Investigation of the Evidence for Jesus* (Grand Rapids, MI: Zondervan, 1998), chapter 4.

54. Winfried Corduan, *No Doubt About It: The Case for Christianity* (Nashville, TN: Broadman & Holman, 1997), 196–197.

55. Paul L. Maier, *Josephus: The Essential Writings* (Grand Rapids, MI: Kregel, 1988), 264–265.

56. Robert E. Van Voorst, *Jesus Outside the New Testament: An Introduction to the Ancient Evidence* (Grand Rapids, MI: Eerdmans, 2000).

57. John A. T. Robinson, *Redating the New Testament* (London: SCM Press Ltd, 1976).

18

Living in a Postmodern World

Under the post-modern onslaught, all boundaries and distinctions
rapidly fall. Some of the losses associated with the collapse of
traditional distinctions have been trivial, but others have been
earthshaking, and there seems to be no way to distinguish
between the two in the post-modern context. People no longer
know where the lines fall.[1]

"**B**eauty is in the eye of the beholder." Many of us have uttered
these words at some point in time. But few of us have really thought
about the implications of this little phrase. Its message is that objective
standards for beauty do not exist and that virtue is arbitrarily defined
by individuals. What may be beautiful to you may not be beautiful to
someone else, and what one perceives as ugly may be truly exquisite to
another.

Perhaps this criticism simply nit-picks an innocent phrase that has
seen many adolescents through the more insecure years of life. However, the *implication* of this phrase—the supremacy of subjectivity and
relativism—is becoming the worldview of many Americans today. Modern society generally believes that *truth*, as well as beauty, is in the eye of

the beholder. Truth is not objective, something that exists apart from us; rather, truth is "what works for us." This emerging perspective denies *standards* and argues that truth is relative to individuals or cultures.

The Objection of One Truth

The greatest offense to the unbeliever is the Christian's insistence that there is only one truth. The statement that Jesus is the *only* way, the *only* truth, and the *only* light seems rather closed-minded. For secularists, it seems reasonable that if there *is* a "God," people should be able to worship him (or her or it) however they choose. In fact, George Barna of the Barna Research Group found that 62% of all Americans believe that all religious faiths teach the same lessons about life. Barna also found that while 60% of all Americans believe that the Bible is totally accurate in all of its teachings, 70% believe that there are no absolutes! This general lack of foundation is reflected in the title of Barna's current book on what people believe, *Absolute Confusion.*[2] Indeed, confusion is the spirit of the age.

A new worldview is emerging, a worldview that calls into question all traditional notions of truth, structure, and reality. It is called *postmodernism.* Postmodernism removes the anchor of objective truth and pushes human experience into the chaotic sea of human preference and subjectivity. Postmodernism says that while absolute truth was once a viable belief, it has turned out to be little more than a passing fad.

What is the source of this absurdity? For many of us, the notion that there is no objective truth is foolish, and yet this idea is becoming increasingly entrenched in our society. Who would question the scientific truth that light travels at 186,282 miles per second, or that the law of non-contradiction is a fundamental rule of logic? Better yet, who would question that 2 + 2 = 4, or that Jesus is the only way to the Father? Answer: people who seek more consistency in their rejection of God. Fact and certainty are not acceptable to people who deny universal standards. What we are seeing today is a worldview shift, from the modern to the postmodern.[3]

Postmodernism's History

Shifts in worldview are nothing new. Western thought has undergone continual change. As Gene Veith puts it, "One worldview follows another. In the eighteenth century the Enlightenment challenged the Biblical synthesis that had dominated Western culture. With the nineteenth century came both romanticism and scientific materialism. The twentieth century has given us Marxism and fascism, positivism and existentialism."[4] But before we can discuss postmodernism, we need to first take a look at the periods that preceded it: the *premodern* and the *modern*.

The Premodern Age

The premodern age, as it is condescendingly called, is the period in intellectual history that encompasses all thought from ancient Greek philosophy, through the Renaissance and the Reformation, up until the dawn of the Enlightenment. Of course, not every one agrees with when the premodern era concluded and the modern era commenced. A great deal of overlap is present in any worldview transition.

Premodernism, like modernism after it, was a multi-faceted phase of Western culture that cannot be characterized by any one worldview. As Veith puts it, it was a "complex, dynamic, tension-filled era [which] included mythological paganism and classical rationalism, as well as Biblical revelation."[5] But for all of its diversity, the period is marked by a strong belief in the supernatural and in absolute truth.

For example, Plato believed that the natural world manifested so much diversity and change that a supernatural world must exist to establish coherence and meaning. During the Medieval period, the Christian worldview came to dominate this pursuit of the supernatural. This worldview stated that God is the foundation of truth and the purpose of man is to discern his relationship to God. Throughout this premodern period, great Christian theologians flourished, men such as Augustine, Thomas Aquinas, Blaise Pascal, Martin Luther, and John Calvin. Belief in absolute truth and the supernatural was non-negotiable. Premoderns acknowledged that God's unifying truth was the basis for understanding reality as a *universe*, not a *multiverse*.[6]

The Modern Age

The fallen nature of humanity, inclining towards autonomy, made a shift in worldviews inevitable. Man no longer needed to be bound by the superstitious, out-dated beliefs of the past. Modern man did not need the supernatural to guide him; reason and science alone could give him the answers he needed to understand the universe. This paradigm shift from premodern to modern was realized in the period historians have referred to as the Enlightenment.

For many, the Enlightenment was the birth of the "modern" period in intellectual history. Some historians date this period as beginning with the French Revolution in 1789, and ending with the fall of the Berlin Wall in 1989.[7] While many Enlightenment thinkers did not completely reject belief in God, they banished Him to the remotest corner of the heavens. If God did exist, He was neither concerned nor involved in His creation. Reason and science were now the objects of worship, and redemption for mankind was to be found in their study and application.

Others believe that the modern age commenced even earlier, with the Copernican revolution. Both Aristotle (384–322 B.C.) and Claudius Ptolemaeus (A.D. 90?–168?), widely known as Ptolemy, had maintained that the earth was the physical center of the universe. Even the church adopted their views. The Polish astronomer Nicolaus Copernicus (1473–1543) questioned their cosmology and the church's support of it. In the case of Copernicus, and later Galileo (1564–1642) and Johannes Kepler (1571–1630), mathematics was the governing principle to understand the movements of the planets around the sun.

While Copernicus, Kepler, and Galileo all believed in God, they inadvertently set in motion a purely mechanical understanding of the working of the universe. Their emphasis on mathematical applications, as well as Isaac Newton's geometric interpretation of the universe, allowed modernists to embrace a purely mechanistic explanation for all of life. "Science inclined increasingly toward God the Watchmaker," and in time "suggested that God did not have to wind His watch after all—the universe more and more seemed given over by its Maker to impersonal natural laws."[8] The idea that the mechanistic world is governed by impersonal natural laws with no need of divine operation affected thought beyond the mathematical and theoretical.

> The transformation appeared everywhere. Montesquieu explained the development of institutions and national character as resulting from climate. Adam Smith expounded laws of political economy governing the wealth of nations. Gibbon, disinclined to sweeping general laws, nevertheless refined a historiography of purely natural causes, from which all trace of divine purpose vanished. Voltaire speculated on the social origins of morality. The greatest audacity was reserved for David Hume, whose "Natural History of Religion" calmly put religious belief on a par with other natural phenomena and traced its genesis to human efforts to quell fear of the unknown and allay anxieties over the uncertainties of life.[9]

For scientists and social theorists, God was not denied; He was simply redefined. Where He once providentially guided His creation and creatures, "He now appeared to have left the running of the world to impersonal laws."[10]

Now that God had been given the role of the Divine Engineer who was removed from any meaningful contact with the universe, a new paradigm (worldview) was needed to make sense of the world. Modern worldviews such as *positivism* sought to unify the sciences and order human life by finding the basic pattern to explain human nature.[11] *Secular Humanism* emphasized the autonomy of the individual and the primacy of the intellect. Man could solve the problems of society through his own efforts, especially through education and technology.[12] Modernism taught that certain knowledge of ourselves and the world was possible because nature was a closed, static system of natural laws waiting to be discovered. Modernism did not deny certainty or fact, but made man his own god, to determine those truths for himself.

Unlike premodernism before it, modernism rejected the supernatural and proclaimed the sufficiency of logic and normal sense experience. Even biblical scholarship was tainted by this high evaluation of man; reliance upon *reason* instead of *revelation* became the basis for so-called higher criticism.[13] These higher critics rejected miracles, the incarnation, and other supernatural doctrines. Modernist scholars sought to "demythologize" the Bible and free it from the superstitious shackles that had bound it for so long. As Diogenes Allen observes:

> In time some went so far as to claim that the Bible was not needed at all. It was useful to the human race in its infancy, but now that we have achieved enlightenment, we can read the book of nature and avoid all the blemishes, distortions, and absurdities that are found in the Bible.[14]

Eventually this new "naturalistic" religion removed God from the picture altogether and attempted to produce a just and egalitarian social order that would embody reason and social progress.[15]

As it turned out, modernism did not produce the harmony that its prophets predicted. After slavery, two world wars, communism, Nazism, and nuclear bombs, people began to wonder whether the modern mind was really the road to paradise. They questioned modernism's confidence in reason, technology and science. In addition, the belief that nature is inherently orderly and governed by fixed, natural laws came under strong scrutiny. Scholars began to question the idea of absolutes in science[16] and logic[17] and became convinced that nature seems to be inherently disorderly and illusive.[18]

Postmodernism grew out of disillusionment with modernism's failure to produce a perfect, rational, planned, and compassionate world. The dreams of modernity were admirable but in the light of contemporary history seem naive. Loss of faith in society's perfectibility through centralized planning and technological development arose in Europe and the United States throughout the mid-twentieth century, and by 1990, with the collapse of centralized communism in the Soviet Union and Eastern Europe and the push toward deregulation and privatization in the United States and Great Britain, modernism was no longer a central force in economic planning or political thinking.[19]

In addition to admitting a chaotic universe, modern scholars began to criticize the idea that man is simply an unbiased observer of nature: "The mind is not the passive reflector of an external world and intrinsic order, *but is active and creative* in the process of perception and cognition. Reality is in some sense constructed by the mind, not simply perceived by it, and many such constructions are possible, *none necessarily sovereign.*"[20]

Modernism's idea that man is simply a uniform product of nature was dying fast. By reducing the human condition to logic and scientific method, modernism denied the human *spirit*. Man was simply the result of a random assimilation of atoms, subject to the laws of nature in a closed universe. Freedom was an illusion, and determinism was reality. In fact, modernism could not account for the complexity of man's immaterial tendencies other than by appealing to bio-chemical reactions.[21] Darwinism, itself the child of modernism, has turned on its parent and killed modernism. As Legal scholar Phillip Johnson observes:

> Modernism is the condition that begins when humans understand that God is really dead and that they therefore have to decide all the big questions for themselves. Modernism at times

produces an exhilarating sense of liberation: we can do whatever we like, because there is no unimpeachable authority to prevent us. Modernism at other times is downright scary: how can we persuade other people what *they* want to do to us is barred by some unchallengeable moral absolute?[22]

Modernism had delivered the very opposite of what it had promised. Its promises of liberation turned out to be masks for oppression and domination. By removing God and enthroning reason and science, man was now free to do all of the unrestrained evil he was capable of—all in the name of scientific progress. He soon discovered, however, that his self-made liberation had become his prison. Modernism, like premodernism before it, was now vulnerable. Reason and technology were really not messiahs, and the human spirit was still striving for its freedom and autonomy. Disillusioned by modernism, secular scholars were ready to consider a new system.

Defining Postmodernism

What is postmodernism? The system is both complex and ambiguous, but, basically speaking, postmodernism is anti-worldview.[23] It denies the existence of any universal truth and questions every worldview. The postmodernist will not tolerate any worldview that claims to be universal in application. But this is not enough. The goal of postmodernism is not only to reject worldviews as oppressive, but also to reject even the possibility of *having* a coherent worldview.

There are many worldviews around today, and the postmodernist believes that it is his responsibility to critique each one. Worldviews must be "flattened out," so that no one particular approach or belief is more "true" than any other. What constitutes truth, then, is relative to the individual or community holding the belief.

Whereas modernism and Christianity clashed by each claiming truth, postmodernism attacks the concept of truth itself. For postmodernism, truth is simply "what works for you." Postmodernism, then, claims to be not so much an *orthodoxy* (a positive belief system or worldview), as an *orthopraxy* (a series of methods for analysis).

In the postmodern world, man does not sit back and passively receive knowledge about the world; rather, man's interpretation *is* reality. This confusion of subject and object has correctly labeled postmodernism as nihilistic and relativistic.[24] Nothing is absolute; logic, science, history, and morality are merely the products of individual experience and interpretation.

The postmodernist will declare that reality is only what we perceive it to be. By adopting such a view, however, he now has a problem. As such, reality is unknowable. Charles Mackenzie observes: "If in knowing an object the human mind virtually creates knowledge, the question has been raised then, What is the external world when it is not being perceived?"[25] For the postmodernist, the only thing that can be known is personal experience and interpretations of that experience. Man can know nothing in any absolute sense. All one has is his own finite, limited experience. Logic, science, history, and ethics are human disciplines that must, and do, reflect human insufficiency and subjectivity.

In issues of morality, no one particular view is foundational. Rather, each culture's, and ultimately each individual's, view of ethics is just as valid as the next. This view is the basis for "multiculturalism" and the "political correctness" movement in today's society. Rather than affirming any one morality as absolute, every person's moral persuasion must be respected no matter what it is, and language must be revised so as to erase all offensive and narrow-minded perspectives.

Assessing the Postmodern Worldview

Postmodernism correctly questions modernism's reliance upon logic and science as certain paths to truth. The fact that philosophies of logic, science, and ethics are constantly changing shows that man without God cannot attain uniformity or ultimate standards. Modernism's unswerving faith in man was a foolish extreme. But postmodernism, even with its rejection of modernism's claims, pushes another extreme. Postmodernism's rejection of "absolute truth" undermines its own position. On what basis ought the postmodernist view be taken as *true*? Is its denial of "absolute truth" itself absolute? In other words, how can the postmodernist claim that his way of looking at things is "true" all the while denying the concept of truth?

The fact is that even as postmodernism denies all worldviews, it is itself a worldview. It is not just a system of analysis, because it must have a view on reality, knowledge, and morality in order to discern and justify its methods. Postmodernism is riddled with assumptions, in need of as much scrutiny and evaluation as any other worldview. The postmodernist must absolutize his claims to get his system going. This kind of extreme relativism is impossible; it affirms what it denies. Likewise, if language is all there is to reality, and all interpretation is subjective, then why do postmodernists write books? Why believe that there is any possible way to *communicate*? How do we in fact know that the reader's interpretation was the author's intent? This view of language, then, becomes the prison house of postmodern thought.

On a societal note, while postmodernism tries to enhance understanding of the diversity among people, it actually creates a new tribalism. Multiculturalism says that the traditional idea of America, as an assimilation of cultures, is false. America is not a "melting pot," but rather more like a "salad bowl." So everything—education, morality, politics, etc.—is defined by cultural interests. History, for example, is no longer an acquisition of knowledge of past events; rather, it is revised so as to enhance the self-image of a particular group that has been excluded or "oppressed." As Veith observes:

Contemporary scholars seek to dismantle the paradigms of the past and "to bring the marginal into the center" (rewriting history in favor of those who have been excluded from power—women, homosexuals, blacks, Native Americans, and other victims of oppression). Scholars attack received ideas with withering skepticism, while constructing new models as alternatives. Those who celebrate the achievements of Western civilization are accused of narrow-minded "Euro-centrism;" this view is challenged by "Afro-centrism," which exalts Africa as the pinnacle of civilization. Male-dominant thought is replaced by feminist models. "Patriarchal religions" such as Judaism and Christianity are challenged and replaced with matriarchal religions; the influence of the Bible is countered by the influence of "goddess-worship." Homosexuality is no longer considered a psychological problem; rather, homophobia is.[26]

It does not matter what *actually* happened in the worldview shift from modernism to postmodernism; that is impossible to know and as such is irrelevant. It is crucial, however, that we recognize the anti-Christian and self-contradictory message of postmodernism: all beliefs must be tolerated except for the belief that denies that all beliefs must be tolerated. In essence, postmodernism is at war with the Christian worldview. Power is its goal—power for man apart from God. Remember, postmodernism rejects the idea of any universal truth, whether it is history, logic, or Christ.

Is Postmodernism All Bad?

Irving Kristol, a fellow at the American Enterprise Institute, describes the current time as "a shaking of the foundations of the modern world."[27] Other scholars agree:

A massive intellectual revolution is taking place that is perhaps as great as that which marked off the modern world from the Middle Ages.... The principles forged during the Enlightenment... which formed the foundations of the modern mentality, are crumbling.[28]

The collapse of Enlightenment humanism is imminent; it is being attacked from all angles. From religious conservatives to scientific liberals, the shared goal is to overhaul the presuppositions of modernism, although their motives differ greatly. Christians welcome the opportunity for credible public discourse, and many scientists are eager to see a shift in scientific outlook that will account for the anomalies that modern science has avoided. These are exciting times, times in which the church should be alert.

The all-sufficiency of human reason and science is now under fire, and the supernatural—that which is not empirical—is once again open to consideration. The marketplace of ideas is wide open. The church must understand the nature of our age and how Christians can respond to a world increasingly steeped in dissolution. In a postmodern world Christianity is intellectually relevant.[29]

Not only has postmodernism opened the cultural door once again to the Christian faith, but with its critical apparatus it also offers a few lessons for the church to learn. Veith likens the current situation to that of the pagans at the Tower of Babel.[30] Genesis 11:1–9 tells us that at one time everyone in the whole earth spoke the same language. As some were traveling east, they stopped in the valley of Shinar to make a name for themselves by building a tower that would reach into heaven. When the Lord saw what they were doing, He came down and destroyed the heart of their unity: language. As a result, they were scattered over the earth without a way to communicate.

Modern man also built his tower of autonomy. He removed God (so he thought) and placed himself on the throne of his world. But postmodernism demanded that this man-based philosophy be taken to its logical extension of nihilism. It is interesting that postmodernism strikes at the very same thing God did: language. Outside absolute standards, language is reduced to pure subjectivity. And, without language, logic and science are meaningless; they have no application. As we have seen, postmodernism isolates each man in his own private world. The arrogant, pseudo-unity that man had claimed to find was now just a foolish dream. Like the people at the Tower of Babel, modern man has been fragmented and scattered. There is no center of discourse any longer.

In this light, perhaps the most significant contribution of postmodernism is that it reminds us of our finitude. It reminds us that without God mankind is relegated to absurdity. By default, it tells us that God must be the beginning of all of our thinking, that apart from Him we can know nothing. It is the fear of the Lord that is the *beginning* of knowledge (Prov. 1:7), not the conclusion of our investigation. In Christ "are hidden all of the treasures of wisdom and knowledge" (Col. 2:3). This does not mean that we reject disciplines such as logic and science. We see them as *tools* to better understand God's amazing creation, not as *ultimate standards* which take the place of God's revelation. After all, the "gift of logical reason was given by God to man in order that he might order the revelation of God for himself."[31] Science is simply the study of God's creation, so that we might better understand how to care for it, advance in knowledge, and fulfill the cultural mandate.[32]

In the same way, postmodernism reminds us that, like logic, theology is not exhaustive but a developing science. There are many approaches to theology, none complete. It is the theologian's responsibility to examine carefully all propositions in accordance with God's Word and press forward to better understand the revelation that God has given. We are to think God's thoughts after Him.

Conclusion

For our personal lives, postmodernism shows us the futility of autonomy. It forces those of us who know Christ back to the basics of depending on Christ for everything—from salvation to social standards. Only in Christ does man have meaning and purpose; He is the vine, we are the branches, and apart from him we can do nothing (John 15:15).

Notes

1. David F. Wells, *God in the Wasteland: The Reality of Truth in a World of Fading Dreams* (Grand Rapids, MI: Eerdmans, 1994), 48.

2. George Barna, *Absolute Confusion: How our Moral and Spiritual Foundations are Eroding in this Age of Change* (Ventura, CA: Regal Books, 1993).

3. For a more detailed examination of the many issues raised by postmodern thought, see Stephen Best and Douglas Kellner, *Postmodern Theory: Critical Interrogations* (New York: The Guilford Press, 1991); Stephen Connor, *Postmodernist Culture: An Introduction to Theories of the Contemporary* (Cambridge, MA: Basil Blackwell, 1989); Jean-Francois Lyotard, *The Postmodern Condition: A Report on Knowledge*, trans. Geoff Bennington and Brian Massumi (Manchester: Manchester University Press, 1984). From a Christian point of view see Gene Edward Veith, *Postmodern Times: A Christian Guide to Contemporary Thought and Culture* (Wheaton, IL: Crossway Books, 1994).

4. Veith, *Postmodern Times*, 19. Worldview shifts are more fully explained and documented in Richard Tarnas, *The Passion of the Western Mind: Understanding the Ideas that Have Shaped Our Worldview* (New York: Harmony Books, 1991).

5. Veith, *Postmodern Times*, 29.

6. See William H. Halverson, *A Concise Introduction to Philosophy*, 4th ed. (New York: McGraw-Hill Publishers, 1981), 413–17. Halverson points out that the study of philosophy encompasses all other disciplines. It seeks to create the concepts which will unify knowledge and provide a foundation for meaning.

7. Thomas C. Oden, *Two Worlds: Notes on the Death of Modernity in America and Russia* (Downers Grove, IL: InterVarsity Press, 1992), 32.

8. James Turner, *Without God, Without Creed: The Origins of Unbelief in America* (Baltimore, MD: Johns Hopkins University Press, 1985), 36.

9. Turner, *Without God, Without Creed*, 36.

10. Turner, *Without God, Without Creed*, 36.

11. For a detailed account of positivism see Michael Corrado, *The Analytic Tradition in Philosophy: Background and Issues* (Chicago: American Library Association, 1975).

12. See Gary Scott Smith, "Naturalistic Humanism," in *Building a Christian Worldview: God, Man, and Knowledge*, edited by Andrew Hoffecker and Gary Scott Smith (Phillipsburg, PA: Presbyterian and Reformed, 1986), 161–81.

13. See Edward J. Young, *An Introduction to the Old Testament* (Grand Rapids: Eerdmans, [1949] 1977), 123–41. In responding to the charge that Christianity and reason are at odds, Young says, "Christianity and reason, of course, are not enemies, for Christianity is the only *reasonable* explanation of life, and true reason, which is derived from God, is both humble and receptive."

14. Diogenes Allen, *Christian Faith in a Postmodern World: The Full Wealth of Conviction* (Louisville, KY: Westminster/John Knox, 1989), 36.

15. Stephen Best and Douglas Kellner, *Postmodern Theory: Critical Interrogations* (New York: The Guilford Press, 1991), 2.

16. See Thomas Kuhn, *The Structure of Scientific Revolutions* (Chicago, IL: The University of Chicago Press, 1970). Kuhn argues that scientists interpret the facts they observe according to their presuppositions about the nature of reality and knowledge.

17. Paul Johnson, *Modern Times: From the Twenties to the Nineties*, rev. ed. (New York: HarperCollins, 1991), 700.

18. "With the developments in Einstein's relativity, Bohr's quantum mechanics, and Heisenburg's 'Uncertainty Principle,' strict Newtonian Determinism in physics was called into question. Subatomic particles didn't seem to follow the physical patterns of their constructs. At times they behaved like particles, and at other times they behaved like waves. In Kuhnian terms, 'Normal science' was not able to account for these anomalies. In the words of Sir James Jeans, the 'physical world of twentieth-century physics did not look like a great machine as it did a great thought'" (Richard Tarnas, *The Passion of the Western Mind*, 356).

19. Herbert Kohl, *From Archetype to Zeitgeist: Powerful Ideas for Powerful Thinking* (Boston, MA: Little, Brown and Company, 1992), 127.

20. Tarnas, *The Passion of the Western Mind*, 396. Emphasis added.

21. This process of the reduction of man is described in excellent detail in William Barrett, *Death of the Soul: From Descartes to the Computer* (New York: Anchor/Doubleday, 1986).

22. Phillip E. Johnson, "The Modernist Impasse in Law," in *God and Culture: Essays in Honor of Carl F.H. Henry*, eds. D.A Carson and John D. Woodbridge (Grand Rapids, MI: Eerdmans, 1993), 181–182.

23. Veith, *Postmodern Times*, 49.

24. Nihilism is the view that human existence is totally and irremediably meaningless, that nothing in the world has any value. The most obvious example of nihilism is found in the works of Friedrich Nietzsche (See Halverson, *A Concise Introduction to Philosophy*, 448, 457–62).

25. Charles Mackenzie, "Kant's Copernican Revolution," in *Building a Christian Worldview*, 1:284 (emphasis added).

26. Veith, *Postmodern Times*, 57.

27. Dennis Farney, "Natural Questions," *Wall Street Journal* (July 11, 1994), A4.

28. Allen, *Christian Belief in a Postmodern World*, 2.

29. Allen, *Christian Belief in a Postmodern World*, 5.

30. Veith, *Postmodern Times*, 20–23.

31. Cornelius Van Til, *An Introduction to Systematic Theology* (Philadelphia: den Dulk Foundation, 1974), 256.

32. Genesis 1:28.